The Accidental Critic
Arch Campbell

№ 2344

NEWS MEDIA

Arch Campbell

NBC NEWS

METROPOLITAN POLICE DEPARTMENT
DISTRICT OF COLUMBIA

To: Vivian — Best Wishes

The Accidental Critic

A Television News Memoir

ARCH CAMPBELL

Arch Campbell

Opus Publishing
Politics & Prose Bookstore
Washington, D.C.

Copyright © Arch Campbell 2024

ISBN: 978-1-62429-538-6

All rights reserved. This book or any portion thereof may not be reproduced or used in any manner whatsoever without the express written permission of the author except for the use of brief quotations in a book review.

Cover design and interior formatting by Ellie Maranda

Editing by Sayan Ray

Published through Opus Self-Publishing Services
Located at:
Politics & Prose Bookstore
5015 Connecticut Ave NW
Washington D.C., 20008
www.politics-prose.com // (202) 364-1919

Politics & Prose is a unionized workplace.

For my father, Miller Campbell, the best friend a boy ever had.

Contents

Introduction	xi

TEXAS

The Accidental Critic	3
Raising My Hand	9
Channel 8 News on the Move	15
Cover The Arts	23
The Road to Washington	29

WASHINGTON, D.C.

Eyewitness News	40
Finding My Place	45
"Turkeys Are Dumb"	49
The News Center	52
Spot the Pig	56
That's News to Me	60
Jim Vance	63
Why I Love the Movies	69
Sunrise Shift	75
The Storm	79
The Weekend Weather	84
The Bottom	88
Star Trek	91
Best Movies of 1980	97
"The World's Worst Film Festival"	100
Rising Stars	106
The Oscars	114

The Monkey vs. Wall Street	118
Movies of the Early 80s	120
I Love L.A.	125
Reagan's Microphone	130
1985—*The Color Purple* and Oprah	135
When the Inmates Ran the Asylum	137
Katie and Other Stars	146
Please Return the Towels	152
Bob Hope and Other Golfers	155
Best Movies of 1986-1989	163
The Worst Premiere of the Best Movie	167
Silence of the Lambs: 1991-1992	170
JFK and the *Citizen Kane* Oscar	174
A Few Stories	178
Spielberg's Sister	185
Carson and Leno and Letterman	189
My Home Town	192
Change	197
Second Chance	202
Movies: 1994-1997	205
Diana and Michael	210
Wright Says Wrong!	213
Movies: 1998-2001	218
Bob Long Hot Tears of Despair	224
The Best Interview I Ever Did–2003	226
Synergy	229
Donald Trump and a Few Apprentices	236
Movies 2002 – 2006	241
The Big C	244
Blindsided	250

Blindsided Part 2	253
Changing Channels	258
A New Start	265
Patton and Me	274
Patton and Me, Part Two	279
Whatever Happened to the Accidental Critic?	282

MY HOMETOWN

The Texas Eagle	290
The Ghost of West Mistletoe	295
Martha's Vacation—1942	302
Dangling from the Family Tree—1946	305
The Woman Who Talked All Night	310
The House on West Mistletoe	313
The Son of a Used Car Salesman	315
Woodlawn Elementary	318
Life With Father	321
Success!	326
Life with Mother	330
Jefferson High	335
Fortune Smiles	339
San Antonio College	343
The Greatest Store	336
Radio	353
I'll Be Back	357
UT Austin	361
KTBC Austin	363
Grad School	368
Exit Stage Left	373
Fast Forward	380

Goodbye Part One 381
Goodbye Part Two 385
Family Reunion 392

MY PLACE
Return 398
Jim Vance 402
Whatever Happened to Arch Campbell? 408
"What's Your Favorite Movie?" 413

Acknowledgements 425

Arch Campbell Biography 427

Endnotes 430

Photo by Bob Casazza

Introduction

"I WANT A MOVIE REVIEWER! WHO WANTS TO DO it?" The newsroom went silent. I took a breath, raised my hand, and said, "I'll do it!"

I was working in the WFAA-TV Newsroom in Dallas in 1973. An ABC affiliate, owned by *The Dallas Morning News*, our newscast struggled in the contest for viewers. Management wanted to change that and brought in a new boss: Marty Haag, former assistant News Director of WCBS-TV, New York. Our newsroom, a bunch of Texas kids just starting out, braced for this East Coast boss.

Every morning Marty burst into the newsroom barking orders, asking questions, laying out the day's assignments. A big tall guy full of energy and a decade older than most of us, Marty aimed to shake things up. The week he shouted for somebody to review movies coincided with the opening of a coming-of-age comedy called *American Graffiti*. I bought a ticket, wrangled a film clip, went on the air, and described the story—a 1962 summer night as kids just out of high school drive around listening to Top 40 radio. In a few days they will step into the next stage of their lives. I gave it three stars out of four and said, "It's got a good beat and the kids can dance to it," the phrase Dick Clark used on *American Bandstand*. The anchor-man laughed.

The next morning, Marty Haag charged into the newsroom yelling assignments. He turned to me and said, "Arch! You are now the station movie reviewer."

Because I raised my hand, I've been writing and broadcasting and podcasting about movies and entertainment and unusual people and oddball places ever since. A series of lucky breaks led me into television news, just as the industry discovered the attraction of local news. We started trying things just to see what worked, or sometimes, just for the heck of it. Newsrooms expanded, audiences increased, and television news performers became local stars.

I worked in radio and television for more than 50 years. For most of those years I appeared on the local news of NBC owned station WRC in Washington, D.C. My friends and I remember those days fondly—so fondly we get together regularly to trade our favorite stories. I'll share some of those tales with you in the pages that follow. I hope they make you smile or even laugh out loud. Time may have dimmed or polished up a few of them. Please forgive the fog of memory.

Early in my reporting days, I interviewed the state historian of Texas at the Hall of State in Dallas' Fair Park. A kindly academic, he showed me a diorama of the transfer of Texas from a republic to a state. The model portrayed a broken flagpole with the Texas flag on the ground. The historian said when the President of Texas lowered the Texas flag for the last time, the flagpole broke, symbolizing the end of Texas as a republic.

"Oh gosh," I exclaimed, "did that really happen?"

The state historian looked me square in the eyes and said: "Son, if it didn't happen, it could have happened, and should have happened."

TEXAS

1
The Accidental Critic

TELEVISION! I should have known. Growing up, television was everything in our house—iPad, iPhone, and TikTok combined. From sign on to sign off, our TV stayed on. I should have known I would find a life in TV. Silly me, I thought I wanted to be a piano player.

It started with my father, Miller Campbell. He never slept. He loved movies, music, and staying up late. He watched Jack Paar's late night talk show, especially for the appearances of Oscar Levant, the hypochondriac concert pianist and wit. I could hear my father laughing as I tried to sleep upstairs. After the Parr Show, Daddy flipped the channel to whatever movie played on the other two stations. He'd seen most of these films in the 1930's and 40's in the downtown San Antonio movie palaces: the Majestic, the Aztec, the Texas, and the Empire. Laughter and TV and old movies seeped into my subconscious.

Like I said, he never slept. As the night wore on, he moved to his upright piano. A natural born musician, he played piano "by ear," a talent he discovered as a child. Night after night, I heard his favorites from the great American songbook: "Stardust" and "Moonglow" and tunes he composed.

I wanted to do that. I wanted the life of a late-night piano player. My father sold stuff for a living—insurance, cars, tract houses—on commission. No sales, no money. As a result, we lived in a world of ups and downs. I asked for piano lessons and had to wait until age fourteen, when the family fortunes picked up a little. My folks happily shelled out a few bucks a week to our church organist, Donna Mae Perry. She taught on a baby grand that smelled like furniture polish, in a house laced with old lady perfume. From September to May, I practiced diligently.

Donna Mae announced the annual spring recital. On the big day my mother and father, sister, friends, and neighbors gathered in the showroom of a downtown music store. My solo came early with the first-year group. That group consisted of over-weight pimply faced 14-year-old me, and a bunch of little kids in the first grade. It never occurred to me I would perform with a group of kids half my age.

I towered over the little tykes, sticking out like a sore thumb. Blushing with embarrassment, I played my dopey little tune. That killed it. I dropped piano lessons.

Defeated by music, I turned to photography, my next step toward TV. I signed up for the high school photography staff.

I joined the camera club, and hung out in the cave-like photo lab that smelled like vinegar. I aimed to join the ranks of the camera-artistes. One afternoon, a fellow shutterbug suggested we roam the campus looking for interesting shots. The Vice Principal saw us in the courtyard. "Where's your hall pass, boys?" he bellowed. We didn't have one.

High school kids didn't just roam around back then. I remember that today when I see kids stream out of high school midday heading to McDonald's. The Vice Principal marched us back to the yearbook teacher and yelled at her.

"What are these kids doing roaming around?" Furious at the Vice Principal's reprimand, the yearbook teacher kicked me and the other guy off the staff.

Having failed at photography and music, I signed up for speech class. Now I was getting somewhere. The semester began with 'after dinner' speaking. I told the comic tale of my week in the hospital after a lawnmower threw a rock into my leg, cutting several tendons. I connected jokes and one-liners about bedpans and hospital food and hopping around in a cast. My classmates laughed. The teacher gave me an A.

Laughter felt good. We laughed at home. My father told jokes and my mother spun outrageous tales. Comedy… that's the thing for me. A pal and I auditioned a two-man act for the annual high school talent show. Our act fell flat.

The school's imposing drama teacher, Miss Jean Longwith, beckoned us to the back of the auditorium. She stood up, stretching about a head taller than my friend and I. She leaned in and boomed: "Boys, you stink. You're not gonna be in MY talent show." Yes, I know you think I'm exaggerating, but I swear, she really said, "boys, you stink." In fact, "you stink," was her signature reprimand. We paused a beat to let that sink in. Then Miss Longwith turned her laser gaze on me.

"YOU," she bellowed, "I want YOU to be my emcee."

I gulped, and said, "OK."

The next week, a dozen other students and I met backstage to write the talent show script. Miss Longwith wanted a *Wheel of Fortune* theme, but couldn't find the prop she thought existed. We rooted around in the flats and costumes backstage. I discovered a cape that looked like the one the *Shock Theater* host wore on our local TV horror movie show.

"Wear that," she growled.

Working with a list of acts, we tossed around ideas for skits and introductions. The material presented in front of the curtain would give the stage crew time to set up behind the curtain. These idea sessions felt grown up. As we spoke, Miss Longwith hunched over her ancient typewriter pecking out the script on a mimeograph master sheet.

In one segment a fortune teller asks, "what do you get when you cross a parrot with a five-hundred-pound gorilla?"

I answer, "I don't know, but if it talks, you better listen." The crowd roared. The laughter washed over me like a healing balm. I discovered a new love: performance.

After the show, my classmates looked at me differently. I did not play sports. I was not the brightest bulb. However, I could stand on stage and crack jokes. The day I emceed my high school talent show changed my life. At the end of the semester, my speech teacher told me, "you ought to go into radio. You've got the gift of gab."

One of the talent-show judges chaired the San Antonio College speech and drama department. He offered a campus tour. A little booth behind the school theater caught my attention.

"This is our campus radio station WSAC." Then he added, "your drama teacher, Jean Longwith, will join our faculty this fall and teach Radio/TV."

That settled it. I would follow the teacher who put me on stage. I registered for her radio classes freshman year, picking up in college where we left off in high school. My sophomore year she hired me to run the campus station and assist her. My work at the college led to a job announcing records on a local FM station. When I transferred to the University of Texas at Austin, the FM job qualified me for weekend DJ work at KTBC radio in Austin.

I juggled shifts at KTBC with classes in radio and television. My part time job turned into a full-time job. The University of Texas Communications School launched a Master's program and recruited me. With a graduate degree, I could return to San Antonio College and teach broadcasting in my mentor's department. I wanted to work for the woman whose opening line to me was, "you stink." For my Master of Arts in Journalism and Mass communications, I wrote a thesis on the future of FM radio.

Fate intervened. An attractive young woman I knew at KTBC divorced her husband, moved to Dallas, and landed a job as a program assistant at WFAA, a major radio/TV station. WFAA needed a radio announcer. She recommended me. I got the job, moved to Dallas, dated the woman, lost the woman, kept the job.

WFAA felt like college extended, with most of the staff in our mid-twenties. I noticed petite blonde Sheila Moore, who worked in the TV sales department. She was smart and miles out of my league. Somehow, we clicked. We married at age twenty-five.

I approached the WFAA news department. The News Director turned me down. A major Atlanta radio station offered a job in news and programming. I readily accepted, resigning from WFAA radio. More importantly, Sheila resigned. The WFAA sales manager didn't want to lose her. She understood broadcast sales. Her boss treated her like a daughter.

"What will it take to keep your husband here?" the manager asked.

She knew the answer: "Arch wants to work in TV news."

The door opened. Management transferred me to TV news to keep my wife in sales. Travis Linn, the News Director, didn't exactly welcome me. The front office dumped me in his lap, not knowing he'd turned me down earlier. My big break parked me at the bottom, writing copy and running errands.

One afternoon, our crusty assignment chief, a newsroom legend named Bert Shipp, pulled me aside: "You see all these people in here? Every one of them can cover a wreck or a fire. If you can produce a feature, a little human-interest story, you'll find your place on TV." Bert talked the boss into giving me a chance. He collected oddball ideas. In the months that followed Bert sent me in search of fainting goats, cow callers, 70-year-old soda jerks and a variety of bizarre events.

Thanks to Bert, I found my place. Pretty soon the newsroom looked forward to my features, the kind of light stories that once ended local newscasts.

Then, everything changed. Our new boss, Marty Haag, arrived with carte blanche to make WFAA TV News successful. He tossed out several old timers. Somehow, I survived. The morning Marty shouted, "I want a movie reviewer! Who wants to do it?" I remembered my father's late-night movie habit, and smiled as I raised my hand.

American Graffiti opened that week. The 70s ushered in one of the most exciting eras of film. The arts exploded. The baby boom came of age, as did television and television news. Thanks to my restless father, his love of movies, an embarrassing recital, the lack of a hall pass, an intuitive teacher, a smart wife, and raising my hand, I found my place.

The trick was keeping the job, and managing to change as TV news changed. Some lucky breaks helped, beginning with the summer everything changed in the newsroom of WFAA TV, Dallas.

2
Raising My Hand

WHEN PEOPLE ASK, "HOW'D YOU GET THAT job going to the movies?" I sometimes say, "luck," other times I say, "I raised my hand." Only occasionally I tell them the rest of the story:

WFAA Radio, Dallas

I landed in the WFAA TV newsroom on a fluke. Newly married and ambitious, I was working as a disc jockey for Dallas radio station WFAA AM. I was pretty good as an easy listening announcer: deep voice, sly humor. "… And now *The Carpenters* hammer and saw their way through 'We've Only Just Begun.'"

Not many deejays worked into retirement age. News looked more promising. I sent an audition tape to WSB radio Atlanta. The program director called: "we need someone to work half time as an announcer and half time as a newsman." I told him I wanted to move into news. The offer sounded great. We struck a deal. My wife Sheila and I viewed the move from Texas to Atlanta as a great adventure. I resigned from WFAA radio, and Sheila resigned from WFAA TV sales.

Sheila worked for a talented Sales Manager named

Ward Huey. She developed the ability to price commercials in a complicated system based on audience ratings and availability, sort of the way airlines price tickets today. WFAA TV's ratings often fell below the other stations, but Ward Huey's salesmanship and pricing system made WFAA the most profitable of the major Dallas-Fort Worth channels. Sheila's resignation meant her boss would lose time teaching a newcomer. If he could keep me happy somewhere in Dallas, Sheila would stay, and he wouldn't have to replace her.

Ward Huey pitched a scheme to WFAA TV Station Manager Jack Hauser, another tough cookie who rarely took no for an answer. The two managers summoned Sheila. "What would it take to keep Arch in Dallas?" Hauser barked, "how about if we get him a job in another radio station in town?" Sheila told them I just completed a Master's Degree in Journalism at the University of Texas. She uttered the magic words: "he wants to work in Television news."

The next day, Hauser ordered me to his office. "How'd ya like to work in our TV newsroom?" I paused. Of course, I wanted to work in TV news, but I didn't want to ride into the newsroom on my wife's coattails. Hauser was vague about exactly what I would do. I doubt he gave it any thought. The WFAA news department produced four hours of programming a day. All those local commercial breaks brought in buckets of money. The newsroom kept adding people. I think he figured they'd find something for me to do.

Hauser enthused, "you have a Master's in Journalism. You'll be great." I wanted to succeed on my own. I turned him down. I think it shocked him.

The next day, Hauser commanded me back to his office. "I told Ward you're feelin' bad about gettin' into TV on account of your wife. Don't worry about that. Take the job. This is a golden opportunity."

I interrupted: "I've already accepted the offer in Atlanta."

"Gimme me that guy's number!" Hauser said, "let's call him right now." Hauser got WSB Radio on the line and handed me the phone. I told the manager in Atlanta, I had an offer to join the WFAA TV news department, and remain in Dallas.

The WSB guy was furious. "What do you mean you have another offer?" The phone was on speaker. Hauser cut in, "you listen here. This is a big break for Arch. He's going to work in television news. We're keeping him." The alpha males shouted a little more until Hauser added, "that's it, good bye." I laugh remembering this, although the conversation unnerved me at the time. Hauser grinned and shook my hand. "Welcome to WFAA TV News." In all the confusion, I forgot to ask for a raise.

Sheila seemed to like the way things worked out, possibly relieved her new husband could climb the ranks beyond disc-jockey. A few months earlier she was Sheila Moore, a cute girl standing in a crowd talking and joking in the parking lot after work. A Louisiana native, she worked in New Orleans for a year after college, then moved to Dallas. We talked a little and flirted a little and I said, "hey, how about we get a beer?" Sheila responded, "hey everybody, Arch and I are going to get a beer. Come on." I muttered, "I meant just you and me." She giggled. Off we went with a gang and by the end of the night Sheila and I were a couple.

We split pitchers of beer at a favorite bar or crashed at each other's apartments. We attended weekend parties at "The Dorm," a house rented by four producer/directors where they hosted regular weekend BYOB bashes. We watched the latest movies and dissected them afterward. A favorite restaurant became "our place." Sheila was small, slender, smart, funny, and beautiful. I was lonely, insecure, living in a strange city without many friends. I couldn't live without her. We married in August, 1971. She was 24 and I was 25.

Hauser jumped on an assignment for me. A local minority owned business group challenged WFAA's license. The Federal Communications Commission (FCC) required station owners to renew their broadcast license every few years, demonstrating efforts to serve the community. The A. H. Belo Corporation owned WFAA TV and Radio and *The Dallas Morning News*. Station lawyers fretted over the issue of concentration of media, that is a newspaper also owning a television and radio station in the same city. The lawyers working on the renewal application told Hauser to include a history of WFAA-TV in the application. When Hauser heard "station history," my name flashed in his brain.

"We've got this guy Arch Campbell. He has a Master's degree in Journalism from the University of Texas. He'll write our history!"

Hauser assigned me to work for one of the management's right-hand guys, known as "The Fixer." People at the station whispered about The Fixer, speculating he rummaged through desks and trash cans and spied on employees. I gave friendliness a try, suggesting we have lunch and talk over my assignment.

"I don't go to lunch," he growled, "what do I wanna go to lunch for?" With that he took an apple out of a paper bag. "This is my lunch, an apple."

We did not go to lunch; however, The Fixer found me a desk and phone in a vacant dressing room behind the switchboard. He piled several folders of company archives, mostly press releases and newspaper clippings, on the desk. His parting words to me were, "get going." One day I walked into my office as Ben Barnes, then Lieutenant Governor of Texas, changed his pants to prepare for an interview, a reminder I was working in a dressing room.

Nobody asked, but I love stories about the early days of radio and TV. WFAA was a landmark radio station licensed in the 1920's. When I joined the radio station, I made friends with several old-timers who shared stories about radio's golden age and the early days of live television.

Ward Huey, my wife's boss, began his career on the TV studio floor crew. A live commercial called for a demonstration of a Sears power saw. The crew elected Ward to operate the saw. While the announcer extolled the saw's virtues, Ward started the machine. Sawdust sprayed everywhere, and flew up Ward's nose. Ward started sneezing uncontrollably while the crew doubled over with laughter.

WFAA veterans helped me contact former employees. A senior manager recalled WFAA's first remote broadcast of the Cotton Bowl football game in 1950. The event required days of planning and a bus load of equipment and personnel. A retired program director proudly remembered shooting silent 16 mm film of an airplane crash. After airing the footage on WFAA-TV. He airmailed the film to NBC New York where the footage aired on the network newscast, *The Camel News Caravan.*

Television's arrival after World War II represented a miracle as great as today's Internet or iPhone. Viewers thrilled at any picture received over the air, even a test pattern. WFAA's General Manager, Mike Shapiro, had a vision beyond pictures and a good signal. WFAA was the third station on the air in Dallas-Fort Worth. The FCC consolidated Dallas and Fort Worth into one market, awarding the sought after NBC affiliation to Fort Worth station WBAP. WFAA affiliated with ABC, the least successful of the three networks at the time.

 Mike Shapiro believed strong local programming would overcome a weak network. He starred in his own program, *Let Me Speak to the Manager,* answering viewer questions and complaints, earning him recognition and status. Shapiro encouraged the A.H. Belo Corporation to build Communications Center, a state-of-the-art broadcast facility, in 1961. Locals nicknamed it "Shapiro's Shack."

My report highlighted Shapiro's vision and WFAA's leadership in emerging technology, including installing the earliest videotape machines. WFAA TV produced more news and local programming than any of the other stations in the Dallas-Fort Worth market. I listed numerous awards and citations, and assembled the record of a model station. The history project kept me busy for six weeks. It helped me transition from radio announcer to TV Newsman. I used research skills from college with reporting skills I would need in the newsroom. Not long after I turned in the report, the FCC renewed WFAA TV's license. I moved to the newsroom where my new boss didn't want me.

3
Channel 8 News on the Move

Travis Linn graduated from Harvard on scholarship, a credential that raised eyebrows in 1970s Texas. A brilliant man in his thirties from the small city of Temple, Texas, I found Travis very smart and somewhat distant.

The front office moguls dropped me into the newsroom not knowing Travis didn't want me. When I approached him about a job in radio news a few months earlier, he listened to my tape and grimaced. "I don't like the way you sound," he sniffed. Now I returned, dumped in his lap. Travis told me, "I don't see you working on the air." That felt like a knife in the gut. TV news professionals looked down on radio disc jockeys, some of whom waltzed onto the air as anchors with little or no experience.

"Train this guy, will you?" Travis said as he handed me off to a young producer named Lee Salzberger[1], known in the newsroom as "Newsburger." Lee loved piecing together the 6:00pm news, choosing and arranging stories, placing filmed reports around weather and sports, and making sure everyone met his or her deadline. Lee laughed and shouted and jumped out of his chair like a jack-in-the-box. His rundown and news scripts went to a director, as well as several technicians, and to the news anchors. Lee sat next to the director during the broadcast changing and rearranging stories up to the final second.

Newsburger showed me newsroom writing style and format. Copy covered the right side of the page while tech instructions such as voice over film or sound on film took the left side of the page. Newsburger handed me a few wire stories to rewrite. He read and approved my copy, as well as my typing. Later that afternoon Lee led me to film editing. Fortunately, I had learned the mechanics of splicing film in college. Writers often edited film to go with their copy. Our mission: "write to the visuals." Newsburger told me anchors read aloud at the rate of 120 words a minute. Writers use that formula to match film to copy. Thirty seconds of film covers 60 words, etc.

With those instructions, my job as a writer began. I rewrote wire copy, edited film, and showed up rain or shine from 2:00pm to 11:00pm Sunday through Thursday. One assignment involved news stories from Houston. WFAA and the Houston ABC affiliate KTRK arranged to share stories with the help of Southwest Airlines. Either station could hand a video tape of the days hot story to the flight attendant on the Houston-Dallas shuttle.

As the rookie writer, I would drive the station van to Love Field, walk onto the tarmac, and bounce up the steps to greet the always beautiful young woman who opened the airplane door. She would smile and hand me the tape, which I drove back to the station. Today, video moves in an instant. The Southwest Air hand off was the fastest we had in the 70s.

The WFAA TV newsroom teemed with characters. Herb, an older bachelor writer, previously worked in Democratic U.S. Senator Ralph Yarbrough's office. Herb theatrically slipped into imitations of the creepy Hungarian actor Peter Lorre. "I'm Peter Lorre, I'm Peter Lorre," Herb croaked. His hijinks disgusted his fellow writer Doris, a middle-aged former newspaper crime reporter. Doris would bristle and scream, "shut up! Herb." Doris and Herb's nerves frayed as 10:00pm got closer. Herb amped up the anxiety sputtering, "we're not gonna make it. We're not gonna make it."

Of course, Doris and Herb loved the deadline pressure, writing copy, editing film, assembling the film reel, distributing the evening scripts, and breathlessly charging into the studio with new or updated copy. They also loved egging each other on.

I knew two of the other writers from our days as UT Austin journalism students. John Sparks, Bob Crook, and I bonded during our dinner break at *the Dallas Morning News* cafeteria next door. At the time, *Dallas News* retirees received free meals in the company cafeteria. John and Bob and I consumed the cafeteria's famous chili alongside retired *Dallas News* employees decades older. Many of our dinner mates lived just above the poverty line in the Lawrence Hotel, a seedy building nearby. Most of them remembered the Great Depression, when a free meal represented a valuable perk.

Bert Shipp fit the bill as the quintessential assignment chief. A newsroom legend, Bert covered the Kennedy Assassination in 1963. Rumor had him possessing a top-secret copy of the Zapruder assassination film. Bert intercepted Abraham Zapruder when he walked into the station November 22, 1963, with his 8mm home movie footage of the motorcade. Zapruder, brought to the station by Secret Service agents, thought the station could process the film. WFAA processed 16mm, not 8mm. Bert called the local Kodak chief and arranged for urgent processing. The camera Bert used the day of the assassination, a 16mm silent wind-up Bell and Howell, has a prominent place in the Sixth Floor Museum next to the assassination site.

Bert Shipp—WFAA-TV

Bert smoked a pack of Salem Cigarettes daily, lining the butts upright on a shelf above his desk. He growled orders in a cloud of smoke. Sometimes, he wandered in late at night rip-roaring drunk after roaming the city in a crew car, looking for wrecks and fires. Sending a reporter out on a hot crime story, Bert would scream, "ask him if he feared for his life."[2] Shipp published a hilarious memoir *Details at Ten* recounting his adventures during the Kennedy assassination, his coverage of Ross Perot's mission to save American POWS in Vietnam, and his exclusive interview with the Beatles in 1964 when he barged into the group's dressing room with a help of a friendly security guard.

Bert frightened me. My fear prevented me seeing his sense of humor. He assigned a young woman the job of reporting on a pet steer that liked to watch our newscast. I still remember the shots of the owner leading the steer into his house and the TV room in time for the 6:00pm Channel 8 News. The young woman misidentified the steer's gender (steers are castrated cattle) and left the business after much teasing.

When Bert told me to pursue features it gave me the courage to go back to Travis Linn. "How about letting me do some feature stories?" Travis wasn't impressed. "I need you on your writing shift." Then he pivoted: "If you want to film a story on your own time, I'll look at it."

Bert kept a thick file of oddball stories, some jotted down on envelopes, others clipped from newspapers. He handed me a clipping about an elderly man working behind the soda fountain of the Highland Park Pharmacy.

"See what you can do with this, Hoss." Everyone was "Hoss" to Bert, possibly a reference to the classic TV western *Bonanza*. Bert would further explain I might be Hoss but he was "The Stallion." Bert gave me more good advice. "No matter what the story, start with a strong open, use sound, and finish with something memorable."

The old soda-jerk agreed to an interview. The Highland Park Pharmacy hadn't changed much since the 1920s.

I put a script together before filming as a planning exercise. Bert suggested I wrap the story sucking the final drops of an ice cream soda with a loud gurgling sound. A friendly film editor helped assemble the piece. Travis watched the finished work and to the surprise of both of us gave it his ok.

Newsburger said he only had space for the anchorman's commentary or my feature. The anchorman said, "run the feature." At the end of the newscast, I left the newsroom, and watched in an empty office. The anchorman came on when it finished and said, "Arch Campbell does good features." His ad lib made my career possible.

That ad lib changed Travis Linn's opinion. Soon Travis was saying, "I want you to be my Charles Kuralt," referring to the CBS reporter whose *On the Road* features often concluded the *CBS Evening News*. Bert's files and a few of my own ideas led to stories about an old man and his model railroad, an interview with David Guion, who transcribed the folk song "Home on the Range," and a feature on a farmer who claimed his goats fainted whenever they heard a loud noise. I banged and chased and of course the goats didn't faint which made an even better story. A year and a half after landing unwanted in his newsroom, Travis promoted me to full-time feature reporter. The move came with the raise I forgot to ask for when I transferred to news: $207.50 a week.

My big break at WFAA TV survived Sheila's departure for a better job in the advertising department of a Dallas Insurance company. Fortunately, Ward Huey, who engineered my move into the newsroom, didn't transfer his hurt feelings to me.

The WFAA newsroom, full of talented, ambitious performers, produced enough drama for several novels. A few years before I started, Murphy Martin returned to Dallas as anchorman after five years with ABC in New York. A big Irishman with a deep voice and dominating presence, Murphy signed off each night with, "that's my time, thank you for yours." He gave WFAA a commanding, old school, network news presence. Paired with longtime newsman Bob Gooding, the two anchors often won the Dallas-Fort Worth news ratings.[3]

Murphy caught the attention of Ross Perot while covering one of Perot's early missions to negotiate information on American POWs in Vietnam. Perot convinced the anchorman to leave Channel 8 and work for Perot's United We Stand organization. Murphy's departure in January, 1970, threw the newscast into turmoil.

Travis tried several anchor teams without much success. Ultimately, he elevated a feisty newsman named Don Harris, host of the morning show, to co-anchor the 6:00pm and 10:00pm news.

Sports anchor Verne Lundquist and weatherman Dale Milford added pizzazz to the 6:00pm news. Lundquist would leave in a few years for CBS Sports. Milford sometimes discussed his political philosophy leading into his weather. A candidate for the Democratic nomination for Congress accused Milford of using his position to promote an undeclared candidacy. Milford resigned the next day, and announced for Congress. Milford won the race for Congress in November, 1972, and served three terms. His departure left WFAA without an established weatherman.

Murphy Martin returned to WFAA from United We Stand in 1972. Murphy's third stint didn't increase the ratings. The team of Murphy Martin and Don Harris lacked chemistry. Harris loved to tweak the Dallas establishment.

Murphy Martin identified with the Dallas establishment and the moguls in Ross Perot's circle.

Don Harris preferred reporting to anchoring. He negotiated a special report unit. His investigative pieces aired in prime time "News 8 Reports" as well as on the 6:00pm and 10:00pm news. One story showed the ease of smuggling drugs across the Mexican border. When Delta Airlines installed the first metal detector at the Dallas airport, Love Field, Harris arrived with a camera crew.

Harris brought two newsroom employees with him, one carrying a shopping bag with a .38 taped to the bottom, the firing pin removed. The other hid a Derringer in a shoulder bag, again, with the firing pin removed. They breezed through without setting off the alarm. The report infuriated and embarrassed Delta.[4]

Don Harris wrote and delivered commentaries on subjects including open housing, enraging the Dallas establishment. Although Don Harris loved controversy, he did not love defending his work to management. During one of these sessions Harris copied the inscription chiseled onto the edifice of the Dallas News Building, owners of WFAA-TV. He shouted the words at his bosses:

> "BUILD THE NEWS UPON THE ROCK OF TRUTH AND RIGHTEOUSNESS. CONDUCT IT ALWAYS UPON THE LINES OF FAIRNESS AND INTEGRITY. ACKNOWLEDGE THE RIGHT OF PEOPLE TO GET FROM THE NEWSPAPER BOTH SIDES OF EVERY IMPORTANT QUESTION."

Don Harris' recitation did not win the day. Not long after the encounter, Harris departed for KNBC-TV in Los Angeles. A few years later, he joined NBC News where he reported on the fall of Vietnam, escaping from the American Embassy in one of the last helicopters. In November, 1978, Don Harris traveled to Jonestown in Guyana with California Congressman Leo Ryan to investigate Jim Jones' religious cult. Jones' supporters shot and killed Harris and Congressman Ryan and several others as they were boarding an airplane to return to Los Angeles. Later that day, Jim Jones massacred his followers instructing them to drink Kool Aid laced with poison. 918 people, including Don Harris, died that day. Jones was found dead of a gunshot to the head.

Don Harris was the anchorman who said, "run the Feature," and ad-libbed, "Arch Campbell does good features," after my first story. He showed kindness to a rookie trying to move forward. I wince when I hear the phrase, "drink the Kool-Aid," out of respect for Don Harris.

We signed off our reports, "Channel 8 News on the Move." "On the Move" also described the turmoil in our newsroom. The soap opera of revolving anchormen and off the air drama caught up with Travis Linn. In the summer of 1973, Travis called a newsroom meeting to announce his resignation. "I can't tell you where I am going at this time, I can only tell you I plan to work in education." Travis joined the Dallas Community College District as head of the Instructional Television Center. Three years later, CBS News hired Travis to head their new Dallas bureau.

A few days later, we gathered to hear from our new boss, Marty Haag, coming from the CBS owned station in New York City. To calm our fears Marty said, "I'm not coming in here with a machete."

And then he fired half the staff.

4
Cover the Arts

Marty Haag—WFAA-TV

MARTY HAAG HIT the newsroom like a tornado. A big guy in his late 30s, I can still see him in motion: talking, yelling, screaming. His career matched his whirlwind nature. He wrote and produced for NBC in New York. He earned a promotion to News Director of the NBC owned station in Cleveland. He moved on to L.A. and made it back to New York as assistant News Director of WCBS-TV. He had roots in Dallas, beginning his career as a reporter for *The Dallas Morning News*. I think his wife came from Dallas and didn't like New York. To please her, Marty took the job at WFAA.

Station management introduced Marty at a mass meeting in production studio A, the largest at the station. The firing began the next week. I saw Marty fire a guy walking down the hall. The guy thought Marty was joking and started laughing. Marty doubled down, screaming, "you're fired!" Twice as loud. The rest of us got the message.

A bunch of new people joined the staff. Marty put us on a beat system. One reporter would cover crime, another education or government or consumer affairs. My beat was features, and thanks to raising my hand, movies.

One dramatic afternoon, Marty stormed into the newsroom. Our furious typewriter pounding stopped.

Red-faced, Marty screamed, "I have fired Murphy Martin. I don't wanna hear any of you gossiping about it." With that, he stomped into his office. The move shook the newsroom. Murphy had worked for a national network. Murphy possessed the highest name recognition in Dallas. The shocking move paved the way for Marty to pair Tracy Rowlett, a new hire from Oklahoma City, with Iola Johnson, a recently hired charismatic African American woman from Tucson, Arizona. Tracy Rowlett and Iola Johnson worked together for a dozen years, forming a dream team few thought possible.

One morning Marty looked at me and said, "Arch, you now cover not just movies, but also, the arts!" He steered me into his office and started reading a letter from a viewer who liked my movie reviews. He quoted her, "the arts deserve a daily segment on the news, the same as sports and weather." Haag looked me in the eye and ordered: "Arch, get out there and dig up stories about the arts. Go to it!"

Marty Haag gave me the keys to the coolest job in local TV. In the 1970s, movies pushed the envelope, telling stories and showing things you couldn't see on TV. If you missed a movie in first run, years passed before it made it to TV. My new assignment licensed me to recommend what's good. How great is that?

The 70's arrived on the heels of Mike Nichol's *The Graduate* (1967) in which Dustin Hoffman as Benjamin Braddock returns to his parent's affluent home with a college degree and no direction. His parent's friend, the bored housewife Mrs. Robinson, seduces him. The plot thickens when Benjamin falls in love with Mrs. Robinson's daughter. *The Graduate* defined movies as the creative voice of my generation.

An upcoming group of young directors launched the movies of the 70's. Francis Ford Coppola created *The Godfather, Godfather Part Two* and *Apocalypse Now*. Martin Scorsese added *Mean Streets, Alice Doesn't Live Here Any More,* and *Taxi Driver* to the classics list. Steven Spielberg invented the summer blockbuster with *Jaws* in 1975, and George Lucas followed *American Graffiti* with *Star Wars*, arguably the most important series of the 20th century. 1973 and 74 produced some timeless classics, including *The Exorcist, Paper Moon, Chinatown, The Sting, Serpico, Day for Night,* and *Blazing Saddles.*

When Marty Haag told me to cover the arts, he expanded my universe. I found stories in the local theater community. The Dallas Theater Center created a sensation on the tenth anniversary of the Kennedy assassination with *Jack Ruby: All American Boy.* The play recalled Jack Ruby's world of strip clubs and characters and 1963 underground Dallas. A breathtaking scene recreated Ruby shooting Lee Harvey Oswald in slow motion. I produced a feature, interviewing Dallas wise guys who knew Jack Ruby, including Artie Brooks, the emcee of Ruby's Carousel Club.

Director Brian DePalma came to Dallas to film *Phantom of the Paradise*, his remake of *Phantom of the Opera*. I received permission to bring a camera crew and watch DePalma film inside an abandoned downtown theater. I observed bright lights, a lot of running around, and a couple of scenes that made it into the film.

Braniff Airlines hired Alexander Calder, famous for his modern art mobiles, to paint an original design on a DC 8 jetliner. Braniff's fleet came in psychedelic colors—pink, blue, and green. The ad agency, Wells Rich Green, recommended the outrageous paint to enhance the once stodgy airline's image. Now, a Braniff jet would fly with an original Calder on the fuselage.

I arrived with a cameraman at Love Field to a hangar full of reporters. The elderly Calder climbed up a scaffold. Workers handed him a spray gun. He began blasting red paint on an unvarnished jet, laying down a background for his design. The wind blows in Dallas. I looked at the guy next to me. His white shirt was turning pink. The cheap grey suit I put on that morning was turning red. As Calder worked the spray gun, a mist of red paint fell on all of us watching.

Calder climbed down and started wandering around. I trotted over with my microphone and blurted, "how do you like painting an airplane?" He answered with a one-word grunt, barely acknowledging my dumb question. That night I told viewers Calder painted not only the airplane but also most of the reporters watching him.

The Metropolitan Opera arrived in Dallas. I received permission to film a rehearsal and attended Joan Sutherland's performance of Offenbach's *The Tales of Hoffman*. On the air, I related the story of the opera fan who hollered, "yahoo" rather than, "bravo" with the other opera fans during the performance. Joan Sutherland and the cast bowed toward him during their curtain calls looking highly amused.

In addition to my arts reporting, Marty wanted stories that captured local color, much as Charles Kuralt captured rural America in his *On the Road* series. I roamed the little towns surrounding Dallas and Fort Worth during a time Texas was transforming from a rural state to a cluster of urban centers.

The WFAA Fort Worth bureau told me about an old timer who didn't own a car, choosing instead to travel by horseback. My film footage of the elderly gentleman navigating city traffic on a horse made viewers smile. That day I heard about a blacksmith, working under a giant oak similar to the chestnut tree in the poem, whom I featured in a news segment.

A viewer called to report a gathering of six generations in one family. I rushed to a Dallas nursing home and lined up the family's five women and a newborn. I interviewed the mothers in order. When I got to the eldest, the Great-Great-Great-Grandmother I asked, "what is it about your family that makes everyone run off and get married?" The almost 100-year old woman replied, "I didn't run. I walked."

Every night at six, the newsroom gathered in front of three black and white 19-inch TV sets to watch our news and the competition. We cheered each other's work, like family.

In November 1973, I traveled with a cameraman by private plane to Terlingua, Texas for the annual Terlingua chili cook off. The event began a few years earlier as a goof, inspired by *Dallas Morning News* writer Frank X. Tolbert's columns about Texas chili. By 1973, the chili cook-off looked like a beer drinker's Woodstock. In my chili and beer fueled haze, I somehow identified the contest winner and other assorted characters present. The Chili Appreciation Society International has kept the Terlingua chili cook off going ever since.

I traveled to Ponder, Texas, the location of the Ranchman's Café, a little spot profiled in *The Dallas Morning News*. When you ordered a steak, the waitress fired up a power saw, cut a T-Bone off a side of beef, and cooked it. The menu offered meat, potatoes, salad, and pie. They operated with water from a well, and no public restroom. I know it's hard to believe, and certainly not legal today, but I swear: in 1973, the Ranchman's Café did not have a restroom. None of the reports on the Ranchman's Café mentioned this. I asked the owner about the lack of facilities. She told me: "if you have to go, you can go to the barn, or go down to the filling station about a mile down the road."

The story finished with a shot of me walking out of the café, turning down the dusty road out of town. In voice over I signed off, "this is Arch Campbell, Channel 8 News, looking for that filling station, about a mile down the road." The anchor team howled. I didn't know it then, but this corny feature would propel me all the way east to Washington, D.C.

5
The Road to Washington

With TV commercial star Rodney Allen Rippey, 1974

MY OLD BOSS—TRAVIS LINN—INVITED ME to breakfast at the Fairmont Hotel. His call, several months after he left WFAA, surprised me. Travis possessed a quiet introspective nature, the opposite of Marty Haag. That morning, he looked over his scrambled eggs and said, "they're not paying you what you're worth. You need to move to a bigger station in a bigger city."

I thought about saying, "why didn't YOU pay me more?" But I didn't. After all, Travis changed his mind, gave me a break and upped me from writer to reporter. I don't know what caused him to offer that advice. I decided to take it as a signal to think bigger. The WFAA newsroom churned through an alarming number of people. Travis told me one of his best friends ran WGN-TV news in Chicago. A few weeks later, I took two weeks off.

I produced a series of reports on Amtrak when passenger service returned to Dallas after a five-year hiatus.

The assignment renewed my love of trains. I booked my wife and me on the *Southern Crescent* passenger train from New Orleans to Washington, D.C. We rode Amtrak to New York, Chicago, and back to Fort Worth.

I sent tapes to New York and D.C. without much success. I cooled my heels in the lobby of WTTG-TV in Washington without an appointment. The News Director refused to see me. In New York, a kindly gentleman at NBC showed me around the network newsroom but promised nothing. I sent a tape to an executive at ABC not knowing he worked in radio instead of TV and that he hated TV. When I delivered my TV tape, he blew a gasket, screaming: "This is a TV Tape!" He threw me out of his office.

Travis' friend, the WGN News Director, gave me a tour, pointing out his long-time employees. "That guy's been here thirty years and the guy over there twenty-five and this one a mere twenty-two years. None of them plan to leave. Thanks for coming in, but we won't have an opening until one of these guys die."

Back in Dallas, I marched into Marty Haag's office. "Marty, I'm under paid. I deserve a raise." Instead of throwing me out, Marty nodded and said he'd get back to me. A few days later he handed me a two-year contract for $15,000 a year. The contract called for thirteen-week cycles. The station could fire me at the end of any cycle. I could resign if I gave thirteen weeks' notice. I signed, smiled, and shook Marty's hand.

Marty Haag's encouragement made me a better reporter. The opportunity to report allowed me to show my true self as I met quirky people, went to oddball places, and found interesting things.

I rode the first airplane to land in the new D-FW Airport January 13, 1974. My cameraman and I flew to Little Rock and boarded the American Airlines jet scheduled to arrive a minute after midnight. Chaos broke out as the plane touched down. Passengers unbuckled and rushed the exit door, desperate to win the honor of first passenger to step in the new facility. My cameraman and I elbowed our way in the thick of it, so we could capture film of the first passenger, recently identified as husband and wife J.W. Parker and Patricia Allen. I remember their athletic efforts elbowing their way off the plane.

For the series on Amtrak, I rode from Chicago to Fort Worth, roaming the train and exploring the return of rail transportation. I covered the problems of aging in America in a five-part series. Marty assigned me to fill in for the morning show host on his two-week vacation. I loved the early morning free-wheeling ninety-minute live program. My new contract and the opportunities coming my way made WFAA feel like home.

Then, everything changed.

I was taking a break in the morning show office. A news aide shouted something about a long-distance call for me. She said a guy named Bruce MacDonell in Los Angeles was on the line. I said, "I don't know any Bruce MacDonell." She held the phone to her ear and said, "he says you want to take this call."

Bruce MacDonell ran the Special Projects unit for KNBC, Los Angeles. Don Harris, the WFAA-TV anchorman who liked my work, left Dallas for KNBC-TV, and went to work for Bruce. NBC was promoting Bruce to Washington, D.C. to shake up WRC-TV News. Bruce asked Harris if he knew any offbeat reporters. Harris mentioned me, specifically the story on The Ranchman's Café. Bruce asked for a tape including that piece. A week later he called back offering a three-year contract: $23,000 the first year, $25,000 the second, and $27,000 the third. NBC would pay for my move to Washington, D.C., and assign me to their local owned station WRC-TV.

At that time, networks could own a limit of five VHS (channels 2 through 13) stations. ABC, CBS, and NBC all owned stations in New York, Chicago, and L.A. ABC also owned a station in Detroit and San Francisco, CBS in Philadelphia and St. Louis, NBC in Cleveland and Washington, D.C. Landing in one of those fifteen owned and operated facilities put a reporter in the major leagues.

Marty Haag took the news stoically. Ward Huey, the station manager who engineered my move from radio to TV news, called me into his office. He told me he wanted me to stay and would come close to the offer. "How close?" I asked. The answer didn't sound close enough. The next day I wrote a resignation letter, giving thirteen weeks-notice per my contract. I would leave in late September, 1974. I kept working without incident. In fact, I produced some of my best work during those final 13 weeks. To his everlasting credit, Marty Haag told me, "that's a big station. You can do things there you can't do here." I still marvel at Haag's kindness and generosity.

Suzie Humphreys, the actress who co-hosted the morning show *News 8 Etc.* scheduled a series of stories in Ruidoso, New Mexico. The resort community wanted to promote a new million-dollar quarter-horse race, as well as other aspects of the area. Susie, reeling from multiple changes in her professional and personal life, canceled at the last minute. Bert Shipp grew up in New Mexico and, who knows, might have had a connection to the big horse race. He told Marty to send me.

A privately owned Cessna transported a cameraman and me five hundred miles to New Mexico. We left Dallas on a blistering hot 100-degree day. When we set down in the Sierra Blanca mountains, the thermometer rested in the 70's.

We traveled to Ruidoso Downs and filmed preparations for the big race.

We gained entry to the Inn of the Mountain Gods, a resort/casino under construction on the Apache reservation, one of the first gambling facilities to open on reservation land. I interviewed the Chief of the Apache nation about his idea to open a casino.

As part of this trip, I profiled the artist Peter Hurd, a Western landscape painter and student of N.C. Wyeth. Hurd won the commission to paint the official portrait of President Lyndon B. Johnson in 1967. For reasons few understand, Johnson hated the finished portrait, calling it "the ugliest thing I ever saw." Hurd donated the work to the National Portrait Gallery where it enjoys a position of prominence today.

My cameraman and I filmed Peter Hurd in his studio, watching the artist at work. We shared dinner some miles away at a beloved restaurant named for and located on Coe Ranch. This gentle artist treated my cameraman and me as old friends. He laughed recounting LBJ's dislike of his portrait.

I fondly remember those days in the beautiful New Mexico mountains and desert.

Whenever I visit the National Portrait Gallery, I stop to admire Hurd's portrait of President Johnson, which I do not find ugly.

Back in Dallas as my departure date grew closer, my friend Bob Crook came over to my desk. "Let's go out front a minute." We stepped into a sparkling September day. "Look at that sky," Crook said. With mischief in his eyes he exclaimed, "you'll never see a sky like that up East. You'll be sorry you left Texas!" Crook laughed, and I laughed, trying to ignore the little voice expressing doubt inside my head.

Leaving Texas, I didn't expect the emotional pull of my home state. When I traveled to the little towns around

Dallas and Fort Worth for human interest stories, I remembered my father talking about his father and uncle and his grandmother's stories of ranch life in West Texas. My Texas roots go back five generations.

My wife and I collected a circle of unique friends. One of my favorites lived in a mansion on Swiss Avenue, a once grand boulevard fallen into disrepair. I met her as the neighborhood applied for historic preservation status. I produced several stories on the effort to save the neglected estates of the Swiss Avenue Historic District.

Mary Ellen Bendtson moved to Dallas in the 1930's after modeling in New York.

She told lusty stories of youthful pursuits: dating oilman Sid Richardson, and posing for the art deco statues on the grounds of Fair Park, site of the 1936 Texas Centennial celebration. She and her husband Christian, who claimed to be a Danish Count, took Sheila and me under their wing, inviting us to their crumbling Swiss Avenue palace for drinks. Christian would match Mary Ellen's outrageous stories, dropping sentences such as, "when I was in Paris running around acting crazy with Scott and Zelda." Their living room held two baby grands and a mirror the size of a garage door.

We attended parties with the Bendtsons and their friends. Wide-eyed, I watched distinguished adults consume stunning amounts of alcohol. I found respected citizens passed out on various couches and beds.

Mary Ellen encouraged Sheila and me to buy a house on Swiss Avenue. We found a kindly real estate agent who specialized in the area. We looked at several run-down mansions at the cut rate price of around $50,000. The week I accepted the WRC offer, the agent called with news of an owner ready to make a deal: $45,000 for a four-bedroom, three-bathroom brick and stone mansion, with a garage apartment on Swiss Avenue. I told her we were leaving town. The house is worth millions today.

Dallas represented Texas in all its contradictions. Rednecks mixed with sophisticates. One of the most enlightened men in America, Stanley Marcus, oversaw Neiman Marcus, one of the world's most luxurious department stores. He worked in harmony on community issues with stone faced conservatives. They shared a love for the city and the state. WFAA TV gave me access to this potpourri. Because I appeared on television, people knew my name, watched my reports, laughed at my jokes, and took my phone calls. Now, I would leave. Our friends threw us a little farewell surprise party. I felt a knot in my stomach.

The morning in September, 1974, we set out for Washington, I carefully placed most of my clothes on a hanging bar stretched across the back seat. We pulled out of our driveway. The car hit a bump. My clothes fell in a heap. I stopped, and screamed, "this is a sign! We're not supposed to leave!!" My wife was not about to give up this adventure. "Shut up and drive!" she yelled. We accelerated up the Interstate 30 ramp and headed east.

Marty Haag remained at WFAA as News Director from 1973 to 1989. His energetic newsroom and a boost in ABC's prime time ratings made WFAA the most watched and ultimately dominant Dallas-Fort Worth news organization for a generation. WFAA's parent company promoted Haag to Senior Vice-President of News Operations, where he oversaw up to 20 stations as well as two regional 24-hour cable news operations. Marty Haag retired in 2000, receiving the broadcast industry's highest honor, the George Foster Peabody Award for lifetime achievement. He taught journalism at Southern Methodist University and worked as a consultant. He died of a stroke January 20, 2004.

Travis Linn opened the CBS News Dallas bureau in 1976. In the 1980's he moved to the University of Nevada-Reno where he served as Dean of the Journalism school for twenty years. He died in 2004, age 64, in Reno, Nevada.

The A.H. Belo Corporation, owner of WFAA-TV, expanded into a major television group of as many as twenty stations. A.H. Belo sold their television properties to Gannett Corporation in 2013. In 2019 *The Dallas Morning News* sold their newspaper headquarters, the landmark building next to the WFAA studios, with the quote Don Harris used for arguments sake on the front. A builder is considering converting the space to condos or offices. I wonder how it will feel to walk into your apartment beneath

BUILD THE NEWS UPON THE ROCK
OF TRUTH AND RIGHTEOUSNESS etc.,

Mary Ellen Bendtsen died in 2005, age 88. Her will touched off a spectacular legal drama over ownership of her mansion on Swiss Avenue. Two middle aged male antique dealers cultivated a friendship. In return for what they described as caretaking, they expected Mrs. Bendtsen to deed the house to them, and videotaped her signing a will giving them her mansion on her death. Mary Ellen's daughter sued for elder abuse. A lengthy court case ruled the will invalid.

A series in *The Dallas Morning News* described this once-fascinating personality in her final days wandering the decayed unheated rooms of her mansion, staring at dusty portraits of her as a stunning young beauty. The court case and a fire kept the mansion empty for a decade. In recent years, a wealthy businessman bought 4949 Swiss Avenue and restored the home to its original grandeur. Locals refer to the former Bendtsen home as "The Queen of Swiss Avenue." Some say Mary Ellen haunts the property. I believe it.

WASHINGTON, D.C.

6
Eyewitness News

A GENIUS NAMED AL PRIMO MADE TV NEWS cool when he created the *Eyewitness News* format. In the early years of television, most stations presented local news as a fifteen-minute program: News, Weather, and Sports. The local news led in to fifteen minutes of network news. In 1963, CBS expanded the *CBS Evening News* to thirty minutes. NBC followed. The half hour network newscasts encouraged local stations to expand to a half hour as well.

In the late 1960s, Al Primo worked as News Director of KYW-TV Philadelphia. He noticed the union contract allowed a writer to appear on air if he or she read copy they wrote. Primo called in his writers and asked about their interests. Based on their answers, he assigned them "beats" much like a newspaper. One KYW writer covered city hall, another education board events, or museum openings. Beat reporters developed sources and contacts over time. The writer/reporters would return to the station, write a story, and appear on set talking about their report with the news anchor. The exchanges became known as 'Happy Talk." The format upended the formal radio style presentations of previous years.

Eyewitness News reports made space for unpredictable fun ad libs.

Primo perfected his formula at New York station WABC-TV. Soon *Eyewitness News* dominated New York television, making tons of money as ratings skyrocketed. Channel 7 *Eyewitness News* featured men and women from diverse backgrounds (Geraldo Rivera, Rose Ann Scarmadella, Kaity Tong). The reporters looked and talked like New

Yorkers. My former boss Marty Haag made similar moves at WFAA, including a beat system and a diverse team.

Eyewitness News made NBC local newscasts look stodgy. The competition cut into NBC owned station ratings and profits. NBC needed to catch up. They planned to re-brand their five owned station newscasts as *The News Center*. Stations would receive new sets, new anchors and reporters and create unique segments. The plan paved the way for my job.

My new boss, Bruce MacDonell, wanted to shock stuffy Washington, D.C. He arrived with a reel of about a hundred outrageous stories produced at KNBC Los Angeles. He would rerun them on WRC, seeding the newscast with features about calendar girls, trained bears, and car salesmen.

A wiry wisecracking guy, Bruce MacDonell peppered his conversations with "asshole," "jackass," and "bonehead." The week I arrived, Bruce and I talked about Don Harris, the anchor who recommended me, and my story at the café without a restroom.

Bruce called me "Starchy" and informed me I would fill the role of resident zany. When the revamped news began in a few months, I would appear every other day, alternating with human interest reporter Mary Ann Maskery.[5] We would both share a cameraman assigned to a newly created special projects unit. In Dallas, Marty Haag expected reporters to produce two stories a day. Bruce laid out a slower pace which he assumed would produce higher quality work.

WRC News lacked the zip we had at WFAA. The anchors sat behind a collection of stainless-steel cylinders. Bruce said they looked like garbage cans.

The Moog synthesizer opening music sounded like burping. Co-anchor Jim Vance sported a wide screen Afro.

His partner, Glenn Rinker, resembled an airline pilot. Together they looked like a street dude and a country club banker. Reporters never appeared on set, glimpsed only in their filmed stories.

Even more unusual, a corny comedian reported the weather. Willard Scott went by "Willard!" with an exclamation mark. Middle aged and balding, Willard! didn't look like the kind of hipster who would attract a new generation. The sports anchor, Bud Katz, called himself "the Old Buckeye." Bruce MacDonell fired Katz his first week as News Director.

"Don't pay any attention to what you see on the air," Bruce said, "I'm going to clean house." WRC aired a half hour newscast from 6:00pm to 6:30pm and a second thirty minutes from 7:00pm to 7:30pm with *NBC Nightly News* sandwiched in between. The other stations produced better newscasts.

Channel 9 WTOP (owned by The *Washington Post*) dominated the ratings. The station adapted the *Eyewitness News* format under the direction of Jim Snyder, a visionary leader hired as Vice President of News in 1968. Snyder paired Max Robinson, one of the first black anchormen in D.C., with Gordon Peterson, a former Marine who began his Washington career reporting for WTOP radio as well as television. Robinson possessed a commanding voice filled with authority and poise. Peterson's Marine bearing gave him presence and integrity. The two men synced.

Jim Snyder

Ironically, Robinson worked at WRC for three years before joining *Eyewitness News*.

A longtime beloved weather anchor named Louie Allen handled weather. The anchor team rounded with one of the most unusual talents in broadcasting: Warner Wolfe, a sports savant whose recall of trivia and statistics made him a star on a call-in-sports show on WTOP radio. Wolfe easily transitioned to television. He didn't know how to type, therefore worked with a hand written outline. When Warner wanted tape in his segment he cued the director with the phrase, "let's go to the videotape." The phrase became Warner Wolfe's trademark.

Jim Snyder possessed an extraordinary sense of talent. He gave prominent anchor posts to J.C. Hayward, a Howard University graduate with a big personality and the ability to thread the needle between serious news and fun. Snyder hired Maureen Bunyan as a reporter and weekend anchor, promoting her to lead co-anchor when the ABC network hired Max Robinson. Channel 9's movie reviewer, Davey Marlin Jones, appeared on set with long hair and a hat, sometimes performing magic tricks while reviewing. Henry Tenenbaum held down the last spot in the news, producing creative funny human-interest stories. Within a few months, Henry Tenenbaum became one of the best-known personalities in Washington.

Other legendary presences at WTOP included veteran crime reporter Mike Buchannan, former *Washington Daily News* reporter Pat Collins, Andrea Mitchell, Susan King[6] and many others. I watched Channel 9 and liked them much better than Channel 4, the station where I worked. Channel 9 produced a compelling, habit-forming daily broadcast.

The competition also included WMAL Channel 7, an ABC affiliate owned by *The Washington Star*. Channel 7

News looked young and hip in the style of the emerging ABC network. Fred Thomas, a wry erudite African American, led a team of young attractive people. Ed Tierney provided memorable features. WMAL's special project unit headed by Paul and Holly Fine dominated the local Emmy awards.[7]

As ABC's prime time ratings increased, WMAL TV seemed on the cusp of overtaking Channel 9, but never did.

Independent station WTTG, Channel 5's 10:00pm News attracted an audience wanting news earlier in the evening. Handsome D.C. native Maury Povich anchored. Well known as the son of revered *Washington Post* sports writer Shirley Povich, Maury oozed confidence. A phrase used to describe anchor Tom Snyder also applied to Maury. He could strut sitting down.

Bruce MacDonell was convinced he could beat the competition. "Those boneheads are a bunch of assholes," Bruce said, "I'm gonna blow 'em off the map."

7
Finding My Place

Almost everyone at NBC belonged to a union: engineers, editors, photographers, writers, and on the air talent. I could not appear on air until I joined AFTRA, the American Federation of Television and Radio Artists. AFTRA did not come cheap. I think it cost me $500 to join. Given the jump in salary, I didn't mind. Over the years I appreciated the benefits of union membership.

Houses cost twice what they cost in Dallas. For $62,000 my wife and I settled on a run down 1930's side hall colonial in Chevy Chase, D.C. The radiators creaked, the kitchen sink leaked, and the doorbell screeched. At least it was close to the station and the neighborhood had giant trees and quirky neighbors.

At work, I learned a reporter could not offer to carry equipment, or do anything other than report. Three men (and they were all men) made up a film crew: camera, sound, and lights. In Dallas, I worked with a one-man crew. The two of us improvised, like jazz musicians. Working with the big union crew slowed the process and worked against spontaneity.

NBC film crews alternated assignments between local and network. Some of the older guys worked as newsreel photographers in the 40s and 50s.[8] Many of them covered House or Senate hearings. Those crews arrived at a hearing room early so the light man could hang lights. The cameraman set up a tripod and rolled until the film ran out. The sound man sat in a chair and often fell asleep.

At age 28, hired to produce zany features, I was working with men more than twice my age. The crews generally were good sports, and rarely resisted an idea. However, moving around with three men proved cumbersome. When I asked to film a stand-up, the light man set up a light and took a reading. The sound man performed an audio test and wired a microphone to my shirt. The cameraman set his tripod. For a feature on a Friday night fire station bingo game, the light man insisted on hanging dozens of floodlights, turning the place into a blinding sound stage, and of course, intruding on anything natural.

WRC News shared a large open space with NBC network news. The local newsroom carpet, stained and worn, joined the network carpet, clean and plush. The border between the two carpets formed a literal line of demarcation. Local news people jumped and yelled as they worked. Network news-people maintained decorum as they quietly read *The Washington Post* or afternoon *Star* cover to cover.

Walking the halls, I encountered some of the biggest names at NBC News, including Tom Pettit and Carl Stern. One day in the men's room, David Brinkley stood at the urinal next to mine. I stammered something like, "great kidneys move alike." Brinkley ignored my stupid comment.

Adding to the culture clash, local news people worked at a communal baby blue Formica counter top. A producer named David Nuell would stand on the counter and drop his pants to get our attention. Ultimately the massive piece cracked when someone jumped on it to yell something.

Betty Endicott ran the WRC assignment desk. Energetic, funny, and a trailblazing woman in broadcasting,[9] Betty handed me a folder full of ideas left behind by a former News Director. A few days later she assigned me a feature on a ballroom dancing class at Catholic University taught by Vic Daumit, the old-style pomade haired owner of the Vic Daumit dance studio. In 1974, most students were protesting or blasting rock music in their dorm rooms.

Washington, D.C.

It looked unusual to see long haired kids learning the box step. The crew managed to dance around me as Vic's assistant Mauve gave me instruction. For the big finish I stepped on her foot. Bruce thought this was funny and I seemed to be off and running.

I caught an assignment every few days. Betty sent me out to report on the high cost of Halloween. On Halloween night, Bruce told me to take a video crew and go trick or treating at 11 pm news anchorman Glenn Rinker's house. His wife opened the door and snapped, "shut that camera off! I don't trust the media!" And then slammed the door in my face.[10] When the encounter aired on the news that night, Rinker, the dignified airline pilot looking newsman, seemed genuinely surprised as he said, "hey! That's MY house."

I made the front page of the Style Section of The *Washington Post* November 23, 1974. Betty Endicott received a press release from the St. Andrews society announcing Ian Campbell, Duke of Argyll and leader of the Clan Campbell, would attend their Tartan Ball, and was available for interviews.

I arrived with my large crew at a hotel reception filled with upper class Scots drinking single malt whiskey. The Duke looked uncomfortable. I began an interview in which, trying to build a zany image, I asked if, "all Campbells are heir to vast soup fortunes?" The Duke replied, "I hope so." I followed with, "are Campbells different?" To which the Duke replied, "not at all." For some reason I blurted ,"then why are we here?" *Washington Post* writer Paul Richard repeated my cheeky comment in his hilarious article "A Campbell for All U.S. Campbells"[11], adding, "it seemed like a reasonable question." I did not run the interview or the footage of me wearing a kilt that fell down around my ankles. My prominence in the paper surprised me. Then again, it was publicity and they spelled my name right. [12]

The Scots were not amused—Courtesy WRC-TV

8
"Turkeys are Dumb"

Courtesy WRC-TV

I THUMBED THROUGH A FOLDER FULL OF STORY ideas and found a note titled: "Turkeys are Dumb." Research showed turkeys don't know how to fly, walk around in clumsy herds, and when it rains, look up at the sky with their beaks open until they almost choke. I located a turkey farmer on the eastern shore of Maryland willing to let me come out for a story.

The farmer obviously had appeared in dozens of Thanksgiving stories. He told me, "the only thing dumber than a turkey is the guy who raises them."

For B-roll[13] or cover footage, I started walking in the herd of turkeys. I discovered turkeys follow humans. I literally led a herd of them. When I made a sound, they gobbled in unison. I turned around and yelled, "War!" They responded:

"GOBBLEGOBBLEGOBBLEGOBBLEGOBBLE."

I threw my arms in the air as I yelled, "Inflation!" and again received:

"GOBBLEGOBBLEGOBBLEGOBBLEGOBBLE."

I screamed, "Turkeys are dumb!" the Birds said:

"GOBBLEGOBBLEGOBBLEGOBBLEGOBBLEGOBBLE."

Inspired, I turned to the camera and as if talking to the turkeys said, "thank you." Adding, "I'm Arch Campbell, NBC News." The turkeys started gobbling again and I turned and screamed, "I wish you turkeys would SHUT UP!"

On the fly, just like that, I produced the elements of a perfect 1970's news feature, with a three-man crew following. I had the turkey gobbling and some funny close ups for the open, I had the farmer and his quip for the middle, I finished with an off the cuff stand up close. "Turkeys are Dumb" hit every note Bert Shipp taught me about features in Dallas.

Dave Nuell, WRC's executive producer, wanted to run it on the Thanksgiving newscast. There's not much news on Thanksgiving or other holidays, so I understand the decision. However, Thanksgiving viewers watched football, not local news.

Even so, when "Turkeys are Dumb" aired, it produced a lot of reaction. Nuell liked it so much, he shipped the film to *The Today Show*. Of course, *Today* didn't want it the day after Thanksgiving. Still, it made me feel great that Nuell sent it.

Washington, D.C.

A few days later in a department store, a guy came up to me and said "Weren't you that guy with the turkeys?"

The Today Show never returned the film. I imagine they threw it away. So many people remembered the story Dave Nuell told me to recreate it the next year. Not only did "Turkeys are Dumb" run Thanksgiving, 1974 and Thanksgiving, 1975, it also ran in various versions for the next fifteen years. Once I earned enough vacation time, I made sure to take Thanksgiving off, to escape "Turkeys Are Dumb"—the story that refused to die.

9
The News Center

Bruce MacDonell told me to hold my work for a few weeks. He wanted to stockpile material to run once *The News Center* debuted. The NBC owned stations were moving ahead with their plan to compete with *Eyewitness News*.

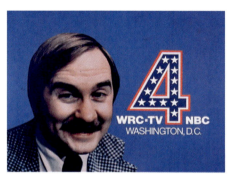

Courtesy WRC-TV

Designers produced a hexagon set, painted beige, with a soffit overhead proclaiming *The News Center*. The redesigned newscast would air from 6 to 7:00pm. *NBC Nightly News* would move to 7:00pm, following *The News Center*.

Bruce went on a hiring spree. New people showed up every week. Bruce worked in Detroit at WXYZ, and brought in friends from that station including reporter Kelly Burke and a producer named Jim Van Messel. Bruce lured Fred Thomas away from Channel 7, and found a deep voiced young guy named Jackson Bain in Atlanta. *The News Center* would feature a different anchor team at 6:00pm and 11:00pm. Bruce would shuffle Vance and Rinker, Fred Thomas, and Jackson Bain.

I stacked up several features over the next few months. I would film one day, work on a script a second day, and turn it over to an editor on a third day, then wait a couple of days for the editor to finish. Then, I'd start the process again.

Washington, D.C.

My stories included a feature on a local bar serving more than a hundred brands of beer, and a feature on the legend of a giant snake slithering around central Pennsylvania. I found a man who collected model trains and owned his own Pullman rail car. In the roughest part of downtown D.C., a character out of central casting operated a tattoo parlor. During my interview he rolled up his sleeves and pulled up his pants revealing a body completely covered in tattoos. Although not unusual today, a man covered in skin art shocked viewers at the time. I wrapped the story with the artist giving me a fake tattoo, which I discovered said: "CBS." The executive who owned the ad agency promoting the station had a bomb shelter in his house. We went into his hole in the ground and found stacks of canned rations. "They look pre-eaten," he rasped, adding, "if the A bomb falls, I'll be at the office. The maid will survive."

The News Center premiered in January of 1975 and fell flat. The anchors hunched around the hexagon set looking ashen against the beige background. *The News Center* intro, which Bruce promised would jolt viewers out of their seats, consisted of a collection of slides of local landmarks, changing every second or two set to generic electronic music. In a medium driven by video, the still shots looked tired.

Bruce hired esteemed *New York Times* food reporter Marian Burrows, and assigned her to investigate hamburger meat served at downtown fast-food outlets. Burrows and her team produced a report of almost fifteen minutes, discussing bad meat in stomach turning detail. The hamburger investigation belonged on an investigative program, not the first story on the local news. *The News Center* debut went downhill from there.

In the 70s, D.C. newscasts leaned on sports anchors for ratings success. Channel 9's Warner "let's go to the videotape" Wolfe dominated with hilarious asides and features such as the "Boo of the Week." WRC's assignment editor Betty Endicott, a Minnesota native, remembered an entertaining sports anchor on Minneapolis radio named Dave Sheehan. She sold Bruce on hiring Sheehan. As Bruce and Betty talked about the guy, Bruce decided to promote him as Dave "the Mouth" Sheehan. No one bothered to explain the strategy to Sheehan. On the air his first night, a new guy in town trying to find his way, Dave Sheehan delivered the sports in the usual jock style. Viewers thought, "where's the mouth?"[14]

Willard! Delivered the weather on debut night with a tuxedo clad violinist performing next to him. The bit felt forced. When Bruce arrived from L.A., he wanted to fire Willard. Cooler heads prevailed. Willard's long career including a stint as Bozo on afternoon TV, and as co-host of *The Joy Boys* on WRC radio, made him indispensable, even when his gags flopped. [15]

One of the anchors introduced a story about a serious crime. The director cut to film of some alligators in a pond at the zoo. Both *The Washington Post* and *The Washington Star* jumped on this goof in their review of *The News Center*. Because of the long investigative piece, I did not appear that first night. Normally I might have felt slighted. Watching, I felt relief.

The News Center lacked one of the most important elements of *Eyewitness News*: the reporters. On Channel 9, a varied group of people came on set to introduce and field questions about their stories. On Channel 4, reporters appeared mostly on film. A story aired and ended and the anchor went on to the next thing. NBC preferred formal news presentations, even on their local stations.

Beyond the gaffs and miscues, moving *NBC Nightly News* to 7:00pm enraged D.C. news junkies. Before the change, Washington's elite could watch NBC's network newscast at 6:30pm, and then catch Walter Cronkite on CBS at 7. Now NBC and CBS aired opposite each other. Viewers complained.

Years later, Channel 9's News Director Jim Snyder told me he and his staff watched the first *News Center* with jaws dropped. Jim turned to his staff and said "I hope they do this every night!" Channel 9 held first place in the ratings, with Channel 4 in second as 1975 began. By the end of February, Channel 4 had fallen somewhere between third and fourth.

Bruce approved the stories I produced in advance. He also vetoed several. One afternoon, I heard him coming out of the editing room after watching one of my stories. "I don't think he knows what he's doing." Depressed, I went home, sick to my stomach, convinced I made a terrible mistake leaving Dallas for WRC.

10
Spot the Pig

Courtesy WRC-TV

Bruce MacDonell handed me an article from *The National Observer*.[16]

"The USDA has been breeding miniature pigs for research purposes for several years, but now they don't need them, so they want to promote them as house pets. Go get one, train it, and do a story about it."

Think about that assignment. I was to obtain a miniature pig, train the animal, and report.

So, I called the Department of Agriculture and sure enough, I could purchase a miniature pig for about 80 bucks. The day he arrived, my crew and I traveled to College Park, Maryland. A USDA spokesman said, with a big smile, that a miniature pig could be just as loyal and loving as a dog. An assistant, wearing a standard issue white lab coat, wheeled out a wooden crate, opened it and said:

Washington, D.C.

"This is your pig."

I pulled out a little animal about the size of a puppy weighing 4 or 5 pounds. At Bruce's suggestion, I named him Spot. Following the advice of *The National Observer* article, I put Spot in a little room in our basement. I arranged Spot's food and water at one end, and put newspapers down in the opposite corner. As every farmer knows, pigs are smart, clean animals. By instinct Spot used the newspaper as his bathroom, and ate his food (multi grain pellets from a pet store) and drank his water in the clean corner opposite. You have read correctly. I paper trained Spot with little difficulty.

However, I didn't exactly think this all the way through. My wife and I easily bonded with Spot, taking him to the back yard to run and play. After a while, I put a collar on Spot and walked him on a leash. Sometimes as we watched TV upstairs, Spot would escape his basement room and scamper up the stairs, using his snout to bang on the door, his way of saying he wanted to be with us.

The saga of Spot aired in three parts. In the first episode, I introduced viewers to Spot, including film receiving him and an interview with the grinning USDA spokesman. In the story, Spot and I ran in the back yard, and I took him on a leash for a walk on the National Mall. To end the piece, I put on my pajamas, mentioned something about a long day, said good night to the viewers as the camera pulled out to reveal Spot in bed with me. The light went out and Spot squealed. Back in the studio, Jim Vance and Glenn Rinker's jaws dropped. They were literally speechless.

A few days later, on March 6, 1975, the Solo Dog Food company announced a singing dog contest in the Mayflower Hotel. Our assignment editor Betty Endicott grabbed the press release and ran into my office insisting I enter Spot. When the crew and I arrived, fifty-five dogs and their owners wandered around, waiting their turn in the spotlight. Some dogs sang, others whimpered. Then came my turn. An announcer said:

"Arch Campbell and Spot."

Pigs squeal when you pick them up. I'd been listening to Ethyl Waters sing "Am I Blue?" on an album of 1920's recordings. I got down on one knee, launched acapella into the first line of "Am I Blue?" Then I picked up Spot who squealed in perfect time to the song. I sang a phrase, let Spot squeal, put him down, sang the next phrase, picked him back up and so on. Our performance went something like this:

Am I Blue?
SQUEAL
You'd be too…
SQUEAL
Now he's gone and we're through…
SQUEAL
Am I Blue?
SQUEAL

Spot's performance created pandemonium. The crowd screamed with laughter and applause. That night, footage of me and Spot showed up on the *CBS Evening News with Walter Cronkite*, as well as *ABC News with Frank Reynolds*. Ironically, NBC, stepped out of the room for a break and missed my performance. However, my WRC crew got it all. When it aired on *The News Center* that night, the anchors laughed long and loud.[17] Henry Tenenbaum, Channel 9's ace feature reporter and one of the most talented competitors I ever faced, sat out the news that day. He told me later I completely scooped him.

Miniature or not, Spot kept growing. The USDA predicted he would reach twenty percent the size of a regular pig. That mean he might hit 120 pounds. The nights when he scampered up the basement stairs and banged on the door weren't quite as cute as he gained heft. I called around and found a pet boarding facility on acres of land in rural Columbia, Maryland. The Preston Country Club for Pets agreed to take Spot. I brought him out, and turned him loose. He ran across a field of tall grass as the cameraman filmed him in slow motion.

The camera crew and I spent many hours at Maggie's Goal Post on Wisconsin Avenue, thanks to the mandated union lunch break. The owner, Maggie aka Phillip Manganello, allowed us to use his bar as a setting for the third chapter of Spot the Pig.

I ordered a beer and explained to the audience that I had said good bye to my best friend. In the story, I reprised Spot's early days, including walking him on a leash in front of the Washington Monument. I showed his appearance in the singing dog contest. At the moment I let him go, footage of Spot running in slow motion aired over the Ray Conniff Singers version of "Born Free." The effect was laugh-out-loud hilarious.[18]

Washington stand-up comic Mark Russell was on set that night. When the piece finished and the camera came up on the studio, he and the anchors faked weeping, as if they had watched the saddest Hollywood tear jerker. My boss Bruce loved it. I took his idea, ran with it, and lived up to my assignment as resident zany. Maybe moving to D.C. would work out after all. Then again, maybe not.

11
That's News to Me

Grape stomping at the Roma Restaurant

Spot the Pig took weeks to research, shoot, and assemble. Bruce MacDonnell wanted the special project unit to work on that schedule. However, because I appeared only occasionally, viewers hardly knew me. Every now and then, a stranger would come up and ask, "didn't you used to work in Dallas?"

On Channel 9, Henry Tenenbaum appeared Monday through Friday, always at the end of *Eyewitness News*. His fans knew to wait for Henry's payoff. Fridays, he highlighted weekend events. For a story on a steam train excursion, Henry shoveled two loads of coal into the trunk of his car,

Washington, D.C.

and drove off sounding like a steam engine. For a story on a Renaissance fair, Henry jousted an old tire hanging from a tree.

Tenenbaum possessed tremendous talent and the ability to create a hilarious story every day. It took him only a few months to become one of the most recognized names in town. He won a local news Emmy for feature reporting his first year.

In an effort to expand his range, Tenenbaum produced a four part behind the scenes series on the Channel 9 news operation *That's News to Me*. The segments showed the story assignment process, reporting, editing and presentation. The station reassembled the hit series into a half hour special. *The Washington Post*'s fearsome television critic Tom Shales reviewed the special, indicating he didn't think much of the program, and thought even less of local TV feature reporters, especially me.[19]

Shales described Tenenbaum as "…one of the fairly new breed of reporter-comics enlisted to add still more entertainment to news programs." Shales continued:

"Tenenbaum has had himself tumbled into a swimming pool, showered with leaves, and subjected to other indignities to get laughs."

Then the article discussed the other feature reporters in town. "Channel 7's Ed Turney did a boat show bit that consisted mainly of his leering at a bikini clad model."

And finally, this. "Channel 4's Arch Campbell, described by a station spokesman as the resident 'zany'—and the most pandering of the lot—took a frightened squealing baby pig to a singing dog contest and thereby created the true repugnant model for adding comic relief to comic relief."

Shales wrapped up his review with a suggestion. "Perhaps it is time TV news people took a deeper look at what they do and how they do it."

My description as "pandering" and "repugnant" in *The Washington Post* didn't exactly help my prospects. I'm pretty sure the article got the attention of the big wigs in New York. During my series on Spot the Pig, I brought Spot to visit the newsroom. Spot took off running down the NBC halls, as people screamed with laughter. At the other end of the newsroom, the network people were not amused. Betty Endicott told me that an NBC producer sputtered the word "shameful."

As *The News Center* ratings dropped, I noticed more consultants and news executives from New York in the building. One afternoon I overheard one of the consultants tell Bruce MacDonell, "the problem with Arch Campbell is he stops the show." In today's corporate world, that assessment probably would produce a pink slip. Fortunately, this happened when companies resisted firing employees. Bruce called me in and pitched a new assignment. Channel 4 planned a second hour of news at 5:00pm. I would move to the new hour, anchored by Jim Vance.

"I want you to go out and find all the interesting places around our area. We might call it *Serendipity* or *Discovery*." My reports would air at 5:25pm Monday through Friday. The consultants hoped a 5:00pm newscast could boost the ratings for the 6:00pm News Center. I asked to call the segment *Discovery*.

I told Vance I'd been assigned to the 5:00pm. Vance nodded and said, "be cool."

12
Jim Vance

VANCE WALKED TALL, WITH GREAT POSTURE and an Afro so high it almost brushed the ceiling. He took his time making up his mind about the various characters who came in and out of the WRC newsroom. Vance looked askance at me, but liked my story on Spot the pet pig. I think he admired that I had the nerve to go all in on a bizarre undertaking. He talked about Spot for decades, sometimes mentioning in an aside, "you know, Arch Campbell used to have a pet pig." I watched him mention me and the pig during a newscast years after I left. His co-anchor Doreen Gentzler threw him a puzzled look.

I never knew what to expect from Vance. He criticized stories he didn't like—right on the air. He lobbed a dart at me for including the theme from *2001 A Space Odyssey* in a feature. "Shame on you, Arch Campbell, for using that cliched music." I didn't dare complain. Vance was his own man.

He began receiving hate mail as soon as he arrived at WRC in 1969. Government pressure on broadcast license renewals led networks to promote diversity. WRC hired him with only a year's TV experience. Vance moved up quickly from reporter to weekend anchor, replacing a white man. In 1972, he moved to weekday anchor with Glenn Rinker. Each promotion increased his hate mail.

When Jim Vance was nine, his father died. His mother left him with grandparents and family in Ardmore, Pennsylvania while she worked and lived in Philadelphia. The family encouraged him to go to college, although he wanted to be a plumber like his father. At Cheyney State College, Vance earned a degree in English. After graduation, he taught high school English, then moved into newspaper reporting and radio work and ultimately a small TV station.

I always assumed NBC found Vance as the network began recruiting diverse hires. Vance's widow, Kathy McCampbell Vance, tells me Vance found WRC. An employment agency told him about the opening at WRC. Vance applied and got the job.

By 1974, Vance had established his credentials. However, the assignment to anchor the new 5:00pm News was not exactly a promotion. The 6:00pm and 11:00pm were considered more prestigious. I can only guess the bosses moved Vance to 5:00pm to round off some of his edges.

Bruce MacDonell suggested Vance write commentaries, to give him a presence at 6:00pm. Vance, with his English degree and love of writing, embraced the idea. His first commentary made fun of his frustration trying to put together a playhouse for his daughter on Christmas Eve.

Washington, D.C.

The serious guy with the big 'fro showed he could make viewers laugh. In another commentary, Vance recalled seeing his father weep when the plumber's union refused to let him join because of discrimination.

Don Harris, the anchor I knew at WFAA in Dallas, delivered commentaries at KNBC TV when he worked with Bruce MacDonnell. Both Harris and Vance loved language and relished agitating viewers. I watched Vance hang around the newsroom delighting in taking the angry calls that often followed his comments. Don Harris did the same thing in Dallas.

In the years that followed, Vance's commentaries gained him a unique position. He managed to thread the needle, sometimes angering viewers, just not quite so much they stopped watching. Vance also contributed another element to WRC's eventual success. As a courtesy the Friday 6:00pm News ran credits of all the technicians involved in the newscast. Bruce asked Vance for some music. Vance had been listening to an album by MFSB-Mother-Father-Sister-Brother. He liked a cut titled "My Mood." WRC has played "My Mood" ever since.

The *Discovery* assignment came with a regular Monday through Friday schedule, although the 5:25 time slot wasn't great. I bought a bunch of Washington guidebooks and read up on unique places within driving distance to profile on the new series.

My stories included a visit to the Ladew Topiary Gardens on the estate of a deceased eccentric millionaire in Monkton, Maryland. The guy liked hedges trimmed to look like animals and other things. His gardens included a fox hunt carved out of bushes and a Chinese junk, all shaped from greenery. The state of Maryland inherited the place, left by Mr. Ladew to use as a park.

Other segments showcased the monuments at night, in the days when you could park in front of the U.S. Capitol or the Lincoln Memorial and visit any hour. I hunted the location of boundary stones set in 1791 by Benjamin Banneker to mark the border of the District of Columbia. A few of the historic stones sit in suburban front yards, others in parking lots or public parks. One stone sits in a river wall in the Potomac.

I visited ethnic restaurants and sampled food from Thailand, Russia, Argentina, and any other country with a restaurant serving its food. I profiled a men's gourmet club and featured unusual houses, including the renovated gatehouse of a long-gone castle. I fondly remember a profile of The Southern Railroad *Crescent*, one of the last non-Amtrak streamlined trains. The *Crescent* traveled from Union Station to Atlanta every day and onto New Orleans three times a week. Fans boarded downtown and got off in nearby Alexandria, just so they could eat in the dining car.

Discovery saved my scalp. It also dove-tailed with Bruce's interest in the quirky details of Washington. Bryson Rash, a pioneer broadcaster, early TV anchorman, and old school gentleman, collected stories about D.C. oddities. Bryson, then working as WRC's editorial director[20] caught Bruce's attention, stopping in to drop bon mots and vignettes about the town's oldest elevator or ugliest statue. Bruce decided to turn Bryson's stories into a one-hour special titled *Washington Odyssey*. Everyone on the air appeared with one or two stories. Possibly sensing his time as News Director coming to an end, Bruce turned running the newsroom over to Dave Nuell, and holed up with Bryson editing his stories into a television script. Bruce rented a tour bus, put the staff on board, and filmed us riding around town in segments used between stories.

One of my *Odyssey* segments took me to the top of the U.S. Capitol where designers called for thirteen columns to hold up the base of the top statue: Lady Liberty. It turns out when you count the columns, they only number twelve. A crew and a producer and a U.S. Capitol guide and I climbed up the creaky sideways steps inside the capitol dome to reach the balcony under Lady Liberty. I looked west toward the Washington Monument at a view few will see. I can thank Bruce and history buff Bryson Rash and *Washington Odyssey* for my unforgettable climb to the top of the U.S. Capitol to film a 30 second stand up about a missing column.

Washington Odyssey provided the greatest success of Bruce MacDonell's tenure. It won multiple awards and glowing press.[21] Bryson Rash retired not long after the program. He published his material as *Footnote Washington*, a guidebook still listed on Amazon.

The inevitable shake up began. Bruce didn't renew Glenn Rinker's contract. Jim Snyder, the guiding hand of Channel 9, now elevated to Vice President of News for the *Post-Newsweek* television stations, immediately snapped up Rinker to anchor the *Post-Newsweek* station in Miami, WPLG. Meantime at the NBC network, executives replaced Jim Hartz on *The Today Show* with Tom Brokaw and Jane Pauley. The change sent Hartz to replace Rinker at WRC.

Cut-backs followed. A year and a half after it began, the 5:00pm news struggled to find an audience. *News Center 4* often fell to third place behind Channel 9 and Channel 7. NBC higher ups stepped in. They moved *NBC Nightly News* from 7:00pm back to 6:30pm, and cut *The News Center* to an hour from 5:30pm to 6:30pm. The promotion department tagged the new line up "The Ninety-Minute Day." Sometimes the anchors mangled the phrase to "The Ninety-Minute Hour." Often the broadcast felt like it. Consultants chose Vance and Hartz to anchor.

Fred Thomas, one of the first anchors Bruce hired, moved from anchoring to reporting. Jackson Bain, another

The Accidental Critic

Bruce MacDonell hire, moved to NBC News as a correspondent and later to Channel 5 as an anchor. The cut-backs eliminated a roster of contributors including Nicholas Van Hoffman, Jeffry St. John, Mark Russell, and movie reviewer Judy Bachrach. My segment *Discovery* ended. Nuell put me back on the features beat.

During my first years at NBC, the rumor circulated that WRC didn't have to make a profit because NBC operated it to cement good relations with the FCC. Unlike other local stations, the General Manager did not control the news department. NBC News managed the five network owned affiliate newsrooms. Bruce could thumb his nose at anything the General Manager didn't like, and often did. As *The News Center* struggled, and NBC Network programs struggled, things changed, beginning with the organizational chart.

NBC owned station managers gained control of their news departments. A new General Manager arrived at WRC. He and Bruce didn't like each other. Soon, Bruce announced his departure for the NBC Asia Bureau in Hong Kong. A few days later, the General Manager, a homesick Chicago native, returned to his home town. At the time I remember Bruce saying, "If I'd known he was leaving, I would have stayed."

Every now and then, Marty Haag called from Dallas, asking how I liked WRC and did I want to move back to Dallas? By this time, WFAA's ratings had jumped with an assist from the success of ABC network programming and a revamped energetic news team. My heart said, "yes," however I knew Dallas offered limited opportunity.[22] Dave Nuell, whom I liked, took over as News Director. Jim Van Messel, who produced the 5:00pm news, moved up to executive producer. I knew I needed to stay at WRC, even though I really wanted to go back to Dallas.

13
Why I Love the Movies

American Film Institute - Silver Spring, Maryland

THE YEAR I TURNED FIVE, A COUPLE OF GUYS lugged a massive mahogany cabinet into our house. The console came with radio, phonograph, and best of all: a 17-inch television screen. I settled right in front of the glowing black and white images. Growing up, I discovered the movies on local TV. My father shared his favorites. One Friday night, KENS TV premiered *Shock! Theater*. A host wearing a black hat and cape introduced horror classics from the laboratory of an imaginary castle.

My father and I watched *Frankenstein, The Mummy, Dracula, The Wolf Man,* and the sequels that followed. KONO-TV offered Frank Capra stories including *Mr. Deeds Goes to Town, Meet John Doe,* and *Mr. Smith Goes to Washington*. Afternoons, WOAI-TV served up Busby Berkley musicals: *42nd Street, Footlight Parade,* and *Dames*.

Dick Powell and Ruby Keeler turned *I Only Have Eyes for You* into a hallucination. Instead of running home to play baseball, I ran home to watch movies.

I discovered film noir; Orson Wells' *Citizen Kane,* Joan Crawford as *Mildred Pierce,* and Humphrey Bogart in *The Maltese Falcon* and *Casablanca*. My father pointed out the Hitchcock thrillers, the Preston Sturges comedies, and Frank Capra's *It's a Wonderful Life*, which we watched every Christmas Eve, the only night TV showed it.

The Repertoire movement arrived during my college days at the University of Texas. Theaters booked classic films, attracting students like me to movies made before we were born. A screening of W.C. Field's *Never Give a Sucker an Even Break* sold out an Austin theater. Even though I'd seen it many times on the late show, a midnight screening of *Casablanca* in a packed theater felt like seeing it for the first time.

In March of 1972, my job as a WFAA-TV news writer helped me wrangle a press pass to the SMU USA Film Festival honoring Frank Capra. Every morning at ten, Professor Bill Jones introduced a Capra classic, followed by a Q and A with Frank Capra and some of the stars of his films, including Claudette Colbert, Jean Arthur, and Donna Reed.

That week at SMU, I watched *It Happened One Night, You Can't Take It with You, Lost Horizon, Meet John Doe, Mr. Smith Goes to Washington,* and a festival concluding screening of *It's a Wonderful Life*. I knew these films having seen them as a kid on our 17-inch screen, but viewing with an audience gave Capra's work new life. The mostly student crowd cheered the ending of *Mr. Smith Goes to Washington*. Long haired hippies wept during *It's a Wonderful Life*.

The classics connected me to my father, who died when I was 23. In Dallas I frequented the Granada Theater and the

Washington, D.C.

renovated Lakewood theater. On any night I could watch The Marx Brothers comedies, *Duck Soup* and *A Night at the Opera* or the Fred Astaire/Ginger Rogers musicals, *Top Hat* and *Swing Time.*

When Marty Haag anointed me the WFAA movie reviewer, I subscribed to *New York Magazine*. I loved Judith Crist's movie reviews. I met and interviewed her when she came to Dallas promoting a book. She smiled when I brought up her controversial lampoon of *The Sound of Music*. She mercilessly panned Julie Andrew's beloved musical on *The Today Show*. Judith Crist laughed recalling her reasons for hating one of the most successful films of all time.

I subscribed to *American Film Magazine,* the publication of the new American Film Institute.[23] When I moved to Washington, I arrived in the AFI's home city. My subscription included AFI membership and a discount at screenings in the AFI theater at Kennedy Center. Two or three times a week I joined a crowd of movie geeks.

One night at *Double Indemnity*, a surprise guest rose to speak. James M. Cain, author of the novel, shared a few tidbits about the story that became the movie. Cain, whose work included *Mildred Pierce, The Postman Always Rings Twice*, and several other pulp thrillers lived in nearby Hyattsville, Maryland. Disillusioned with Hollywood, he moved to the east coast to research a Civil War novel, which he never finished. He said a few words without a microphone which I couldn't hear. Later, I discovered Cain's books and beautiful hard-boiled prose.

An AFI employee named Mike Clark wrote many of the program notes. Mike composed beautiful essays about the night's film. He made the connection to James M. Cain, inviting him to the *Double Indemnity* screening. *USA Today* hired Mike as senior film critic. Mike also contributed annually to *Leonard Maltin's Video Guide,* the vast expanding compilation of mini reviews of films available on videotape and later DVD. In later years, Mike and I chatted before and after screenings. I always got a little tongue tied around Mike Clark because I admired his work so very much, beginning with his AFI Program notes.

An Orson Wells series included *The Lady from Shanghai,* a gem I'd always wanted to watch. On the way into the theater, the usher said "We have a pristine nitrate print." Film buffs know nitrate film projects the ultimate crisp black and white images. Studios stopped producing on nitrate because the film is highly flammable. I'd seen selected scenes from *The Lady from Shanghai* on *The Dick Cavett Show* during one of his interviews with Orson Wells.

The movie began and I watched Orson Wells as a lowly sailor, with an annoying Irish accent, hired to work on the yacht of beautiful Rita Hayworth and her husband Everett Sloane, whom I recognized as Bernstein in *Citizen Kane.* During a voyage, Rita appears to like the sailor better than the husband, leading to a murder plot and a possible frame job. The projectionist made the switch to the final reel. On screen, Rita Hayworth drove a gleaming '47 Lincoln Continental convertible up a San Francisco hill.

The film jumped. The picture froze. The frame melted inside out. The audience groaned. I heard a, "whoosh" and turned around. I could just see inside the booth as the top reel on the projector burst into flame. It was true. Nitrate film looked great. It also catches fire. The lights came up and somebody said, "everybody leave now." We calmly moved toward a series of large sliding doors.

The AFI operated in a backstage space Kennedy Center didn't use. The heavy doors—designed to load in sets—slid open. Out we went. The crowd stood and watched as firetrucks arrived. Somebody said, "anybody know how the movie ends?" Years passed before I saw the finale of *The Lady from Shanghai*. If this happened today, everyone with a cell phone would post. In 1975, nobody reported the event. An old movie on fire at the AFI didn't qualify as news that year.

Not only did Washington film buffs have the American Film Institute, we also filled the Circle Theater on Pennsylvania Avenue. Brothers Jim and Ted Pedas loved movies and knew real estate. Gradually they bought various theaters in town creating the Circle organization, a real estate and theater empire.

Ten dollars bought ten tickets to the downtown Circle Theater. I fondly remember a screening of *The Third Man* and the audience's delight at the film's final scene, a funeral service much like the one as the story began, and Joseph Cotton's romantic snub accompanied by the zither music that made *The Third Man* so unique.[24]

The Biograph on M Street in Georgetown showed foreign and American classics, and fun stuff. During the Watergate scandal, the Biograph scheduled midnight screenings of Richard Nixon's 1952 "Checkers" Speech. Audiences laughed at a young Nixon responding to charges of financial improprieties during his Vice Presidential campaign. Nixon concluded saying his daughters received a Cocker Spaniel, named "Checkers;" a gift, by golly, he intended to keep.

Later, the Biograph scheduled midnight shows of *Bedtime for Bonzo,* an embarrassing 1950 Ronald Reagan comedy featuring the future President and a chimpanzee. The Key Theater in Georgetown introduced me to *Jules and Jim*, Francois Truffaut's very French romance between Jeanne Moreau, Oskar Werner, and Henri Serre. I still remember the audience gasp at Truffaut's tortured ending. The Key became known for years of midnight singalongs of *The Rocky Horror Picture Show.*

I reminded both Bruce MacDonell and Dave Nuell that I reviewed movies in Dallas. I knew Bruce wanted to add reviews to either the new 5:00pm or the 6:00pm news. On Channel 9, Davey Marlin Jones' popularity soared. With long hair and a floppy hat and occasional magic tricks, Davey mesmerized viewers. Some nights he would run through a series of film titles, reviewing them by either keeping the ticket stub, tearing it in half, or tossing it over his shoulder. The effect was genius, although sometimes Davey got so wild, viewers often didn't know if he liked a movie or not.[25]

Bruce watched my audition tape and shook his head. "I don't see you doing this." He hired *Washington Post* writer Judy Bacharach to review movies. When the cut backs came and the 5:00pm newscast vanished, movie reviewing went with them.[26] My return to the movie beat would have to wait.

14
Sunrise Shift

WITH MY *Discovery* segment canceled and the news reduced from two hours to one, I struggled for airtime.

A few months before NBC transferred Bruce MacDonell, he hired one of his old pals named Ken Reed. A news veteran about twenty years older than me, Ken possessed a deep voice and a wicked sense of humor. In the early 1960s, Ken, as Program and Operations Director, helped turn New York radio station WINS into the first all-news radio station in America. I don't know what changed Ken's fortunes. I only know he wound up in Tulsa, Oklahoma where he managed a liquor store. One of the Tulsa television stations hired him as a feature reporter.

I watched some of Ken's audition tape. He painted unique inspirational pictures set to music. He produced good stuff. I expected we would compete. Instead, we became fast friends. We both had to fight to get anything on the air because of the reduced news time. Ken reminded me of my father, with the same mix of humor and hard luck.

One morning a female colleague arrived visibly upset. She delivered details of the young man who anchored the early morning news on Channel 7. Driving to his shift, possibly asleep at the wheel, the newsman hit a tree and died. Our colleague, in great distress, grieved the loss of a young life, and of all he might have accomplished. As she wailed, tears falling from her eyes, Ken wrote a note, folded it, and passed it to me. I opened it and read:

"I understand there is an opening at Channel 7."

I think Ken called in a favor from our boss Bruce Mac-Donell. I came to know Bruce a little better as I worked for him. Bruce grew up in Detroit, entered broadcasting as a radio news writer. He landed a job at WXYZ-TV Detroit, the ABC owned affiliate. Bruce wrote gags for comic Soupy Sales, host of a national children's show carried from WXYZ on the ABC network. Soupy ended each show with a pie in the face. Bruce followed Soupy to New York, and later worked on *Don Ameche's Showtime,* a TV circus show. Ultimately Bruce moved to Los Angeles to head the KNBC special projects bureau. His showbiz background informed his news experience.

Bruce and I shared a connection to Don Harris, whom Bruce worked with in L.A. Harris recommended me to Bruce. I read the shocking details of the Jonestown massacre, in which Don Harris died, in the November 21, 1978 Sunday edition of *The Washington Post.* The next day I walked into Bruce's office, and found him slumped at his desk with tears running down his cheeks. "I can't believe it," Bruce whispered. We hugged and said little else. I regret I never had the chance to thank Don Harris for his generosity. The next month Bruce left for the NBC Hong Kong bureau.[27]

Bruce's departure left Ken Reed on thin ice. The new boss, Dave Nuell, barely knew Ken. Nuell assigned Ken to

Washington, D.C.

anchor the morning news cut-ins for a week. Everybody hated that assignment, especially Ken. You had to arrive at 5:00am, write a 15-minute newscast using video tape from the night before, and produce and anchor at 6:45am plus two five-minute cut-ins at 7:25am and 8:25am. The newsroom rotated the cut-in assignment because of the exhausting schedule. You had to hang around the newsroom until at least 1:00pm. Inevitably the cut-in person caught an assignment keeping him or her working until early evening. Dave Nuell considered me apart from the regular reporting staff, so he left me off this rotation.

I figured if Ken Reed could do it, so could I. Plus, volunteering might justify my existence. I marched into Dave Nuell's office and said, "why don't you let me anchor the cut-ins." Nuell, who laughed as he talked said, "hah! You want to do the cut-ins? Be my guest. Start Monday." That week, I came in, wrote the news, pulled video, went on the air, and turned in a story for the 5:30pm News. Thursday of my first week, Nuell said, "why don't you just keep doing this for a while."

I caught more assignments because I was in the newsroom before the rest of the staff arrived. As the weeks passed, people started to recognize me. I kept the schedule for a year and a half. I made a ton of extra money because anything past eight hours paid time and a half. That bonus kicked in at 1:00pm. I sometimes worked until 6:00pm.

The schedule had me in bed by 8:00pm, out of bed at 3:45am, and in the newsroom by 5:00am. On the air in basement Studio F, I read my newscast with Columnist George Will on my left waiting to appear on the national *Today Show*. One morning I told him I enjoyed his column in *Newsweek*. George Will gave me a withering look and said nothing.

The studio cameras remained stationary. The operator rarely moved the device. The union mandated stage manager sat in the corner sound asleep, snoring so loud I wondered if my microphone picked up the noise.

One morning Ken Reed sat down at the desk next to mine looking ashen. I remembered that look from my childhood when my father came home with bad news. Ken wrote another note, folded it, and handed it to me.

"I have been fired."

The standard NBC contract, under which both Ken and I worked, stipulated four 13 week cycles a year. At the end of any of those cycles, the company could discharge us. The Union mandated three weeks severance for every year worked.

Ken left a few days later. I organized a goodbye party and kicked in some money to buy him a pocket watch. I think I ordered something sloppy and sentimental engraved on the watch, or maybe it was just Ken's name.

15
The Storm

THE ALARM WENT OFF AT 3:45AM MONDAY, February 18, 1979. I shaved and showered and looked outside. It snowed a few inches overnight. The snow stopped, the sky cleared and the moon was shining. I started my drive to WRC about 4:45am, and noticed my Cadillac Seville (purchased with all of the overtime I made on this schedule) slipping and sliding as I nudged it up the hills on Nebraska Avenue. It started to rain and the rain turned into a light snow as I drew near the station. I pulled into the parking lot on what looked like a chilly winter day.

It kept snowing. Kenny Gamble, who ran the morning news desk, came in muttering expletives as he shook the snow off his coat. Paris Kenna, just beginning her career as a news aide[28], walked over from a house she shared with several other young people near the station. Kenny shouted out anything important he picked up from a crew or the police radio. Paris kept up with the wires, made phone calls, and did everything to help make our deadline.

I turned on the radio to catch the WMAL 5:30am newscast. WMAL TV's overnight stringer Larry Krebs roamed the city with a silent camera looking for wrecks and fires and crime. He always stopped by WMAL radio to update Bud Steele,[29] a radio newsman with a voice so deep it rattled the speaker on my receiver. Krebs reported several cars stuck in the snow. Steele added the snow coming down had not been forecast. I started writing for the 6:45am newscast. As the snow came harder, the technical director told a studio crew member to push one of the giant floor cameras into the lobby and point it out the door. The tech director turned on the camera and put the picture on a monitor. Now we could see the beginning of a major snow storm.

Paris ran the script down to the control room and I went on the air at 6:45am. We used the shot from the lobby camera to lead the newscast. I mentioned the weather and driving problems, and some car crashes we confirmed on the police radio. By the time I got off the air at 7:00am, the snow was coming at the rate of two to three inches an hour. Kenny picked up police reports of impassable streets. The blizzard of '79 arrived as a complete surprise. Given today's weather technology, it's hard to imagine, but true, that nobody saw this major blizzard coming.[30]

The daytime news staff usually arrived between 8:30am and 10:00am. Dave Nuell, Joel Albert, and Jim Van Messel called to say they couldn't get out of their driveways. Kenny and Paris and I plus a handful of engineers and technical people had the station to ourselves.

Nuell told me to go on the air and ask anyone with a four-wheel drive vehicle to come to WRC. The station would hire drivers and their cars for the duration. NBC kept two or three couriers on call. I think one of them drove a Jeep, the original kind from World War II, capable of getting through the snow. Nuell began making arrangements to bring some staff into the office by Jeep or four-wheeler.

Meanwhile, *The Today Show* in New York, where it did not snow, gleefully took our camera pictures from the lobby. My cut-ins at 7:25 and 8:25 turned into announcements to stay home and stay off the roads and can we borrow your four-wheel drive car? Fortunately, February 18, 1979 was President's Day, a holiday.

Over an 18-hour period, National Airport recorded almost 19 inches of snow. Downtown saw depths of 23 inches. Neighborhoods east of D.C. measured 25 inches. The blizzard of '79, somewhat forgotten today, held the record as the second biggest snowstorm in the area for thirty years.

The courier picked Dave Nuell up at his home in Rockville and got him to the station around 10:00am. A bundle of energy, and loving every minute of this weather crisis, Nuell wrangled his team of Jim Van Messell and Joel Albert into the building. I stayed doing cut-ins beyond the usual times until one of the drivers managed to bring Vance and Jim Hartz to the station.

Channel 4's best-known personality and 6 and 11:00pm weatherman, Willard Scott, presented a problem. Willard lived on a farm in rural Paris, Virginia, sixty miles from the WRC studios. Willard had no chance of making it to the station. That night Vance and Hartz described a city stopped in its tracks by a surprise storm. Willard called in by phone, yukking it up with Vance and Hartz for several minutes.

Snow and ice completely covered my car in the parking lot. A volunteer took me home and picked me up at 4:00am the next day. Tuesday, February 19th, the area remained at a standstill. Nuell's volunteer drivers brought more people into work on the Tuesday morning cut-ins.

One of the bosses insisted we put a spokesman from the mayor's emergency preparedness office on the phone. The morning crew, used to the normal sleepy routine, struggled. I'm not sure the morning audio man knew how to patch a phone call to the air. On my shift, I introduced the spokesman, and put the phone to my ear. He started talking and none of what he said made it on the air. The shot on camera showed me with a phone to my ear nodding my head saying, "un huh, un huh." That week Tom Shales in *The Washington Post* poked fun at what he called my "report," quote unquote.

Nuell and his team worked alongside me and I think appreciated that I gave it my best. They saw another side of the former "resident zany." Nuell even overlooked the embarrassing silent phone call.

That Tuesday, Paul Anthony, a talented voiceover announcer and long-time Washington personality who anchored the weekend weather, volunteered to walk to the station. Paul would give the official weather report on the 6 and 11:00pm news. Paul lived three miles away in Chevy Chase. It must have been quite a slog through all that slush and ice. Nuell gratefully welcomed Paul's offer.

That afternoon, Anthony prepared maps and drawings and put together a detailed explanation of what happened. When the news began at 6:00pm, Vance and Hartz described the aftermath of the big storm. Nuell, aware of Willard's popularity, set up another phone call between Vance and Hartz and Willard at his farm. The anchors and Willard laughed and joked in what writer John Carmody called a "marathon phone call." The anchors and Willard went on so long, the producer cut Paul Anthony's segment. Paul didn't get on the air at all.

With steam coming out of his ears, Paul Anthony quit on the spot, walked out of the station and never returned.[31] John Carmody in *The Washington Post* reported the incident the next week. In the article Dave Nuell said:

"Paul's probably pretty sore at me…He did a fine job for us over the years and I kind of understand the situation… But he's gone…"[32]

The next morning, Nuell came in about the time I finished my third cut-in. He yelled across the newsroom, "Arch." Then he laughed. "Have you ever done the weather?" Something told me to say yes. I sort of lied. The month after *The News Center* began, Willard went on vacation. Bruce MacDonell put various people in Willard's place including me. Yes, I did the weather—once. But I didn't say that. I just said, "yes."

Nuell continued, "Arch. You are now the weekend weatherman!"

16
The Weekend Weather

WILLARD Scott took a little getting used to, but once you got to know him, he became your friend for life. As I've told you, Willard lived on a farm between Paris and Delaplane, Virginia, sixty miles west of the station. Because of the distance, Willard went to a restaurant for dinner, usually taking someone with him. I got in on many of these crazy excursions.

One night Willard had a taste for German food, so we went to the Old Europe, an old school Georgetown establishment. Willard blew into the joint, ordered the first of multiple rounds of drinks, and started telling stories and jokes. A crowd gathered around our table. A boisterous German tune started playing, prompting Willard to climb on a chair and dance like a go-go girl. Two and a half hours of beer, mixed drinks, and wienerschnitzel later, we poured ourselves into Willard's car, lurching back to the station in time for Willard to laugh his way through the weather. The Old Europe waved us out at no charge—just another night with Willard.

Washington, D.C.

Willard grew up in Alexandria, Virginia, attending college at American University. He started at NBC in 1952, in the days when NBC hired kids as pages and put them in uniforms to do odd jobs and give tours.

At American University, Willard met Ed Walker, AU's first blind student. Ed loved radio, and came to study broadcasting. Willard and Ed teamed at the campus radio station. Their act improved so quickly, Washington station WOL hired them. Thanks to Willard's job as an NBC Page, WRC gave the pair a try out and ultimately a regular show. Management moved Willard and Ed from afternoons to nights, a move at first considered a demotion. However, nights gave them delicious freedom. Ed performed impersonations, and Willard made wisecracks. They produced parodies of television shows and created chaos, throwing trash cans full of rocks around the studio just for the fun of making a loud noise.

Jim Vance told me when he first came to WRC, the late news team would go down to the basement radio studios to watch Willard and Ed work, barely making it back in time to deliver the news. Willard and Ed filled their studio with friends and fans laughing at their antics.

Channel 4 tapped into Willard's popularity and hired him to deliver the weather, a subject about which Willard knew nothing. He wore a toupee, and promised viewers he would throw it at the camera during the rating period. And he did.

Willard raised chickens on his farm. Once a week he hauled dozens of eggs to the station. "Egg Man! Egg Man!" he shouted as he ambled up the NBC hallways, his regular customers rushing out to buy his wares.[33] Vance once asked Willard why he bothered to sell eggs. "If this TV thing doesn't work out, I've always got my egg money." At the end of 1979, NBC tapped Willard to bring his act to *The*

Today Show. In a familiar pattern, Willard's co-anchors and the national audience resisted him at first, then came to like him, ultimately turning Willard into a beloved national figure.[34]

I did not ask Willard how to report the weekend weather. He didn't know anymore about it than I did. The weekend news producer buttonholed me with instructions. She said a picture of the evening weather map came across the faxsimile machine[35] about 4:45pm. Get the map, take it downstairs, put the major weather fronts, the high-and low-pressure systems and a few temps on the national map. I would receive the afternoon forecast on the 5:00pm news wire summary, give it to the graphics person. As the weather reporter, I would sit next to the anchor on the set, ad lib a weather headline, walk over to the national map, show the weather patterns,and give the local forecast. My final instruction? Remember weather systems generally move from west to east.

The News Center updated Willard's weather map to a velcro backed sketch of the continental United States. The forecaster chose from a collection of huge child-like images to illustrate weather patterns. The sun, the rain, the snow decals, the temperature numbers were the size of my hand. It only took a couple of fronts, some sun in the west, a rain storm down south, and a few snow icons to completely cover the national map.

After getting up at 3:45 every morning, the weekend weather schedule felt great. Arrive at 3:30 in the afternoon, get the weather map the next hour, go to the studio and Velcro together the icons. On set at 6:00pm or so, laugh with the anchor, walk over to the map, make a few jokes, go back to the set. Leave at 6:30pm, come back about 9:30pm, do it all over and go home at 11:30pm.

Washington, D.C.

Sue Simmons anchored the weekend news. She brought just the right amount of wise cracking to make the segment fun. A sophisticated New Yorker and daughter of jazz musician John Simmons, Sue oozed talent. I got through my first weekend thanks to her, expecting to go back to my sunrise schedule the next week. It turned out nobody in the station wanted to do weekend weather. I filled in for eight months.

Moving around in different jobs somehow improved my feature work. For the last day of February 1979, I produced a piece titled "So Long Febraury". The surprise snow storm, the unusually cold weather, plus a farm protest blocking traffic, turned February 1979 into one long annoyance. I pulled tape of all the terrible things and listed them in order by date. I shot footage of a desk calendar ripping the pages, throwing them over my shoulder, as I recounted frozen pipes and canceled events and potholes big enough to swallow a Honda Civic. I put the piece to march music and narrated in newsreel *March of Time* style.[36] For the finale, I held a giant calendar and said, "and now I'd just like to say," and then I gave a big raspberry, "PLLLLLLAAAHHH to February." With that I threw the giant February page into the trash.

"So Long February" played just before 6:00pm. When it ended the anchors and floor crew and everyone in the studio screamed with laughter. I think it captured the frustration of a trying month. A few weeks later, I won my first local news Emmy for "So Long Febraury." Henry Tenenbaum won an Emmy his first year. It took me four years.

17
The Bottom

WRC's prospects looked grim at the end of 1979. I never imagined a decade of bad luck would lead to a golden age, transforming WRC into a dynasty.

Nobody gave much thought to a trade *The Washington Post* made with *The Detroit News*. *The Post* exchanged ownership of ratings leader WTOP Channel 9, for WDIV-TV in Detroit. *Post* lawyers feared a potential FCC concentration of media rule might require breaking up ownership of both a newspaper and television station in the same city. *The Detroit News* faced the same fear. The two corporations received permission to exchange stations.[37]

Channel 9 dominated Washington TV news in the 1970s. Anchors Gordon Peterson and Maureen Bunyan formed a powerful team, aided by a brilliant staff of reporters and producers. The switch dispatched Channel 9's beloved News Director Jim Snyder to Detroit. His staff admired him so much they paid for his goodbye party themselves. Snyder built Channel 9 News from scratch, finding and developing extraordinary talent. Once he left, his staff began drifting away. Significantly, Channel 9's lead anchor Gordon Peterson felt so unhappy he considered switching to Channel 4.

NBC sent a new General Manager to WRC. John Rohrbeck learned broadcasting as a salesman at KABC-TV and later KNBC-TV in Los Angeles. Rohrbeck arrived in Washington as Bruce MacDonell departed for Asia. In one of his first moves, Rohrbeck promoted Bruce's second in command Dave Nuell to take over the News Department. Nuell knew D.C., and knew the staff. He liked us and we liked him.

Washington, D.C.

Rohrbeck took some time to learn the city, and watch our competition. He dropped into the newsroom often to visit. During one impromptu meeting, he said we might not beat Channel 9 one on one, but we could win as a team. The team idea raised morale.

After ten years at the anchor desk, Jim Vance emerged as our newsroom leader. Strong and opinionated and not afraid of speaking truth to power, Vance connected to a young diverse audience. He partnered with Jim Hartz, former host with Barbara Walters of *The Today Show*. In 1976, Barbara Walters departed to anchor the news on ABC. The first female evening network news anchor, ABC reportedly paid Walters a million dollars a year. Her move shook up NBC's morning show. NBC replaced Hartz with Tom Brokaw, and sent Hartz to WRC.

Jim Hartz possessed impressive credentials as a network correspondent and anchor. However, it would take years to overcome Gordon Peterson's standing at Channel 9. John Rohrbeck, intent on shaking up the market, came up with a big idea. He would lure Peterson away from Channel 9 and create a dream Washington TV news team: Gordon Peterson and Jim Vance. Peterson, unhappy with Channel 9's new owners, accepted Rohrbeck's offer. Peterson's lawyer claimed his contract with *The Washington Post* corporation didn't transfer to *The Detroit News*. The Detroit ownership disagreed. Peterson and *The Detroit News* went to court.

While Peterson's case dragged on, word arrived that Jim Hartz would no longer work for Channel 4. Hartz' departure shocked the newsroom. Some felt Rohrbeck dismissed Hartz to make the case that Channel 4 expected Peterson to make the move. The gamble failed. Peterson lost his case, compelled to stay at Channel 9. The Detroit owners signed Peterson to a lucrative long-term deal. However, Channel 9 never quite recovered from the change in ownership and

The Accidental Critic

the magic touch of Jim Snyder and *The Washington Post* corporation.³⁸

For a time, Jim Vance anchored with Sue Simmons. The pair created something remarkable: a strong Black man and a sophisticated funny Black woman in a city sensitive to race. Unfortunately, the Vance/Simmons team didn't last long. WNBC offered Sue an anchor job in New York, her home town, a move she readily accepted.

Visiting Willard at The Today Show, 1980

The biggest blow came to Channel 4 in December 1979, when *The Today Show* announced Willard Scott would leave Washington to anchor the weather on the national morning show. *The Washington Post* put Willard's departure on the front page.³⁹ Television critic Tom Shales described Willard as "endearing" and quoted Scott saying, "the way I look at it, I'm there to fill the void created when J. Fred Muggs left."⁴⁰

Vance and Willard fought back tears during their last broadcast together. Willard would replace the current *Today Show* weatherman Bob Ryan, a physicist and licensed meteorologist, who considered weather a serious subject. Ryan arrived at WRC, somewhat displeased with NBC for sending him to Washington, and replacing him with a comedian. No one guessed the importance of this trade or that Bob Ryan would become the keystone of Channel 4's success.

18
Star Trek

Hollywood came to Washington December 6, 1979. *Star Trek: The Motion Picture* brought the stars of the highly anticipated space adventure to town for the world premiere. Director Robert Wise personally carried the print to the MacArthur Theater in the Palisades neighborhood of Northwest D.C. Paramount wanted to tie the film in with the relatively new Smithsonian Air and Space Museum. The *Star Trek* event benefited the National Space Club, an organization promoting space careers for young people.[41]

Movies entered a new era when Steven Spielberg unveiled *Jaws* in 1975. The shark themed horror/adventure jammed theaters. *Jaws* attracted lines that stretched around the block, creating the buzzword "blockbuster."

Star Wars upped the ante in 1977, introducing the multi-episode movie. *Star Wars* took fans into space. After *Star Wars*, Hollywood embraced space, and naturally *Star Trek*. The new film would build on the success of the NBC series with the cult following. Now fans could see the *Starship Enterprise* plus Captain Kirk and Mr. Spock and the rest of the characters on the big screen. The Washington location also created a perk for Congressmen, Senators, and lobbyists. Inviting politicians to a gala premiere might gain a legislative favor in the future.

The premiere fit my new gig. After eight months fronting the weekend weather, the station found a replacement. As the fill in weather guy, I showed some personality. *The News Center* moved back to the hour between 6 and 7 with *NBC Nightly News* afterward. Grateful that I covered his weather problem, Dave Nuell told me to go back to the feature beat on the revamped newscast.

The new general manager, John Rohrbeck, recognized one of the missing ingredients of *The News Center*—the reporters. For years Channel 9 showcased reporters live on the set. Now Channel 4 would do the same, and that included me. My new gig placed me on the end of the 6:00pm news, talking to the anchors, reading my lead-in, and laughing on return. I produced stories about classic cars and a bar that only served bottled water, and a woman who dressed as a Christmas tree, branches and all, for the holidays.

The camera crew and I arrived for the *Star Trek* premiere. A Paramount pictures film crew lit the MacArthur Theater entrance like a sound stage. Hundreds of Trekkies spilled into the street, including a fan who turned an old U.S. Mail delivery truck into a street version of the Enterprise.

The stars began to appear, their arrival timed for maximum effect. Fans screamed as if at a football game. The roar increased for William Shatner. The loudest cheers were for Leonard Nimoy. Nobody thought to set up a press line or mark camera positions. As each star approached, a half dozen film crews rushed the actors. I elbowed my way right into Shatner's and Nimoy's face. I yelled, "Doctor Spock!" to get Leonard Nimoy's attention. He laughed and answered my dumb question.

I returned to the station with a new kind of footage for the 11:00pm news. Celebrities, crowds, bright lights, a red carpet, with cameras bouncing and reporters jostling. I told Vance I expected to find Rona Barrett, the premiere Hollywood gossip of the time, lurking in the bushes. Vance laughed.

Washington, D.C.

John Rohrbeck, the new General Manager, began to build a team to replace the loss of the three major players—Jim Hartz, Sue Simmons, and Willard Scott. Rohrbeck found a young guy from San Diego named Marty Levine. Marty and John shared a California outlook. Young, good looking, and full of energy, Marty put new life into the news as Vance's co-anchor. Marty moved into a house about a block away from mine. We became neighbors and friends.

Rohrbeck tackled Channel 4's sports problem. Channel 9 dominated local sports starting with Warner Wolf. The ABC network lured Wolf to New York. Channel 9 found another Wolfe, named Mike, who favored open shirts and a boisterous delivery. Jim Snyder, the genius behind Channel 9's success, cut Mike Wolfe after a year,[42] quickly promoting Glenn Brenner, from weekends to week days. Brenner brought a mix of humor and memorable bits that won broad appeal. He showcased a local nun to pick football games, produced bits driving the Oscar Meyer wienermobile, and announced a "Weenie of the Week" award. Brenner created a loveable hilarious sportscast. He presented sports for people who didn't like sports.

WRC ran through a series of sports anchors, without success. The most recent, Nick Charles, went on to a successful career at the new national cable channel CNN. Rohrbeck decided to try a guy he found in New York. Over a drunken dinner fueled by the sweet Italian liqueur Sambuca, Rohrbeck hired George Michael, a rock and roll disc jockey and weekend sports anchor.

As 1980 began, the new team—Jim Vance, Marty Levine, Bob Ryan weather, and George Michael sports—jelled. Vance introduced George on his first night with, "I hear we have a new sports anchor and he's pretty good. Here's George Michael." George and Vance took to each other.

Another key player appeared. Rohrback hired Bob Casazza, a young graphic artist from Channel 9, as promotion director. Working with a Los Angeles advertising agency, Casazza fashioned a series of promotional ads starring the new Channel 4 news team. First came, "*News Center* 4 can't wait to show you tonight," in which Vance, Marty Levine, Bob Ryan,and George Michael plugged their specialties. Later, Casazza added me and consumer reporter Lee Thompson to the mix.

The next promotion began in 1981, inspired by Rohrbeck's speech. "We're the Team" showed most of the on-air staff interacting in fun events. One of the first was a crab fest held in a suburban kitchen. Another ad showed the staff hiking and camping. Still another featured a touch football game. The most lavish ad put us on a massive sailboat in the Chesapeake Bay. We stayed overnight for the sailboat shoot, and brought along husbands and wives. Ironically, the "We're the Team" commercials turned us into a team. The overnight stay, with carousing and drinking and staying up too late, created stories some of us still laugh about today.

The other stations thought our commercials fell somewhere between laughable and demeaning. The Chesapeake sailing spot reminded me of an earlier commercial for, I think, Schlitz Beer: "You only go around once in this life, so drink Schlitz." Some of our competitors sniffed, "they're selling you guys like a can of beer." The more the other stations complained, the most successful the commercials became. By the mid-1980s, WRC TV News progressed from stodgy to fun.

After the *Star Trek* world premiere, I regularly reminded Nuell about me and movies. "I used to review movies in Dallas—let's do it here." This time Nuell said, "what the hell. Let's try it."

Washington, D.C.

American Gigolo opened that week. Richard Gere plays a male escort who starts an affair with Lauren Hutton, a state senator's wife. I think I said it looked like an ad for sheets and towels and bored me silly. I wrapped up my review, giving it one star. Vance looked at me, grinned and said, "my man." Vance's form of approval.

John Rohrbeck (L) - David Nuell (R)

Rohrbeck called me into his office. Nuell was with him. "I want you on the end of the 6:00pm and on the end of the 11:00pm Monday through Friday." I gulped and said, "OK," wondering how I could fill all that time. Nuell read my mind and said, "do your features. Talk about movies." And he added, "go to local theater." I didn't know then that Nuell's wife Betsy acted in local theater. She'd been whispering in Nuell's ear to send me into the local theater scene, not knowing I covered local theater when I worked in Dallas.

For *American Gigolo*, I came up with rationale for reviews: did it deliver what it promised? Was it entertaining? Was it worth the five bucks? And I gave it a star rating—between one and four. Viewers would know where

I stood. These guidelines would make me different from Davey Marlin Jones on channel 9.

My second three-year contract was running out. I told Nuell I wanted a raise. He dragged his feet a little. One night after the 11:00pm News, I drove away from the station. Nuell raced his car behind mine, madly honking his horn and flashing his lights. I pulled over. "I've got your contract!" he shouted. I looked at it quickly. Three more years and a nice raise. We signed on the hood of my car, under a street lamp on Nebraska Avenue.

19
Best Movies of 1980

I STARTED A LIST OF TEN BEST MOVIES OF THE year in 1980. I still do it. Looking back, some movies get better with age, others not so much. In 1980, *The Empire Strikes Back* blew me away. I still believe it's one of the great sequels, along with *Godfather 2*. Watching with a packed preview audience at the KB Cinema's 826 seat auditorium, the crowd squealed as the story began. A gasp filled the auditorium when Darth Vader revealed his identity to Luke.

Eunice Kennedy Shriver welcomed *The Empire Strikes Back* cast to a world premiere at Kennedy Center (where else?) benefitting the Special Olympics. At the reception R2D2 gave interviews, Harrison Ford glared at my microphone, and Carrie Fisher looked glassy eyed as she slurred her words.

Being There remains one of my all-time favorites. Peter Sellers lampooned official Washington, playing a simpleton whose musings about gardening officials accept as metaphorical wisdom. Director Hal Ashby shot much of the story in the Biltmore Mansion in Asheville, North Carolina. I loved *Being There* so much I drove to Asheville just to experience Biltmore in person. I've watched *Being There* multiple times since. I suppose our information age makes the premise a little dated. I don't care. I love *Being There* and Peter Seller's performance.

I bought a ticket for the first matinee showing of *Airplane!* The Zucker brothers packed it with so many jokes, fans returned over and over just to catch all the punchlines. When I think of *Airplane!* I remember that afternoon joining a crowd who possibly sneaked out of work or school to fill the KB Cinema auditorium. The place exploded with laughter. I left the matinee feeling giddy.

I didn't think much of *Caddyshack* the first time I watched it. But then a few years later I took up golf and joined a country club and suddenly got it. Michael O'Keefe plays a poor kid trying to earn a caddy scholarship in order to go to college. Outrageous bits by Bill Murray, Chevy Chase, Rodney Dangerfield, and Ted Knight overpower any plot, other than an under class versus one percenters vibe. It's interesting that the one percenters and country clubbers lampooned seem to love *Caddyshack* the most. I interviewed Michael O'Keefe years later when he appeared on stage at Kennedy Center. O'Keefe who also excelled as the conflicted son of *The Great Santini,* told me people would slide up alongside him and drone, "Noonan—Noonan," drawing out the syllables of his *Caddyshack* character.

Jim Vance wanted to see *The Shining*. I gladly took him along to the critic's screening at the MacArthur Theater in Northwest D.C. As the writer going psycho in an abandoned hotel, Jack Nicholson had the audience on edge. I fondly remember Vance exclaiming, "JESUS!" at the top of his voice when Nicholson axes down a door screaming, "here's Johnny!"

This list from 1980 holds up pretty good. You could easily settle in to watch one of these some night.

Best Movies of 1980:
1. *The Empire Strikes Back*
2. *Being There*
3. *The Great Santini*
4. *Raging Bull*
5. *All That Jazz*
6. *Ordinary People*
7. *Close Encounters*
8. *The Elephant Man*
9. *Airplane!*
10. *The Shining* [43]
Extra: *Caddyshack*

20
"The World's Worst Film Festival"

ALL PUFFED UP, I CHARGED INTO DAVE Nuell's office and said, "I wanna cover the Oscars. Send me to L.A." Nuell glanced at me and said, "nah." Then he added, "I've got something better. Go up to New York and cover 'The World's Worst Film Festival.'" I don't remember if Nuell was serious, or making a wise crack, or read about it somewhere. I did some research, and sure enough there really was a "World's Worst Film Festival" in New York in 1980. I talked my way into some press credentials, hopped on the train, and arrived to witness the creation of the movies so bad they're good movement.

Harry Medved and his brother Michael touched a nerve, or at least a funny bone, when they published *The Fifty Worst Films of All Time*. The graphic sized paperback outlined schlock fare such as *They Saved Hitler's Brain*, in which former Nazis follow commands from Hitler's severed head in a big jar resting in the back of a Mercedes. In *Attack of the 50 Foot Woman*, an extremely tall woman wrecks a small town. *The Terror of Tiny Town* presents little people in the old west fighting a Munchkin villain. Many of these titles played on late night TV horror shows, such as *Shock!* the local show I loved as a twelve-year old in San Antonio.

The Worst Films book included a ballot for readers to nominate the worst of all time. To the Medved's amazement, three thousand ballots poured in advocating *Plan 9 from Outer Space*. Eccentric director Ed Wood stitched this together in 1959, with appearances by L.A. horror hostess Vampira and Swedish wrestler Thor Johnson as well as silent footage of Bela Lugosi and narration by the Amazing Criswell. The response to their book inspired the Medveds

Washington, D.C.

to rent New York's Beacon Theater on the upper west side for this delightful showcase in April 1980.

The trip didn't cost much. NBC traded out rooms with the Essex House. That meant the network ran commercials for the hotel and employees like me stayed free. Nuell called WNBC and arranged to borrow a camera crew for a night and use any footage they shot for their newscast. I turned "The World's Worst Film Festival" into a five-part series. It only cost a train ride and a few dinners at Wolfe's Delicatessen.

How great: a double feature every night: *Robot Monster*, and *They Saved Hitler's Brain*; *Reefer Madness* and *The Terror of Tiny Town*; *The Incredibly Strange Creatures Who Stopped Living and Became Mixed-Up Zombies*, and *Attack of the Killer Tomatoes*.

The week concluded with a screening of *Plan 9*, and a posthumous *Golden Turkey* "Worst in Show" award honoring the late director Ed Wood, presented by the *Penthouse* Pet of the Year. The audience screamed and hollered and threw popcorn at the screen.

"The World's Worst Film Festival" inspired *Mystery Science Theater* in which cartoon characters talked back to the bad movies on screen. *The Golden Turkey* for *Plan 9* inspired the award-winning big budget biography *Ed Wood*, based on Wood's eccentric career making low budget films.

The festival provided a tape of hilarious film clips. For four nights I profiled clunker movies. My series received pretty good response, especially to *Attack of the Killer Tomatoes*. Marty Levine, the news anchor who moved from San Diego, knew the story behind the film. A San Diego advertising man named John DeBello made it on the cheap to book in midnight shows.

Two young guys who ran the Jenifer Theater on Wisconsin Avenue saw my series. They booked *Attack of the*

Killer Tomatoes for a Friday midnight show and asked me to emcee. On the big night, the station sent a satellite truck for a live shot, a rarity in 1980. Kids lined up, some dressed as tomatoes. I held a best dressed tomato contest and awarded tomato plants to the winner, who called herself an "Irish" tomato. The entire anchor team came to the theater after the newscast for the gala sold out screening.

I don't remember anything about the Oscars in 1980, but I do remember "The World's Worst Film Festival", *Plan 9 from Outer Space,* and *Attack of the Killer Tomatoes.*

My visit to "The World's Worst Film Festival" and connection to *Attack of the Killer Tomatoes* caught the attention of some University of Maryland student filmmakers. They called themselves "The Langley Punks" and titled their collective efforts "Travesty Films." They invited me to a house they shared to watch some of their work. I laughed at titles including *Intestines from Space*, aliens who land on earth and digest unsuspecting humans. I marveled at *It Came from Marlow Heights* in which a kid eats too many "deathballs" (slang for hamburgers from a long-gone chain called Little Tavern) and *Alcoholics Unanimous*, a slick all-color production ending in an outrageous singing and dancing version of "When the Red Red Robin Comes Bob Bob Bobbin' Along."

The Langley Punks won fame at the Biograph Theater in Georgetown. Every few months, the Biograph held "Expose Yourself" nights. Anybody with an amateur film could bring it to the Biograph and show it. The night the Langley Punks presented *Alcoholics Unanimous*, the crowd erupted, stomping their feet demanding a second showing, which took place to cheers and applause. The combination of the Langley Punks and "Expose Yourself" gave me an idea. I figured if the Biograph could attract amateur films, why not Channel 4 News. My boss, Dave Nuell, loved the idea. We called it "The Home-Grown Film Festival." I made an announcement on the air and the movies started rolling in.

Some of those amateur films were really funny. One of the greatest arrived with the title *The Adventures of Infant Man*. Two local guys, Bruce Raucher and Tim Davis, turned their toddler into Superman, with the help of a tiny red cape, some stop action photography, and a flying dummy. The night I played *The Adventures of Infant Man* on the news, the studio laughter hit ten on the applause meter. You can see it now on YouTube.

That winter I put together a week of home-grown films. The Channel 4 program department repackaged the films into a half hour special with a studio audience, a musician on a pipe organ to accompany silent footage, and me in a tuxedo. The show concluded with the Langley Punks appearing to introduce *Alcoholics Unanimous*.

"The Home-Grown Film Festival" came at the beginning of the home video revolution that led to *America's Funniest Home Videos*. To me, the three-minute time limit of 8 mm home movies generated more creativity. However, home video offered instant pictures, and unlimited time. As video emerged, I received fewer great home-grown pieces, with one exception.

A ninth grader living in Virginia loved stop animation. He noticed my "Home-Grown" segment and went to work. Gary Waxler created a no budget version of our news set. In his first film, I turn into various characters from current movies. I was eaten by a killer tomato, then I morphed into Yoda, while the anchor team watches. The team loved seeing themselves as cartoon figures.

Gary created an encore. He sent in a film in which Bob Ryan pets Cujo, while I turn into a spaceman from *The Right Stuff*, and Vance morphs into Mr. T from *D.C. Cab*.

Gary's early work showed a sly sense of humor. His early films reminded me of the *Mr. Bill* movies on *Saturday Night Live*.

Courtesy Gary Waxler - Large Paw Productions

Gary went on to study film and animation at The University of Bridgeport Film School in Connecticut. After graduation, Gary worked as a free-lance cameraman and animator. In 1994, Gary called. He produced a grown-up version of his "Home-Grown" work. The new animation's professional backgrounds closely replicated the Channel 4 set. Gary sculpted clay figures that hilariously resembled the news team. In one segment, I turn into the Jim Carrey character from *The Mask*, putting on the mask, spinning my head until I turn green and my tongue hangs out of my mouth like one of Donald Trump's red ties. The images on the cover of this book come from that 1994 production.

Gary sent his Channel 4 masterpiece to Will Vinton Studios, creator of the *California Raisins* commercials in the 1980s. Vinton invited Gary out for professional certification, a big deal in animation. Now living in Florida, Gary formed Large Paw Productions. He's won film festival awards and an Emmy. He graciously gave me permission to use his work on the cover of this book.

Speaking of gracious, Gary gave each anchor the clay model sculpted for the film. I kept my cartoon heads (I had several) in a prominent place on my desk. Sometimes a visitor would jump at the sight of cartoon me in clay.

Courtesy Gary Waxler - Large Paw Productions

21
Rising Stars

Betty Davis swept into town in November, 1980 to promote *Skyward*, an NBC movie of the week. She played an elderly airplane stunt pilot who teaches a young paraplegic woman how to fly. Miss Davis arrived for a tightly controlled press conference where we reporters cowered behind a rope line, half afraid to speak in the icon's presence. I got up the nerve to shout out a question about President Reagan, her co-star in 1939's *Dark Victory*, wondering what she thought of his election to our nation's highest office.

"OHHHHH, I have NO political comment. NO. NOOOOOOOOOOO (she dragged the word out), I have no political comment." Betty uttered the words with the tiniest touch of mirth and a slight smile at the edge of her lips, covered with a gash of bright red lipstick.

The young director of *Skyward* lacked Betty Davis' intimidation factor. Ronnie Howard, then twenty-six years old, met me outside the American Film Institute Theater at Kennedy Center for a one-on-one interview. Known then as Opie from *The Andy Griffith Show*, as well as for his years on *Happy Days* and his role in *American Graffiti*, Ronnie (he answered to a youngster's name in 1980) happily discussed the courage it took to direct Miss Betty Davis. Ronnie went on to say he loved working with her and that he hoped to direct more movies in the future. I remember him as a nice kid. I had no idea he would become one of the most important directors of the coming decades. Whenever Ron Howard came to Washington to promote his many films, I reminded him of our meeting at the beginning of his directing career, which Ron Howard always graciously recalled.

Washington, D.C.

John Waters staged a high camp premiere of *Polyester* at the Key Theater in Georgetown on a balmy June night in 1981. Waters won fame for his edgy yet hilarious underground films such as *Mondo Trasho, Multiple Maniacs,* and *Pink Flamingo*s starring drag queen Divine as a participant in a contest for the title "filthiest person alive." *Pink Flamingos* concludes with Divine winning the title after eating fresh dog poop as the soundtrack plays *How Much is that Doggie in the Window?*

Polyester marked Water's bid for mainstream success. The film starred Divine and former teen idol Tab Hunter. The plot lampooned suburbia and family life, with Divine doing a lot of hyperventilating. Waters filmed the production in "Odorama." Audience members received a card with the numbers one through ten.

When the corresponding number appeared on screen, the audience received instructions to scratch and sniff. I remember some of the smells including roses, pizza, gasoline, airplane glue, and a fart.

The audience screamed in ecstasy when directed to scratch and sniff a fart. Channel 4 went all out, sending a live camera for my report. John Waters arrived, complete with pencil thin mustache, delivering snarky lines to my camera. During my live shot, Divine ran up and down Wisconsin Avenue. Kids on the Georgetown sidewalks gasped with delight. John Water's acting company followed a few steps behind, including Mink Stole, Edith Massey, and Cookie Mueller. I'm not sure Tab Hunter attended, but I think he did and was overshadowed by the nuttiness around him. I don't remember what Divine said into my microphone. I only know the sight of Divine in full make up and drag added some out of the ordinary zip to the 6:00pm news.

John Waters made it to mainstream success most notably writing and directing *Hairspray*, based on his childhood memories of 1950's Baltimore and an *American Bandstand* style local TV show's struggle to integrate black and white teenagers. Waters appeared with great humor on a show I hosted at Channel 4 a few years later. On another occasion he allowed our camera into his apartment for a tour which included his prize possession, the electric chair from the Jessup State Prison.

The Washington theater scene mushroomed in the 80s. Downtown D.C. emptied as shops moved to suburban malls. Dozens of small theater companies took advantage of all the empty space. Cutting edge stage companies delighted audiences. I fondly remember a performance of *Marie and Bruce* at the Woolly Mammoth Theater in the basement of a church on Massachusetts Avenue. During one especially outrageous scene, an elderly couple made quite a show of walking out. I loved it and reported it that night as part of my favorable review.

D.C.'s thriving theater scene led to the founding of The Helen Hayes Awards, an annual ceremony honoring the best work of both large and small stage groups. Richard Coe, *Washington Post* emeritus critic and a very nice man, persuaded his long-time friend and native Washingtonian, Helen Hayes to lend her name and presence to the awards. Miss Hayes attended most of the first gatherings as did her son the actor James MacArthur of the original *Hawaii Five-O*.

A fabulous after party followed the ceremony and became part of the tradition. During the first celebration I noticed a young actress with her parents. We started talking and I learned she graduated from the University of Texas at Austin, my alma mater. I don't remember what production she was nominated in that year, but she didn't win.

I jauntily told her she'd win another year, which seemed to brighten her spirits a little. The actress was Marcia Gay Harden, who went on to star in *Miller's Crossing* in 1990. She won the Best Supporting Actress Academy Award for *Pollock* ten years later.

A few days later, I stood outside the MacArthur Theater about to tape a stand up. Marcia Gay, then in her early 20s, jogged by, turned around and stopped to say hello. In the months to come, I watched her perform in *Equus* at the small Source Theater on 14th Street. Later, she led a performance of *Crimes of the Heart* at the Olney Theater that I remember as fondly as the film version. I still see Marcia Gay Harden as an athletic young woman jogging down MacArthur Boulevard in running shorts, stopping to say hello because I told her she'd win an acting award some year.

Washington radio crackled with excitement in the 80s. Several feisty stations battled for younger listeners not attracted to WMAL's middle of the road music and news, and WGAY's beautiful music. Two local guys named Don and Mike teamed up for mornings on the small WAVA station. Their slogan: "we're white, we're fat, and we're Catholic…and we're just sick about it." They called me at home a few times for bits on the air. One morning they convinced me to come to their studio at 8 am. I walked in and noticed a large woman, completely naked, giving an interview. Don and Mike booked her to discuss National Nudist Day. After she left, they turned to the completely flabbergasted me and also invited listeners to stop by and take off their clothes. A couple of naked kids ran across Arlington Boulevard outside the station. A young man and woman on their way to work came in and took off their clothes. I saw my career ending right then and there.

However, the police did not come and I managed to avoid scandal. I found Don and Mike very, very funny.

WRQX asked me to host their morning show when the regular team of Elliot and Woodside went on vacation. The offer took me back to my own radio days, at KTBC in Austin and WFAA in Dallas. Gary Murphy, the news guy came in and helped. Channel 4 taped my appearance for a story that day.

Howard Stern on my pathetic career— photo by Linda Norton

Howard Stern turned Washington radio inside out during 1981 and 1982, He arrived at WWDC radio in March, 1981 after kicking around several small stations. He brought the news woman hired for his shift into the studio, riffing with Robin Quivers on the news of the day.

He brought his producer Fred Norris in for comedy bits, and made WWDC Station Manager Goff Lebhar a daily punchline. A rock and roll disc jockey turned his shift into a comic talk show.

Howard discussed his wife's miscarriage as a comedy bit. When Air Florida Flight 90 took off during an ice storm and crashed into the 14th Street Bridge, Howard called Air Florida's headquarters asking if they offered direct service from National Airport to the 14th Street bridge. A year after arriving in town, almost everyone in town had heard about Howard Stern and his antics.

He invited me on his show one morning when he broadcast from Garvin's Comedy Club. I was a bit player as part of one of his panels. I can't remember what we judged. I wanted to put together a story on the deejay who came to town and got everyone's attention. Jim Van Messel, Channel 4's executive producer, hated Howard Stern and strongly suggested I include the offense many took of Howard's shock-jock bits. I did, and Stern never forgave me. I ran into Howard at the Oscars a few years later and he launched into a rant on my pathetic career. I laughed because I thought Stern was wildly talented and of course he went on to make hundreds of millions in New York radio and Satellite radio and as a television personality.

A rotund chain-smoking character named Jerry Nachman ran WRC Radio during Howard's reign. I knew Nachman pretty well as we ran across each other in the NBC building. Nachman persuaded WNBC Radio in New York to hire Stern, getting him out of town and off the Washington airwaves. Howard had a few months left on his contract with WWDC. He announced he was going to New York but would stay on the air until his WWDC contract ended. One day after a torrent of criticism about WWDC management, Station Manager Goff Lehbar fired Howard. Some think Lebhar axed him because he had lined up a replacement. Lebhar signed "The Grease Man" to take over the morning show. The Grease Man never achieved Howard Stern's level of popularity.[44]

The greatest radio voice to emerge from Washington began an unlikely climb in the 1970's, first as a volunteer for educational FM station WAMU-FM. Licensed to American University, programmed and staffed mostly by students and volunteers, WAMU broadcast from a sparse studio on campus on the frequency 88.5, the bottom of the dial where it attracted little or no attention.

In 1979, Diane Rehm moved up to host *Kaleidoscope*, a two-hour public affairs talk show that leaned heavily on comments by phone from listeners. Diane possessed no previous broadcast experience, having spent her early married years raising two children. She displayed extraordinary intelligence, good manners, and an ability to listen and respond with questions that moved the conversation forward. Authors, many of them politicians, discovered her show which in turn brought more listeners. Prominent journalists began appearing on her Friday segment discussing national and world events of the week.

Diane liked movies. She often invited Davey Marlin Jones of Channel 9 to discuss the latest. I think one of her producers noticed me and suggested a try out appearance. I did not think much of the invitation, but accepted and came to the studio thinking I was appearing on a student program. Instead, I encountered a trim, attractive, mature woman a few years older than I.

Feeling full of myself, as if I was doing Diane a favor, I answered her first questions with a burst of energy and started banging the table for emphasis. If I did this today, she would correct me on the air and possibly dismiss me from the studio. For some reason my behavior amused her. Toward the end of the hour I said, "you are certainly a surprise to me. I want your listeners to know you are a beautiful woman. I thought you were some old bag." I wouldn't dare make that kind of remark today, but back then Diane's eyes twinkled and she broke out into a big broad smile. After that, I appeared three or four times a year, and loved every appearance. I guess she liked that I was funny and had energy and came across on the radio as having fun.

Diane continued as WAMU emerged as the leading NPR station in Washington. Her show went national in the 90s. She occasionally booked me for her national show as part of a panel of film experts. To my surprise, when I left

NBC after 32 years, she booked me for a farewell appearance heard on NPR stations across America.

Diane included me in her family events including an annual Easter Sunday brunch. I attended anniversary parties for Diane and her husband John. The invitation to her show turned into an invitation for friendship.

Diane retired after thirty-seven years on WAMU, but only from her weekday show. Since 2016 she has hosted a regular podcast. She also advocates for the right to die with dignity, producing and narrating a national PBS documentary on that subject.

She showed her tough side and taught me a lesson I've never forgotten. One night, starting in the middle of the night, a toilet in our two-story house overflowed and kept overflowing. When I woke up, water flooded the bathroom, leaked one floor down into the hall, leaked further into the basement and flowed out of the garage and into the street, producing a small river. I called Diane.

"I can't come today. My house has flooded and I've got to clean it up."

"You made a commitment!"

"I can't come."

"That is crap-o-crapola. You made a commitment."

I went on her show. The first thing she asked was for me to tell the story of my overflowing toilet. She beamed and giggled a little as I told the story. I remembered her lesson, especially when someone canceled on me, although I lacked the courage to challenge them the way Diane challenged me. When you committed to her show, she expected you to show up, regardless.

Washington radio filled the air in the 1980s and 90s with competitive talent. Some, like Howard Stern, went on to make millions. For me, the most important voice to come from Washington radio belongs to Diane Rehm.

22
The Oscars

Jim Van Messel, now the newscast executive producer, walked up with a wry smile on his face.

"My wife and I were standing in line for a movie. Two kids behind us quoted YOU, saying YOU said it was good." I expected him to add they watched and thought the movie stunk. Instead, he raised his eyebrows and sauntered away.

That spring, John Rohrbeck, the visionary General Manager who loved Los Angeles, decided I should report from the Oscars. Rohrbeck caught me in the hall. "Go out to L.A. and give us a presence at the Oscars. I like the Bel Air Hotel—book yourself a room there."

Landing in L.A., I drove up the 405 freeway to Sunset Boulevard, turned on Stone Canyon and ambled past the Bel Air Country Club. "Oh yes, Mr. Campbell, welcome to the Bel Air Hotel." The place oozed luxury with flowers and

Washington, D.C.

gardens, and room service breakfasts. In a few years, the massive GE corporation would buy NBC, abruptly ending this kind of extravagance. In 1981, how sweet it was.

KNBC-TV, the L.A. NBC owned station, assigned a crew to me for three days. I produced a couple of stories on L.A. real estate and famous landmarks. I interviewed a few NBC celebrities. I headed to the newsroom the morning of March 30, 1981, ready for my first in-person visit to the movie industry's biggest event.

I heard shouting in the KNBC newsroom. President Reagan had been shot. Doctors were performing surgery at George Washington Hospital. The network took over programming, thinking this might compare to the Kennedy assassination. The Motion Picture Academy quickly announced they would postpone the Oscar Show, a first. KNBC, so welcoming to me, offered a crew so I could report to Washington on the Oscar delay. I called WRC. My home newsroom was in chaos. "Don't do anything," Van Messel screamed, "just go back to your hotel and we'll call you." I never heard back from anybody, so I went back to the Bel Air Hotel and watched the coverage with everyone else. Reagan's recovery changed everything. The next night, the Oscars began with a videotaped introduction from President Reagan, recorded several days before the shooting. With President Reagan safe and recovering, the Oscar show went forward on April 1, 1981.

The time difference made my Oscar visits a breeze. In California, the show begins at 6:00pm, which is 9:00pm in D.C. My early news live-shots hit between 3 and 4:00pm in California, 6 and 7 D.C. time. ABC, not NBC, broadcast the ceremony. For the WRC late news, I reported from the red carpet around 8:20 L.A. time. I could only talk about the early winners as the show had an hour or more to go. No matter. My Oscar trips gave me credibility. I looked impressive in my tux reporting live from the Dorothy Chandler Pavilion.

After 1981, I made an Oscar trip every year, until budget cuts ended my Oscar visits in the late 90s. My Oscar trips resumed after 2007 for ABC affiliate WJLA. I think I must have attended at least 20 Oscar ceremonies as credentialed press.

In the 80s the parade of red-carpet stars concluded with the appearance of R-rated starlet Edy Williams, a voluptuous actress famous for a series of Russ Meyer soft porn movies. Edy streaked the red carpet in a series of low-cut bikini style costumes. Friendly security guards let her walk into the lobby as if attending. One year an Eric Estrada lookalike jogged up the red carpet, walking inside with no trouble. In the 1970s, a streaker flashed across the Oscar stage behind host David Niven. Oscar night had an anything goes vibe in those much looser pre-security times. The Academy required one rule of decorum. Reporters, camera people, technicians—all of us must wear a tuxedo.

I loved milling around the television press room, where pool cameras fed the backstage press conferences to stations across the country. Winners came backstage first to a print press room and then to the television press room. Monitors played the broadcast, but once the big names showed up, the monitors went mute and the celebs answered the usual array of, "how does it feel?" questions. Backstage at the Oscars I missed much of the broadcast.

One year I found a nice restaurant across from the Dorothy Chandler Pavilion. Wearing my tuxedo, I took a seat at the bar with a perfect view of a large monitor. I ordered a drink, consumed a lovely dinner, and took notes on the show until my 8:00pm live shot. Then I sauntered inside to watch the rest in the press room backstage.

Washington, D.C.

The camera crews I worked with insisted on showing me the "real" L.A. We stopped for chili dogs at Pinks or took lunch at DuPars, the well-known mid 50s coffee shop. We never missed an opportunity to stop at Musso and Frank on Hollywood Boulevard. Ever since, I've stopped at Musso and Frank Grill on every L.A. visit. One technician insisted we eat at a place in Glendale called The Bucket. It looked like an upside-down bucket. Inside, an exuberant Greek guy grilled a combination of potatoes, onions, and Italian sausage. So good. Such heartburn.

23.
The Monkey vs. Wall Street

IN 1980, THE INFLATION RATE HIT ALMOST 15 per cent—for just one year. The basket of groceries that cost $1.00 in January cost $1.15 by the end of December. Many people feared keeping pace.

I wish I could tell you how this next event happened, but I don't remember. It might have come from a session between me and Dave Nuell. I think he suggested a series on inflation and personal investing. Neither of us had any idea the idea would morph into "The Monkey versus Wall Street."

The series began setting up a contest to track what might happen if you invested $1000 four different ways. Certificates of Deposit paid around ten per cent that year. For the series I would compare the interest earned on the CD with the growth or decline of a mutual fund, bought on the same exact day. For the third comparison, I connected with Julia Walsh, founder of Walsh and Sons brokerage. Julia Walsh earned a great reputation in town as the first woman to hold a seat on the New York Stock Exchange. I asked her to pick her three favorite growth stocks. The fourth comparison I came up with as a gag. I found a guy with a trained monkey. We filmed the monkey with a felt tip marker in his paw. The trainer motioned the monkey toward the stock listings in the newspaper. The monkey marked three stocks. Those three picked at random made my fourth comparison. Then, I forgot about the whole thing until a month later, when I compared the four funds.

The monkey's stocks pulled ahead just a little. I think the CD outperformed the mutual fund and Julia Walsh. Over the months to come, the monkey's stocks soared.

Washington, D.C.

For each segment I would interview a financial expert. A few months into the contest, the results had Julia Walsh, whom I truly liked and respected, sputtering. At the end of the six months, nobody came close to the monkey, whose wildly random picks beat the market and everything else. A second stock broker challenged me to do it again. For the next series I threw darts at the stock listings, and won again.

Nuell's assistant Joel Albert loved the way this worked out. Joel brought me the paperwork to enter the Fiscal Policy Council's reporting competition. In February of 1981, I received a letter informing me I won the Martin R. Gainsbrugh Citation of Distinction for exceptional and distinguished economic news broadcasting.

I guess they didn't know I did the whole thing as a joke. I just needed material to fill ten appearances a week. Later, I learned I proved something called the "random walk" theory of investing, in which stocks picked at random often do better than stocks picked by professionals.

Joel Albert and Dave Nuell and many others laughed about my highly unlikely economics reporting award. I kept my award of distinction in a frame over my desk for the next twenty-five years.

24
Movies of the Early 80s

Photo by Bob Casazza

1981: I WALKED INTO THE PACKED OPENING night of *Raiders of the Lost Ark* at the KB Cinema knowing nothing about the movie. As it begins, archeological adventurer Harrison Ford as Indiana Jones enters an ancient cave, making his way to an altar. He accidentally springs a hidden trap and suddenly a boulder that almost fills the screen rolls toward him, coming closer and closer as Ford runs faster and faster. The crowd erupted and the story took off from there. Viewers floated out of the theater knowing we just watched something extraordinary—the start of a series that would last decades.

Body Heat shows up on cable every now and then and continues to pass the test of time with flying colors. The Friday it opened in 1981, I started my review: "in *Body Heat*, a no-good man meets a no-good woman and they get up to no good together. And I love it." I still do. Over the years Kathleen Turner came to town for appearances in various productions at Arena Stage. With her deep voice and blazing eyes, Turner always made for a fun and slightly frightening interview. She worked hard to overcome typecasting as *Body Heat*'s femme fatale. She didn't like it when journalists brought up *Body Heat*, even though her turn as the sultry Maddie made her a star. In 1981, a Washington woman who prefers to remain anonymous formed the *Body Heat* Society. She remains vague about the club activities.

Chariots of Fire remains a timeless story of class, privilege, and strongly held beliefs. I found it interesting to see *Chariots of Fire* referenced in the fifth season of *The Crown*, reminding viewers that Dodi Fayed, Princess Diana's lover who died in the Paris collision that killed her, came to prominence as Executive Producer of *Chariots of Fire*. After the 1982 ceremony, I ran into the director David Putman, at the Bel Air Hotel. Since we were staying in the same posh location, I congratulated him on his Oscar as best director. He accepted the compliment as if I were someone important.

Roger Mudd slipped into the urinal next to mine at NBC. He looked at me and proclaimed, "I watched *Melvin and Howard* because of your review and DID NOT like it." With that, Roger zipped up and left.

1982: The audience squirmed during the preview of *An Officer and a Gentleman*. Watching Richard Gere almost break under Lou Gossett Jr.'s basic training made me sweat. The love scene between Debra Winger and Richard Gere pushed the envelope. Everyone held their breath, making no sound, watching the lovers on screen. When Richard Gere bursts into the factory, picks Debra Winger up in his arms, and sweeps her out the door, the place went nuts. I can still hear the squeals of delight.

1983: Nobody noticed *A Christmas Story* when it opened just before Thanksgiving. The director, Bob Clark, made his reputation with a string of horror movies and the R rated sex comedy *Porky's*. *A Christmas Story* tapped into writer Jean Shepherd's nostalgic story of a kid who wants a Red Ryder air rifle for Christmas, only to hear at every turn, "it'll put your eye out." VHS rentals and the 24-hour TNT marathons turned *A Christmas Story* into a classic, worthy of comparison to *It's a Wonderful Life*. Jean Shepherd narrates his own story. He worked many years as a late-night host on New York Radio station WOR delivering monologues based on his stories about growing up in the 1940s. I think Shepherd's narration takes *A Christmas Story* from good to great.

Not too many remember the film of the opera *La Traviata*. It stays with me because I watched it in the screening room of the Motion Picture Producers Association. I ducked out to pee. As I came out of the men's room, the great Jack Valenti bounced into the lobby, saw me, and said, "what are you watching?" He stuck his head in the theater and stayed for a few scenes. Valenti, an LBJ protégé, will go down in history as the MPAA's greatest lobbyist. He knew politics and he loved movies. It wasn't just business with him.

Risky Business previewed at the K B Cinema on Wisconsin Avenue. Tom Cruise announced his stardom in a hilarious energy filled story of a high school senior left to his own devices when his parents go on vacation. His night of freedom includes major disasters: a wrecked Porsche, an encounter with high dollar escort Rebecca De Mornay, and an entrepreneurial solution to his problems. I remember the audience screaming with laughter when Cruise utters his response to apparently failing his interview to attend Princeton, "well, it looks like it's the University of Illinois."

Washington, D.C.

1984: I teared up at the conclusion of *Places in the Heart*. I didn't know why. Later I learned screenwriter Robert Benton argued long and hard for the final scene in which Sally Field shares communion in a small Baptist church with characters both living and dead, a visual portrait of the Bible's communion of saints. This story, based on Robert Benton's grandmother, of a widow holding her family together in depression Texas, still touches me. I covered the Oscars the year Sally Field accepted the award for best actress and delivered her, "you like me" speech. Wags lampooned her at the time. Sally Field got the last laugh as her career has endured and expanded over the decades since.

Amadeus previewed at the National Theater before opening on Broadway. During the D.C. run, producers rewrote and revised the second act and ending. Watching those performances gave audiences the opportunity to see a masterpiece in development. The film version four years later won F. Murray Abraham the best acting Oscar as the uninspired court composer Salieri unnerved by the genius of the unruly immature Mozart, played by Tom Hulce. I interviewed Hulce not long after the film opened. I found him depressed, and uncommunicative. A decade after *Amadeus,* Hulce (also known for *Animal House,*) switched from acting to directing and producing. In 2007. Tom Hulce received a Tony award as lead producer of the Broadway musical *Spring Awakening.*

I believe viewers like hearing about movies, even if they don't intend to go. Opening day of various blockbusters made a good story, showing the excitement and interviewing kids lined up for hours. Walking along the crowd lined up for *Indiana Jones and the Temple of Doom,* I asked a random teenager how he got his ticket.

"My Dad gave it to me," he said.

"Who's your dad?" I asked.

"Davey Marlin Jones."

That night I put the sound bite of Oliver Jones, son of Davey Marlin Jones, on the air, a playful jab at the big dog in town. Today my friend Oliver works as an entertainment journalist and film professor in Los Angeles. We still laugh about our first encounter. You can hear him on his regular appearances on my podcast.

Washingtonian Magazine sponsored a Best & Worst list every year including Best Local TV Movie Reviewer. Davey Marlin Jones placed first all during the 70s. I received my first mention in 1981. In 1983 viewers picked me over Davey Marlin Jones at Channel 9 and John Corcoran at Channel 7. I placed first every year for the rest of the decade until *Washingtonian* retired the category.

25
I Love L.A.

John Rohrbeck, the genius General Manager who turned third place WRC-TV News into a contender, received his reward in 1984. NBC appointed him General Manager of KNBC Los Angeles, the station and city he loved. Rohrbeck's vision for WRC of a team of unique players came together, especially at 11:00pm. By 1984, our news broadcast knocked Channel 9 out of first place every now and then—a feat that seemed impossible during Channel 9's dominance in the 1970s. NBC's improved network programming ratings helped. Rohrbeck's vision laid the groundwork.

I wanted to move to L.A. with Rohrbeck. I'd already lined up a secret weapon a year earlier: an agent. Several  big names in Washington, including Jim Vance, hired Richard Liebner to represent them. Liebner sealed his reputation when he nailed down the CBS News anchor job for Dan Rather. I sent Liebner a tape. He called, inviting me to New York for lunch with him and his wife Carol. They liked me. I liked them. Liebner said when my contract finished, he'd negotiate the next deal, and I wouldn't pay anything until that happened. We shook hands.

Beginning with the 1981 Oscars, I traveled to L.A. to report from the Academy Awards red carpet and to shoot a few other stories while in town. I interviewed old time stars Pinky Lee and Troy Donahue, and NBC television actors and actresses. I rented a 1960 Cadillac convertible from a classic car company and took footage of me piloting the Caddy around Hollywood. I attended screenings at pristine movie theaters in Westwood near the UCLA Campus. Working out of KNBC-TV in Burbank, I felt comfortable. The KNBC newsroom was laid back and helpful and the people I dealt with liked me and I liked them. I loved L.A. I still do.

I saw Rohrbeck as my big chance. I knew KNBC used network reporter Jim Brown for entertainment behind the scenes coverage. Over time, Brown worked less for KNBC and more for *The Today Show*. For a while KNBC didn't review movies.

Years earlier, on one of my first visits to California, I watched John Barbour give a review on KNBC. He delivered a screed against *The Man Who Loved Cat Dancing*. Evidently, Paramount Pictures barred him from a preview, so he bought a ticket when it opened. He hated it, concluding his review with, "that is why I am the man who HATES *Cat Dancing*. ZERO." I laughed and had a vision of myself doing that someday.

KNBC's News Director, whom Rohrbeck intended to replace, hired a friend from Oklahoma named Dino Lalli to review on KNBC. Rumor had it Dino used to be the News Director's barber in Oklahoma. I met Dino and worked next to him at the Oscars. I liked his enthusiasm, and I liked him. He owned his unsophistication, rating movies with Lalli-Pops. I knew Rohrbeck wanted to replace him. Why not with me? Ultimately Dino returned to Oklahoma and continued a long successful career in broadcasting. I marched into Rohrbeck's office.

Washington, D.C.

"I want to go to L.A. with you." Rohrbeck jerked his head a little and said nothing. "Come on, John, you need a movie reviewer and I can do it. Take me with you." Rohrbeck admitted he planned to replace the News Director and Dino Lalli. Finally, he said, "I'll look into it," nodding and grinning and laughing a little. "Now get out of here."

I really wanted that job. My friend John Corcoran landed a gig in L.A. at the number one station KABC. At least I would have one friend in the press corps if I moved to L.A. Our new boss arrived from the NBC station in Chicago. A warm friendly guy named Fred DeMarco came around shaking hands. He brightened up when he saw me. I responded, "I'm looking forward to working with you."

My contract expired in a few weeks. I called my new agent Richard Liebner and said, "get me the job at KNBC." By this time, Jim Van Messel had moved up to News Director and Dave Nuell was promoted to Station Manager. He and DeMarco rushed into my office. "What are you doing?" Van Messel shouted. I shrugged my shoulders. "You can't go to L.A," DeMarco said, "you said you were looking forward to working with me." I said, "yeah, but I didn't say how long. Besides, Rohrbeck needs a movie reviewer." And then I stretched the truth a little. "HE pitched me." That shut them up, because they knew Rohrbeck wouldn't think twice about anything that would give him a competitive edge. Van Messel said, "I think you're great. We need you HERE. We're going to talk to your agent."

I called Liebner and told him what happened. He said,"Just keep working and don't say anything to anybody." Then he called back and said DeMarco and Van Messel were flying to New York the next day. My little visit to John Rohrbeck's office gave Liebner leverage. The truth is: I really wanted to move to L.A.. I wanted to live in Pasadena, and commute to Burbank on the Ventura freeway.

I won't tell you the figures, I'll only tell you Liebner doubled my salary. He tacked a 7 percent commission onto my pay, but considering the increases he won, I never regretted anything I paid Richard Liebner. He represented me 27 years. He also negotiated a weekly movie review and fee from the network's newsfeed service. The program department wanted me to host a local show to air after *Saturday Night Live*. Liebner negotiated a nice fee for that too. Basically, I hit the jackpot because I wanted to move to L.A.

Rohrbeck hired David Sheehan as the KNBC entertainment reporter/movie reviewer. Sheehan had deep roots in L.A. and the industry, having worked for the CBS owned television station from 1970 until the early 80's. He stayed with KNBC for a decade, then returned to KCBS. I crossed paths with Sheehan many times and respected his talent. He knew Rohrbeck almost hired me, and sometimes gave me the stink eye, which I took as the mark of a great competitor. I think I would have succeeded in L.A. I also think I wouldn't have lasted as long as I did in Washington.

My movie reviews went out once a week to all the NBC affiliates. Sheehan probably hated me for that. Pretty soon my reviews regularly ran on about 50 stations. When I came to L.A. and walked the halls of KNBC, people recognized me. I heard Johnny Carson and his producer Freddy DiCordova, would watch the affiliate feed for story ideas, and liked my reviews, mainly because I wiggled my eyebrows as I finished.

My boundless good luck continued. Kathy McCampbell, a fellow reporter,[45] left the newsroom to take the job of WRC Program Director. I'd enjoyed some success hosting a half hour special of the amateur movies for *The Home Grown Film Festival*. Kathy asked me to produce something light to run during four open half hour weekend spots that fall on Saturday afternoons.

Washington, D.C.

George Michael hosted a local sports show that aired 7:30 Saturday night, and repeated after *Saturday Night Live*. I think he interviewed players for the Washington football team. The season ended and Kathy needed something to replace it. She suggested *The Arch Campbell Show*. She liked what we did so much she suggested airing it again at 1:00am, after *Saturday Night Live*, a perfect time slot.

Kathy put together a small staff. We connected with The Improv and a few other comedy clubs. We taped Thursday nights. One of the comedy clubs sent over their weekend headliner. Our unknown comics included Ray Romano, Yakov Smirnoff, and a kid living with his grandmother in suburban Greenbelt, Maryland named Martin Lawrence.

A new club in Baltimore called the Power Plant pitched a special from their location to promote the new venue. The club bought some commercial time, which gave us a small budget. For $100 bucks plus plane fare, we booked an unknown woman named Roseanne Barr. She performed her "I'm a housewife" monologue to great laughter. Visiting backstage before the show, Roseanne told me she worked all the time, rarely saw her family, missed them, and hoped she'd break through someday. A few months later, she co-starred in a special with Rodney Dangerfield. The special led to *Roseanne*. Ten years later, I interviewed her as part of a promotion for one of her projects. I mentioned the Power Plant, and meeting her on the way up. I'd love to tell you she remembered the show and me fondly. When I mentioned it, Roseanne gave me a blank look and shrugged.

26
Reagan's Microphone

Consumer reporter Lea Thompson received a message to call the White House. Lea thought someone was pulling her leg. It turned out the call was real. President Reagan wanted information about one of her reports. The White House told Lea the President watched the 5:00pm News every day while working out on a treadmill.

Steve Doocy created funny stories to end the 5:00pm News. He produced a story featuring a Ronald Reagan impersonator. The White House called. The President wanted a copy. Doocy made a tape, and personally delivered it to the White House. President Reagan stepped out of the Oval Office to accept, telling Doocy he watched him every day.

Not long after President Reagan's reelection, I heard from Bob Johnston. His brother Ernie Jr, a friend and colleague, ran Allied Advertising, the company that placed most of the movie advertising in town. Bob told me the Reagans wanted me to emcee one of the Presidential Balls the night of January 20, 1985. Wow.

The campaign wanted the 1985 inaugural celebration to contrast with 1981. Rather than the big-name stars of the glamourous first Reagan inauguration, they preferred a local vibe. The other hosts included Willard Scott, Channel 9 Sportscaster Glenn Brenner, local radio personalities Jim Elliott and Scott Woodside, football star John Riggins, and several local Olympic athletes.

The government and Secret Service checked my background thoroughly. When I reported to the Sheraton Park hotel the afternoon of January 20, they pinned a level five badge on my tuxedo and hung a giant red clearance pass around my neck. My duties included making a few announcements, introducing the band, and handing the microphone to the President once he arrived. After he finished his remarks, I would invite the President to dance with Mrs. Reagan. January 20, 1985 ranked among the coldest days in D.C. history, with a high of seven degrees and a wind chill several degrees below zero. The inaugural ceremony moved into the Capitol Rotunda. The committee canceled the Inaugural parade, a first.

At 7:00pm I walked on stage and welcomed the crowd. The great jazz singer Joe Williams performed with the new Count Basie Orchestra. During breaks, he and I stood off stage making small talk. Fortunately, I knew Williams' work, including his signature songs "Every Day I Get the Blues," and "All Right, OK, You Win."

Around 10:00pm the band struck up "Hail to the Chief!" and in walked President and Mrs. Reagan. The crowd erupted. The first couple looked dazzling. Reagan, the consummate performer, waved and let the applause soak in, then gave a quick glance in my direction: my cue to hand him the microphone. I bounded in for the hand off and he began speaking.

He started with a joke, something on the order of, "considering this weather, we thought nobody'd come." Then he bragged about the stock market, and promised some good economic news the next day. He made a few references to other President's inaugural balls, thanked the crowd, and made another quick glance in my direction: my second cue.

I walked up with a second microphone and said, "Mr. President, would you do this crowd the honor of leading the ball with a dance with your wife Mrs. Reagan?" The President handed me his mike, turned to the crowd, threw his hands and arms open in one of his familiar gestures, as if to say, "why, sure." Mrs. Reagan stepped in to him and the couple faced the musicians. The Count Basie Orchestra struck up the Neil Hefti smooth jazz tune "Lil' Darling." After a few swirls, the music ended, the Reagans waved, and off they went to the next of nine inaugural balls.

Channel Four assigned long time photographer Harry Davis to tape the Presidential appearance as well as several other events that night. I watched Harry come in and set up. I couldn't get to him because of the crowd. A sea of people stood between me on the stage and Harry on the other side of the room. We waved at each other. At least I knew a Channel 4 camera would record my big moment. I could hardly wait to watch the footage the next day, when I planned to report on my brush with President Reagan.

The next day, January 21st, I started screening Harry Davis' camera footage. I forwarded the tape and saw the President and First Lady sweep onto the stage. A little later the President glanced to his left. I expected to see me walking into frame to hand the President his microphone. That's what I expected. Instead, Harry kicked in his usual news instinct. He zoomed in, cutting me out of the picture. His tape only caught a shot of my hand sticking a mike in Reagan's direction. When I returned to retrieve the President's mike, again Harry only captured my hand. He thought the station wanted the Presidential remarks, not me. My biggest night, with a Channel 4 cameraman rolling, documented by a frame or two of my hand shoving a mike toward the President.

My story the next day became, "My Presidential Hand Off." I used footage of the President arriving and the crowd frenzy and then at the second my hand came into the frame I stopped the footage. "That's my hand!" I screamed. "That's my contribution to Inauguration Night." I followed with a shot of Reagan handing the mike back—to my hand. Just my luck.

Recently, I discovered the actual footage, taken by the White House pool camera crew, the group that followed the first couple everyplace they went that night. The pool footage shows everything. I'm glad I found the footage because I was beginning to think I dreamed the whole thing. Everybody in the newsroom, including me, loved cameraman Harry Davis. He looked sheepish when I told him he cut me out of my own story. I glared at him and then we both laughed.

Three and a half years later, I received a call from Mrs. Reagan's press office inviting me to a screening of the 1942 Jimmy Cagney musical *Yankee Doodle Dandy*. The caller included specific instructions. I was to arrive at the East Gate at 5:00pm. Wear a coat and tie. At exactly 5:30pm dessert and coffee would be served. At 6:30pm we would move to the family theater for the film. The instructions played out exactly.

I walked in and spotted Willard Scott. An old pro at these things, Willard came over and gave me a bear hug. Tom Shales, the TV critic of *The Washington Post* stood nearby. Bernard Shaw, CNN lead anchor, stood with his wife. The President came over to say hello. I think I asked what he thought of modern movies. He started talking about racy movies and how Hollywood did it on purpose and shook his head. Reagan motioned to his plate of pie and mentioned how much he liked desert at the White House.

Right on schedule, the forty guests filed into the White House theater. We sat in comfortable upholstered chairs. Waiters served popcorn and jelly beans on silver trays. Mrs. Reagan came to the front of the theater and thanked us for coming. She introduced A.C. Lyles, a veteran Hollywood

The Accidental Critic

producer who worked at Paramount Pictures most of his career. I imagine the Reagans knew Lyles when she and Ron worked as actors. Lyles made a speech about *Yankee Doodle Dandy* and how they don't make 'em like this anymore. The 1942 black and white musical captured Jimmy Cagney in his prime as song and dance man George M. Cohan. Corny and sentimental, *Yankee Doodle Dandy* doesn't exactly pass the test of time, however watching Cagney sing and dance was thrilling.

When the credits rolled, we applauded and took our cue to leave. Mrs. Reagan said goodbye to each of us at the door. As I approached, she said, "did you like the movie?" I blurted out, "oh, four stars." She broke into a big grin and laughed.

A photographer told me the White House will not release an unflattering photo of the President. When President Reagan said hello during dessert, the official photographer took several shots of me and him. A package arrived at my office a few days later with some beautiful shots of me and Mrs. Reagan, and none of me and President Reagan. Left out—once again. You'll just have to take my word for it.

27
1985: *The Color Purple* and Oprah

Oprah swept into the less than fabulous Tenley Shopping Mall on Wisconsin Avenue, where one of three small theaters would premiere her movie debut in *The Color Purple*. Her appearance turned what looked like just another preview into an event. Oprah flashed a million-dollar smile and headed right for my camera. She beamed at my question about her rise to fame from local TV to national talk show personality to major film star. Her remarks compared to Muhammad Ali proclaiming, "I am the greatest!"

By this time *Oprah!* had ascended to daytime television's number one position. Her career took off after a rocky start a few years earlier at station WJZ in Baltimore. Co-hosting a morning talk show, *People Are Talking*, with Baltimore newsman Richard Sher, Oprah found her voice, moved to Chicago, went national and now was conquering Hollywood and the movies. Oprah's performance in *The Color Purple* elevated her to superstar or even megastar status. She shared the screen with Whoopi Goldberg as one of two sisters separated in the early 20th century and reunited after lives of hardship at story's end. Oprah held her own among the veteran cast. Not only Oprah, but also Whoopi Goldberg benefited from *The Color Purple*'s success. The project marked a change from director Steven Spielberg's usual blockbuster fare, expanding his reach.

Oprah's former WJZ talk show host Richard Sher attended the screening. Oprah consumed the spotlight. Her former co-host stayed deep in Oprah's shadow. Many remember Oprah's pairing with Sher on the morning show as a last gasp effort to find a place for her. Now the morning team reunited, except this time Oprah had turned into a one-word phenomenon.

Some years later, Oprah hosted a special for NBC. WRC sent me to Baltimore to interview her former partner Richard Sher at WJZ. Sher was friendly and great fun, even though I imagine he was going through another one of dozens of interviews about his early days with Oprah. Richard Sher possessed plenty of charisma and star power on his own. In this case, Oprah landed the big break instead of him.

Courtesy WJZ TV

Gossips whispered that Sher expected to go to Chicago with Oprah, and harbored mixed feelings that she left him behind. Richard Sher stayed at WJZ 33 years. He's hosted several projects in retirement. The day I met him and the time I spent with him gave me the impression he long ago made peace with standing in Oprah's shadow.

28
When the Inmates Ran the Asylum

Courtesy WRC-TV

WILLARD SCOTT EXPLAINED THE SECRET OF his early success: "I worked nights and avoided the management during the day."

Managers and salespeople and News Directors swarmed the newsroom during business hours. At night, we—the newsroom rabble—ruled.

The building cleared after the 6:00pm News, only a few engineers remained. Reporters traveled to story assignments, anchors went to a restaurant or home for dinner. I traveled to a theater performance, a movie screening, or an event. Around 9, the on-air team wandered back.

Occasionally, Vance, Bob Ryan, George Michael, and

I went to dinner. One evening somebody suggested a new restaurant on K Street. Drinks were served, wine flowed. I got back to the station and asked Bob Ryan, "who picked up the check?" He shrugged. Vance and George laughed when I asked. I learned the meaning of the phrase "on the house."

The news editing rooms were on one side of the building, with tape playback on the opposite side. Every night a news aide ran with edited videotape from one end of the building to the other, where an engineer operated the playback machine. News people—most of us drama junkies—work to the last second. Getting the tapes to playback created a nightly marathon race.

The director James L. Brooks observed the network and local newsrooms for several days researching *Broadcast News*. The movie includes a scene of a young woman, played by Joan Cusack, sprinting with a just completed news story. She jumps over file cabinets and pushes people out of her way, making it to playback with one second to spare. I believe WRC inspired that *Broadcast News* vignette.

The NBC News Washington bureau wanted room to expand. The company agreed to build an addition attached to the back of the building and move local news to the new space. NBC would take over our part of the newsroom. A three-story addition went up over the course of several months. Among the first improvements, tapes played back next to the rooms where editors assembled our stories. No more marathon race. The anchors and featured reporters, including me, received private offices. The new building made our team feel important and appreciated.

Vance gained the roomiest space at the head of a row of private offices. He brought in a turntable and played mellow jazz at night. I could hear the music in my office two doors up the corridor. A cloud of smoke drifted from

Vance's office as he sat back, listened to music, and puffed his Camels. He hung a Black Power poster of an athletic nude woman with a giant Afro in a prominent space on his wall. When I walked by, Vance often beckoned me in for a visit with his go to expression, "my man."

I loved Vance's cave of an office. When he was in a good mood, Vance was the greatest company in the world. Sometime his moods turned dark. In the early 80s Vance began disappearing, calling in sick at the last moment. One morning he called me at home asking if I'd lend him a couple hundred bucks. A pair of rough looking dudes drove him to my house. I gave him a check. On a spring day in 1984, a memo announced Vance had left for a rehab facility. I found a check for the money I lent him in my mailbox. Vance would return to rehab in the years ahead. To his credit, he never made a secret of his problems, or his efforts to solve them.

George Michael's sports department occupied a giant space at the end of the hall. His visits to Vance's office doubled the smoke pouring out. I could hear the two of them laughing and cursing and running down various managers. "Bastard." "Bonehead." My favorite insult, given the nature of the business: "Carpetbagger." Their talk reminded me of the big family gatherings of my childhood when my father sat next to his favorite cousin whispering dirty jokes and rehashing the family dirty laundry.

George's beautiful wife Pat worked alongside him as writer and producer. George and Pat drove to the station and back home together. I think working with Pat helped George control his temper, at least sometimes. George could erupt like Vesuvius at anything from a coffee pot to a decision he didn't like. When George's first marriage failed, he raised his three children as a single father. Pat successfully stepped in as George's partner and mother to his son and two daughters. In 2016, George's oldest daughter Cindi Michael disclosed a rocky relationship with her father in *The Sportscaster's Daughter: A Memoir*. In all the years I worked with George, I never knew about his conflict with his oldest daughter.

L-R: Me, George Michael, Pat Michael, Michelle Michael
Courtesy Carol Joynt—Q and A Cafe

I noticed a serious young woman taking over as producer of the 4:00pm News. Michelle possessed great story sense. Her suggestions helped improve many of my segments. After several months I discovered Michelle was Michelle Michael, George's youngest daughter. Michelle remains a long-time friend. She often praises Pat for stepping in to parent her and her siblings, and praises her father for his time as a single father while working as a well-known rock and roll disc jockey.

The syndicated George Michael's *Sports Machine* brought George money, enabling him to buy acreage near South Mountain, Maryland on the Montgomery County line. George bred horses and turned his hobby into a successful side business. I traveled to George's ranch several times, sometimes for a story, sometimes just to visit. He loved showing off his farm and horses.

Washington, D.C.

Bob Ryan became and remains my closest friend at the station. Bob and I often went out for beers after the late news. Later we arranged dinners with our wives. I drove a 1979 Cadillac Seville with solid steel bumpers. Bob drove a Saab. We would race each other out of the parking lot. If he got to the exit first, as he stopped his Saab to check for traffic, I would give him a little tap with my Cadillac. I could see him shaking with laughter as he waved his fist at me.

In the 80s, the weather didn't come from a "storm center." Each puff of wind or drop of rain did not require analysis. Barring something biblical, the weather bureau made a forecast early in the evening and usually it held. When I finished my work and when the weather was calm Bob and I hung around killing time until the news started at 11:00pm.

One night we set up an indoor golf course. It started in the newsroom and went down the corridor by the private offices and out into the hallways overlooking the studios. Office golf went on for several months until I hit down on a five-iron causing the ball to fly up and shatter a glass EXIT sign. As the glass rained down, Bob and I ran back into the newsroom like a couple of high school boys pretending nothing happened. The station didn't have security cameras inside then, thank heaven.

When we weren't playing office golf we sat around gossiping about the usual things—who was sleeping with whom and who was about to get fired. Bob and I shared something essential to friendship. We hated the same people.

Moe Javins presided over Channel 4's Studio B like the concierge of a fine hotel. His official title was Stage Manager. Moe wore white cotton gloves as he pointed us to the correct camera and counted us down to our cut-offs. At the time Michael Jackson was famous for wearing a jeweled glove. Moe claimed Jackson stole the idea from him.

The gloves carried over from Moe's original job as a film editor. In pre-video days Moe pieced together reels of 16mm film commercials in the order they needed to run. Editors wore white cotton gloves to keep fingerprints off the film. When Moe moved to stage manager, he kept the gloves. They gave him elegance and helped us. As we starred into the bright studio lights, Moe's white gloves stood out, especially when he waved them in his whirlwind "hurry up" signal.

The Stage Manager's duties included setting out glasses of water in case an anchor had a cough or dry throat. Moe began a tradition. Thursday nights became "rum night." Instead of water, Moe brought in Meyers Dark Rum and mixed it with a splash of Coke. He served our drinks on a silver tray as we entered the studio. The Thursday 11:00pm news turned into a rollicking affair.

Moe drove to work in an old motor home and parked it in the National Presbyterian Church lot next to the station. Many nights I walked through that parking lot on the way to a screening on Wisconsin Avenue. Sometimes I thought I heard the clink of champagne glasses from the Winnebago as Moe shared a candlelight dinner with a lady friend. Later, on my walk back to the station, Moe's camper appeared to rock gently back and forth. Maybe I was just imagining that.

For most of the 80s Channel 4 News looked like a boy's club. In 1989 Doreen Gentzler brought much needed balance. Her first night on the air she jumped in on a Vance/George Michael sports conversation and held her own to the shock and amazement of the two macho men. Doreen won her place on the team in that moment.

While George sat next to Vance, I shared the other end

of the set with Doreen Gentzler and Bob Ryan. During the break I tried my best to make Doreen laugh. Whenever I heard a new joke, I unleashed it on Doreen hitting the punch line just before we came back on the air. Often the camera came up on Doreen giggling and me smirking.

The actor Hector Elizando came through Washington to promote Gary Marshall's movie *Runaway Bride*. As I started our interview, he informed me he tried to learn a new joke every day. I asked to hear this day's new joke.

"A guy wants to work in showbiz. The only job he can get is preparing an elephant act at the circus—baby elephant, mother elephant, and giant father elephant. The preparation includes giving each animal an enema to avoid any accidents on stage. The baby elephant comes in—the guy gives the baby an enema—stuff spews all over him. Next comes the mother elephant—same thing. The stench is horrible as the giant father elephant arrives. The guy is just about to quit when the father elephant turns to him and says, 'How's the house?'"(an inside showbiz expression meaning do we have a good crowd tonight.)

I can still make Doreen laugh

I laughed long and loud because you expect the hoary punchline, "what? And get out of showbiz?" instead of "how's the house?" That night I regaled Doreen with Elizando's story timing it perfectly. She could barely keep a straight face as we went on the air. A few nights later, I reported live from an opening at Kennedy Center. On live shots, you can't see but only hear the anchor through an earpiece of the newscast audio feed. Doreen proved she could give as good as she got. She introduced me, adding, "how's the house, Arch?"

Many years later in 2015, Bob Ryan nominated me as one of the Washingtonians of the Year. Doreen attended the awards luncheon along with Bob. The honoree before me worked with elephants at the National Zoo. I looked over at Doreen and mouthed the words, "how's the house?" She covered her face with her napkin and shook with laughter. For the record, I told the woman from the zoo the same joke and she laughed as well.

When Doreen Gentzler retired in November of 2022, she told me she used to amaze George, when he bragged about his rock and roll trivia knowledge. Doreen would shock George giving the correct answer to such questions as, "what year did the Big Bopper sing 'Chantilly Lace?'" Doreen would blurt out 1958. George had no idea she received the answers in her earpiece, used by the sports producer to communicate directions and breaking news headlines. I don't know if George ever found out.

Our world moved faster as technology improved. Before computers we banged out scripts on manual typewriters equipped with the biggest possible typeface. We typed on thick multi-page script books with carbon copies distributed to the producer, director, audio engineer, co-anchors, and others. Computers eliminated the script books. With the rundown and instructions transmitted to various computers, we no longer needed all that paper. Everything went straight into the teleprompter.

Bob Ryan understood technology better than most of us. The first night we began writing directly into the computer rundown, Bob went into the system and added a line to Doreen Gentzler's introduction to me. I wrote something like: "Arch Campbell's just back from such and such with a review." At that point I was to begin. As Doreen read my introduction, she hesitated. I looked at the teleprompter and saw Bob had added these words: "Arch Campbell has a review…AND HE'S NOT WEARING ANY PANTS."

    I still giggle at the memory of Bob's silly joke. Bob and I dredge up this infantile story almost every time we see each other. Recently Bob admitted Human Resources called him in the next day for a stern, "don't ever do that again" lecture.

29
Katie and Other Stars

WALKING THROUGH THE NEWSROOM DURING the 11:00pm news, I noticed a new reporter talking on the phone. I nodded because I watched her a little earlier on the news. I said, "hey, that was a good story." She giggled into the phone. "Arch Campbell says I did a good story." I'd just met Katie Couric. She was about 28, an Arlington, Virginia native, with plenty of family and friends in town. The bosses assigned her to the 11:00pm breaking news beat.

The managers who hired her—Jim Van Messel, Dave Nuell, and Fred DeMarco—were unceremoniously pushed out between her hiring and arrival. WRC's new boss Jerry Nachman came from the WNBC TV newsroom in New York. He brought Bret Marcus to run our newsroom. Bret Marcus looked like a New Yorker, with a full beard and all black wardrobe.

A few months into her job, Katie marched into Bret's office and told him she wanted to anchor the news. Bret tugged at his beard, thought a minute, and said if she wanted to anchor, she ought to move to a small market, maybe Casper, Wyoming. He told her to stick to reporting because he didn't see her as anchor material. Bret's response did not make Katie happy.

She kept plugging away, catching the eye of NBC Bureau Chief Tim Russert. Elevated to the NBC Bureau, one weekend Katie filled in on the NBC network weekend news, proving the guy who said she would never anchor dead wrong. Katie loved telling this story, even referring to it in a gag reel when Bret left for another job. The poor guy's snap judgment grew even more infamous when Katie won the host job on *The Today Show*, and then replaced Dan Rather as anchor of the *CBS Evening News*. Bret Marcus has never lived this down. Katie won't let him.

She fit right in at Channel 4, wisecracking and teasing and taking a bit of kidding as well. A popular TV ad at the time featured an attractive young woman walking into various situations. When she appears, all talk stops and everyone turns to look as she says, "Anne Klein Two," indicating the source of her high style. For a while, whenever Katie walked into the newsroom I would shout, "Katie Couric, Anne Klein Two." My fellow wise acre, Pat Collins, joined me in a chorus of, "Katie Couric, Anne Klein Two." The more she hated it, the more we did it, until she stopped paying attention. By then, everybody loved Katie.

During the 1989 inauguration, the newsroom stationed me outside the D.C. Convention Center stage door, to catch sound bites from various celebrities on their way to perform. When I finished, the station told me to hand the camera crew over to Katie and get back to the station by courier. Katie arrived and stood next to me as Kelsey Grammar and Lee Atwater stopped by.

Dan Rather hustled toward the entrance. I shouted, "Mr. Rather, Mr. Rather, got a minute for NBC?" Rather bristled and shook his head. Suddenly Katie yelled like a cheerleader, so loud I jumped. She exclaimed, "come on Dan, you were young once. Give us a break!" Rather stopped, took a deep breath, turned around, and headed right to my microphone. I stammered some inane question. He looked annoyed and answered. Rather left and I handed Katie the microphone. Who knew someday Katie would replace Dan Rather on the *CBS Evening News*? Katie tells me she doesn't remember yelling at Rather. That's OK, I'll never forget it.

My friend Tom Gilday met me in the newsroom one afternoon. Tom was about ten years younger than me, single, and a great looking tall black-haired guy from a big Irish family. More than one woman in the newsroom came up to me the next day saying, "who was that?" Katie marched over and demanded I fix her up on a blind date with my friend. Tom and Katie went out. After, he told me she was way out of his league. "I think she's looking for a member of the Chevy Chase Club," Tom said, referring to D.C.'s old money country club.

Katie married a handsome lawyer named Jay Monahan in 1989. Jay impressed Katie's contacts at MSNBC. They hired him as an analyst. The combination of Katie on NBC News and Jay on cable made them one of D.C.'s up and coming power couples. It didn't take Katie long to move to the top at NBC.

The Today Show was in trouble. An anchor change pushed out beloved Jane Pauly to make room for Debra Norville, a beautiful blond from the NBC station in Chicago. Viewers didn't like the change. Norville went on pregnancy leave in 1991. Katie filled in. Debra Norville never

Washington, D.C.

returned. Katie's fill in turned into a seventeen-year run as *The Today Show* anchor and America's Sweetheart.

Katie and Jay Monahan had two daughters together, then faced adversity. Jay was diagnosed with colon Cancer and died in 1998. She made a dignified return, and demonstrated her own live colonoscopy in a week-long segment in 2000. Millions watched, seeing the examination as simple and painless. Katie's report triggered a twenty percent spike in the procedure. Doctors still refer to colonoscopy's acceptance as, "the Katie Couric effect."

Newsroom people make jokes in response to the tragedy we witness daily. I heard a reporter joke that Couric's on-air colonoscopy proved "…they'll put any asshole on NBC." I chuckled at the time, but stopped laughing in 2005 when my first ever colonoscopy caught an undetected stage three malignant tumor. Katie heard about my diagnosis and encouraged me during my treatment and recovery. She's since used her fame to promote several worthwhile causes, many of them Cancer related.

Katie anchored the *CBS Evening News* for five years. She remarried, started her own company, and produced a hilarious autobiography *Going There*. I never imagined the young woman I saw giggling on the phone would turn into a media dynamo.[46]

Steve Doocy came to WRC in the early 80s to add some fun to the expanded 5:00pm Newscast. Doocy, about 27 at the time, knew how to make people laugh with a light touch and graphics and special effects. Using new technology, Doocy could ski down the Washington monument, or shoot his body from a canon into the Capitol dome. I fondly remember a mock game show called "Wheel of Meat." On another segment, Doocy wrestled high school kids in Jello. His stories had a touch of David Letterman.

I admired his work because I know how hard it is to make something light day after day. I booked him every couple of weeks on my late-night show, trying to tamp down my jealousy. Sometimes I felt like Salieri watching Mozart. NBC Productions tapped Doocy to host an updated version of a 1950's daytime show called *House Party*. In one of the segments, Doocy interviewed small children in a revival of *Kids Say the Darndest Things*. The show ran for a season.

Doocy moved to NBC's new cable channel MSNBC run by Roger Ailes. Doocy went with Ailes when he took over Fox Cable. I remember someone casually mentioning Doocy reported the weather on the Fox cable morning show. That show became *Fox & Friends*.

Now, when Doocy's name comes up, most Channel 4 alumni who worked with him remember a funny young guy we expected to succeed. Nobody remembers Doocy ever discussing politics. I never expected *Fox & Friends* to connect Donald Trump and the Republican Party to Steve Doocy.

Steve Doocy has successfully navigated an enduring long-term marriage to Kathy Gerrity. They met at WRC when she worked in George Michael's sports department. They married in 1986, and have three children. Steve's oldest son Peter covers the White House for Fox.

Savannah Guthrie worked as a free-lance reporter for WRC starting in 2000 while attending Georgetown Law School. On my way to the studio, I would see her quietly gathering her things after turning in her story for the day. I loved to swing by her desk, say hello, and sometimes tease her about her name. A few years earlier *The Washington Post* printed a delightful obit of Patricia "Honeychile" Wilder, a showgirl who married a prince. I loved to mention the story to Savanah, urging her to change her name to "Honeychile" just to make her laugh.

Savannah disappeared when she earned her law degree. A few years later, she returned to NBC News, reported, anchored, and ultimately moved to co-host of *The Today Show*. Savannah reminds me of Katie Couric, including her down to earth friendliness. One night as I stood on a red-carpet line for an event at the Newseum, Savannah walked by. All I had to do was call out, "Savannah!" She turned around, saw me, rushed over and gave me a big kiss. I told her how happy I was (and continue to be) for her.

In 2022, on the occasion of WRC-TV's 75th anniversary, Savannah taped congratulations with her *Today Show* co-Anchor Craig Melvin, who also worked later at WRC. Savannah recalled co-workers at Channel 4 giving her a ride home as an example of how kind everyone was to her. She looked like she needed a friend back then. I imagine that's no problem now.

30
Please Return the Towels

B᠎ob Ryan and his wife Olga live a gracious sophisticated life that includes world travel. One night I told him my wife and I planned to travel to Germany as part of a trip for her business. Bob discussed Munich and the Alps and waxed poetic about the German resort town Baden-Baden, home of the world famous Brenners Park Hotel. Bob's wife's relatives lived near Baden-Baden.

We took Bob's advice. Brenners Park lived up to its reputation: an old school European hotel, spa, and medical clinic. Legend says the Brenners Park staff notes every detail of your stay. When you return, they greet you by name and remember what you enjoy.

We visited Baden-Baden's most famous sight: the Neuschwanstein Castle high on a mountain-top. Walt Disney modeled the Fantasyland castle on Neuschwanstein. We

Washington, D.C.

walked down a steep one-mile path to the hotel. That night my ankle hurt. The next morning, I couldn't put any weight on it. The hotel sent up a very serious doctor and nurse from the clinic. Neither the doctor nor the nurse spoke English. The nurse pulled out a hypodermic and gave me a shot in the rear. As I began to go under the doctor wrapped my ankle. The clinic sent up crutches. I attracted quite a lot of attention as I hobbled around the world class resort: the young American who sprained his ankle at the Neuschwanstein castle. Knowing the Brenners Park, I imagined if I returned a staff member would ask, "how's your ankle?"

Back in D.C., my doctor diagnosed a bruised tendon. After a few weeks I healed. Later that summer a letter arrived from Brenners Park with a Baden-Baden postmark addressed to Herr and Frau Campbell. I opened the letter and read in large red letters:

"PLEASE RETURN THE TOWELS!"

I showed the letter to my wife. In a fury, she sat down at her typewriter and wrote:

> *Dear Sir:*
> *I am very offended by your letter accusing us of taking towels from your hotel. I can't imagine how you would think we are the kind of people who would do that. We went to the Brenners Park because we heard about your warm welcome and personal service. This is obviously not true. WE DID NOT TAKE YOUR TOWELS!*
> *Sincerely, Mrs. S. Campbell.*

Back in the newsroom, Bob and I hung around as usual laughing, joking and gossiping. Time passed. A year went by. One night, during a lull in our conversation, Bob turned to me with a little smirk and said, "did you ever get my letter?" That's when it hit me.

PLEASE RETURN THE TOWELS!

Bob's wife had relatives near Baden-Baden. Bob and Olga attended a family wedding in Germany that summer. He managed to obtain some Brenners Park stationery, sent the letter from Germany, and the rest is history. I think we laughed for fifteen minutes straight, as I told him about our irate response, and the harsh letter we sent.

And that is why I can never return to Baden-Baden, and Germany's beautiful Brenners Park Hotel.

31
Bob Hope and Other Golfers

Courtesy WRC-TV

"How'd you like to play golf with Bob Hope?" teased Pat Gallagher, a bundle of energy who talked her way into a job at Channel 4 setting up stories and segments for me. Pat loved show biz. She worked the phones like a boiler room bond salesman. In October 1985, Pat discovered Bob Hope planned a show at George Washington University. Pat hit the phones, selling Hope's people on the iconic comic playing golf with me, a nervous beginner.

I told my News Director, Jim Van Messel, about the Bob Hope match. Van Messel arranged for us to play at Bethesda Country Club, where he was a member. Of course, Van

Messel included himself in the foursome along with the club pro Jim Folks.

Pat picked up Hope in her husband's Cadillac. It thrilled her to drive him to the suburbs. Arriving at the club, Hope (82 at the time) bounced out of the car, shook hands all around, and we teed off. The old comic made a par on the first hole while I took a five. Hope played well and I managed not to embarrass myself. We stopped for an interview on the fourth tee.

I began with this softball: "What's your advice for a beginning golfer, namely me?"

"Have you tried tennis?" Hope threw his head back and laughed heartily. Then he added, "look, so far, we've played three holes. You made five, four, five. I made four, four, five. For the guy just starting out, you're doing great."

Hope easily took the bait when I asked about his favorite golf jokes.

"Oh yeah, a guy gets married. On the wedding night he tells his wife, 'I'm a golfer, so you won't see much of me on weekends.' She says, 'That's nothing. I'm a hooker.' The guy says, 'No problem, just make your grip a little stronger.'"

Hope played six holes. Pat drove him back to his hotel to prepare for his performance. As he left, Hope said, "Arch, I suggest you go home, break your legs break your arms, get them reset, throw away your clubs and take up tennis."

Then he added, "nah, it was great playing with you. Good luck with the game."

The club pro, my boss, and I finished nine holes. On the 9th hole, I hooked a drive into the club's snack shop, almost making a hole in one in a donut. Too bad Hope missed that. Hope's office contacted me whenever he came to town. Shortly before he died, Dolores Hope donated Bob's memorabilia to the Library of Congress. Several photos

Washington, D.C.

of me and Bob Hope on the Bethesda Country Club golf course now reside in the Library of Congress.

As I write these stories and remember that day, I am stunned that Hope got in a car with a woman he didn't know, and rode out to a golf course to play with people he'd never met. I suppose the idea of a little golf appealed to him. I also think the move reflects Hope's confidence.

(L-R) Bob Hope, me, Jim Van Messel, Jim Folks
Courtesy WRC-TV

Golf opened doors for me, starting with my boss Jim Van Messel, who decided he liked playing golf with me—a good sign in a boss. After the Bob Hope match, whenever Van Messel needed to talk to me, the discussion took place on a golf course.

Van Messel introduced me to his friend Jim Snyder, the news management guru who made Channel 9 unbeatable in the 1970s. Snyder moved to Detroit as News Director when *The Washington Post* corporation traded Channel 9 for the NBC affiliate in the motor city. Jim Snyder returned to D.C. as Vice President of News for all *Washington Post* stations.

I met Snyder at a party not long after he moved back to Washington. He looked at me and said, "you're a real survivor." I told Van Messel about the conversation, indicating I thought it was a wise crack. "Oh no," said my boss, "that's a compliment. He gave you a compliment." Van Messel invited me as the fourth in a golf match with him and Snyder and a mutual friend, television producer Jim Silman. To my surprise, Snyder and I liked each other. In the years ahead, Jim Snyder became one of my best and closest friends, partly because he and I had good luck playing and winning various golf matches. Ironically, when I was working in Dallas I sent him a tape, and never received a response. I loved to remind Snyder he didn't hire me when he ran Channel 9, especially after he and I won a tight golf match against a couple of his frenemies.

Golf connected me with people I never would have met otherwise. In May 1989, the Tantallon Golf Club (now National Golf Club) brought Sam Snead to the property to headline a charity tournament benefitting Hospice of Prince Georges County, Maryland. Snead agreed to play three holes as part of an interview. I found him inside the clubhouse trading stories with his managers and the group that brought him to town. "All right, Archie boy, let's see what you got," Snead said and off we went. He took a wide stance and maintained his smooth swing. At age 77, when he hit the ball, it sounded like a bull whip. CRACK! Snead, like many old-time performers (Chuck Berry comes to mind) insisted on getting paid up front. He could not have been nicer that day, so I assume he had his fee in his pocket probably in cash.

A few years later, Jim Van Messel, Jim Snyder, Jim Silman and I (we called ourselves three Jims and an Arch) arranged a golf weekend at the Homestead Resort in Hot Springs, Virginia. Sam Snead grew up in the area and had a long association with the resort. That day, we spotted Snead in a golf cart, playing by himself with his dog riding alongside. As we stood on the tenth tee, we heard his cart coming up behind us. Without saying a word, Snead got out, stepped in front of us, teed off, and scurried down the fairway with his dog at his side. He studiously avoided eye contact, or saying anything. I told my friends Snead didn't say hello because we didn't pay him an appearance fee.

Somewhere in my closet I have a picture of me and Vice President Dan Quayle on the Lakewood Country Club golf course. The club held a long drive contest for charity. Bob Ryan and I answered the call for contestants. As we stood around waiting to show our stuff, a line of black SUV's rolled into the parking lot. Out stepped Vice President Quayle. In his street shoes, polished black wing-tips, Quayle slammed a drive well over 250 yards, winning the contest and the affection of the crowd. I pulled him aside and asked him the secret of his golf swing. Quayle said, "you don't have enough time," with a wink as he posed for the picture and went on his way.

My friend Alma Viator managed publicity for the National Theater. One of Alma's best friends and colleagues, Susan O'Neill, has a famous father: former House Speaker Tip O'Neill. Alma called one afternoon: "How'd you like to play golf with Tip O'Neill?" I set it up at the relativity new TPC Avenel Golf Course in Bethesda, Maryland on a warm day in November 1989.

A black suburban pulled up, out stepped Tip, looking like a big teddy bear and just as friendly. He shook my hand, started laughing, and off we went. I first met Tip when he appeared at the unveiling of new chairs for Ford's Theater. Many theater goers complained about Ford's uncomfortable historically correct chairs, Tip among them. At a news event announcing the new chairs, Ford Theater's Managing

Director Frankie Hewitt asked Tip to try out her new more comfortable replacements. Tip put on quite a show sitting down and getting up and letting out a big sigh. Tip and I had a good laugh then, and shared another good laugh talking about it on the golf course.

A few weeks later, I answered my phone and heard, "hold for the speaker." Tip came on and invited me to the Burning Tree Country Club one day member guest. At that event, Tip's son Kip came over to me and said, "whatever you do, don't let Tip drive the golf cart—you drive it at all times." I believed Kip, because when I played with Tip at TPC Avenel, I spied Tip more than once driving sideways on slopes with angles violating the laws of gravity. That day, at Burning Tree, other golfers and guests cut over from their fairway to say hello and shake hands with one of America's most beloved politicians.

Tip told me his favorite golf story, about his childhood adventures as a caddy on Cape Cod. One day the player assigned to Tip sliced his ball into the woods. Tip, carrying the golfer's bag, went deep into the forest to find the ball. During the search, Tip hung the golfer's bag on a branch. Finally, he found the ball, then realized he didn't have the golfer's bag. Tip forgot where he hung it. Now he couldn't find it. Tip laughed, ending his story with, "I'm the only caddy who found the ball and lost the bag."

For a shoot in California during Oscar week, I played golf at Wilshire Country Club with Pat Boone, one of entertainment's most polite people. Boone hit a shot into a bunker. As he walked toward the hazard he started singing "Love Letters in the Sand." Sometimes I do the same when I'm in a bunker. Pat Boone patiently listened as I told him the story of a Washington television film editor in the days when stations programmed afternoon movie blocks. Station editors sometimes remove a scene or two to ensure

Washington, D.C.

the film fit the ninety minutes or two hours allotted. The station assigned an editor, newly emigrated from Germany, to cut *State Fair*, Pat Boone's musical from the 1950s. The editor, unfamiliar with American culture, removed all the songs. Pat Boone did not find this funny.

My greatest golf moment came May 30, 2000. The Kemper Open, a longtime Washington D.C. area PGA tournament, created a celebrity/pro match to drum up interest. Former Washington quarterback Joe Thiesmann agreed to play nine holes with three PGA professionals in a skins format—meaning a single player in a foursome must win the hole outright to win a point. If two of the four players tie, the points carry over to the next hole. A skins match can go nine holes with the players competing for as much as 9 points.

Theisman canceled. The tournament director called me. Would I sub for the missing quarterback? The match sounded like a good story and a lot of fun. The afternoon of the event, I met the three pros: Rich Beem, Scott Hoch, and Bradley Hughes. Hoch loved movies. He and I enjoyed a long conversation about his favorites, especially *Gladiator*. At one point Hoch teased me about making a long shot over water. "Come on, play golf like *Gladiator*." I said, "*Gladiator* didn't play golf."

We finished the 9th hole tied. The tournament officials decided we would declare a champion in a winner take all chip off. We set up next to the 9th green. The shot required needed to fly over a rise and then roll downhill to the hole. The pros lofted beautiful wedge shots high in the air, landing on the green and tumbling well past the hole. I went last. Instead of a wedge, I used my putter. I made my stroke and watched my ball climb the rise to the top point of the green and then start trickling toward the cup. As the ball slowly rolled closer, the crowd began to cheer. The cheers turned into a roar. My ball stopped 18 inches from the cup. I almost fainted.

I heard Scott Hoch start to laugh as my ball got closer and closer. He half glared at me with an expression combining disgust and admiration. Shaking his head, he turned on his heel and walked away. I donated the $8,000 to the Just for One Foundation, a charity Channel 4 sponsored to help students attend college.

The Kemper Open invited me back the next year. We played one hole. A thunderstorm broke out, canceling the event.

32
Best Movies of 1986-1989

1986: *A Room with a View* remains one of the best of the Merchant-Ivory films, classic stories produced by Ismail Merchant and directed by James Ivory with scripts by Ruth Prawer Jhabvala. Originally founded in India to make films in English, the Merchant-Ivory productions dazzled audiences with stories mostly set in the early 20th century, including *Howard's End* and *Remains of the Day*. I remember coming out of the theater after *A Room with A View* with my spirits lifted. When Julian Sands sweeps Helena Bonham Carter into his arms spontaneously kissing her passionately—well, heck. That's entertainment. *A Room with a View* played the Key Theater in Georgetown almost two years, one of the longest runs of any movie in D.C. history.

The Color of Money updated *The Hustler*, Paul Newman's great 1961 pool shark drama. The update or sequel takes place a generation later, with Tom Cruise in the role Paul Newman made famous and Newman in the George C. Scott manager/bankroller role. *The Color of Money* won Paul Newman his long over-due best actor Oscar.

I would happily watch *A Room with A View* and *The Color of Money* again, and I have.

1987: Our new boss, Bret Marcus, just arrived from New York to take over as our News Director. I stuck my head in his office and said, "why don't you come along to a screening with me? I think there's a good one this week—*Fatal Attraction*." What might have been an ordinary thriller, had us gripping our armrests. Glenn Close and Michael Douglas meet, flirt, fall into bed, and break up. Except, Glenn Close obsesses. She attempts suicide, then threatens Douglas and his family. I still hear the off the chart screams when Douglas' daughter discovers the family bunny rabbit in a pot of boiling water. The screening shook up my new boss and me. On the way back, Bret and I talked about *Fatal Attraction* as a cautionary tale—even a metaphor for the end of casual sex in the age of AIDS.

Broadcast News received more than the usual attention in television news circles. James L. Brooks stood in the back of the MacArthur Theater during the preview. One of the great workplace comedies, *Broadcast News* tells the story of a driven news producer played by Holly Hunter, and the organization's resistance to William Hurt, whose good looks overcome his lack of journalistic experience. Peter Hackes, a former NBC News reporter I knew and liked, played a prominent role as the head of the news organization overseeing the layoffs of several veterans. In one of *Broadcast News*' best scenes, Hackes casually tells a laid off veteran, "now if there's anything I can do for you…" To which the employee answers, "well, I certainly hope you'll die soon." I hosted a screening of *Broadcast News* at the American Film Institute a few months after my lay off from Channel 4, an irony not lost on the audience that night. Of course, the parallel came up in the Q and A session afterward. I could only shrug and say, "that's the way it is." To me *Broadcast News* captures the real thing.

1988: *Babette's Feast* represents a time when foreign films easily found large audiences. This sly Danish comedy spins the story of a dwindling pious religious community. Needing the services of a cook, they take in Parisian refugee Babette. Years pass. Babette discovers her annual lottery ticket has unexpectedly won ten thousand francs. She uses the money—all the money she has—to prepare a glorious feast, revealing in the process her former life as one of the greatest chefs in Paris. The pious congregation struggle to accept her gift, leading to one of my favorite lines: "We will eat the food, but we will not enjoy it." I watch *Babette's Feast* every few years and it remains as delightful as ever.

I was backstage at the Oscars April 11, 1988 when Cher won best actress for *Moonstruck*. She accepted in what's now known as her "naked" dress. Designer Bob Mackie, who created some of Cher's most outrageous looks, fashioned a long sheer black gown with a bikini bottom and tiny bra top. The effect made Cher appear naked. The crowd roared with appreciation when she won the Best Actress award that night, even as they gasped at Cher's outfit. A few minutes later, Cher arrived in the press room. I stood about ten feet away as Cher entered. I can tell you in person I found the dress quite unsexy.

Courtesy WRC-TV

As for *Moonstruck*, the romantic comedy has certainly passed the test of time. I watch it regularly and find it as charming as ever.

1989: The Food for All Seasons charity asked me to host the premiere of *Driving Miss Daisy* in December of 1989. I expected the usual preview screening in a local movie theater. Instead, the producers, Lili and Richard Zanuck, booked the National Theater—the massive downtown venue used for Broadway try outs. The Zanucks brought major cast members for the night, including Jessica Tandy, Morgan Freeman, Dan Aykroyd, and writer Alfred Uhry.

Backstage, Alfred Uhry and I chatted about his story, based on the relationship of his grandmother and her longtime chauffeur. I traded a few stories from my mother's home town of Athens, Alabama. *Driving Miss Daisy* touches on changes in Southern race relations in the 1960s and 70s. Uhry originally wrote *Driving Miss Daisy* as a play. I think his screenplay surpasses the theater experience because the film recreates the look of Atlanta in the years between 1948 and 1973, especially as Miss Daisy trades in her various cars.

Courtesy WRC-TV

After the screening, the Blues Brothers band, fronted by Dan Ackroyd, played rock and roll in a ballroom off the lobby of the J. W. Marriott Hotel. Ackroyd kept the band going after the 1982 unexpected death of his original partner John Belushi. The combination of a screening in the NationalTheater, the appearance of the cast, and the Blues Brothers after party turned the *Driving Miss Daisy* premiere into an extraordinary event.

33
The Worst Premiere of the Best Movie

P LANS FOR THE NEW MUSEUM OF THE AMERIcan Indian[47] prompted Kevin Costner to select Washington, D.C. to host the premiere for *Dances with Wolves*, his debut as a Director and Producer. Based on a well-regarded novel, Costner starred as 1st Lieutenant John J. Dunbar, a Union soldier sent to a deserted frontier post. Initially fearing the Indigenous tribes in the area, Dunbar earns their respect and ultimately joins the Lakota Sioux, falling in love with Mary McDonnell who plays Stands with a Fist, a white woman kidnapped as a child and raised Native American. *Dances with Wolves* spins a wistful story of the passing of frontier life.

Courtesy WRC-TV

The gala premiere rolled out October 19, 1990, a month before the official movie release. Orion Pictures brought a bus load of national press and critics to interview the cast and attend the screening at the Uptown Theater, Washington's grand art deco 900 seat single screen venue.

Costner and the executives obsessed over making everything perfect. They insisted the projectionist install a new projector bulb for the event. The projectionist, possessing intimate knowledge of the Uptown's ancient machinery, balked, telling anyone who would listen that projector bulbs require a break in period, that sometimes a brand-new bulb would burn out faster than one in use. As you might expect, nobody listened.

I hustled over to the Uptown early, and broadcast live from the theater for the 6:00pm News. Premieres at the Uptown always drew a crowd of neighborhood characters. My friend Bobby Abbo and his mother Anna owned and operated the Roma Restaurant across the street. Mrs. Abbo hustled over to ask, "what's a happening?" "Kevin Costner's coming," I told Mrs. Abbo as she raised an eyebrow, impressed.

Fans cheered as the stars arrived, with the biggest roar for Costner. I asked him about having the power to pick his projects and why he selected this one. Costner said the subject meant something to him and I'd understand when I watched the movie. A member of the Smithsonian's staff introduced the stars and Costner spoke. The lights went down. A hush fell over the packed house.

About 40 minutes in, the screen dimmed and then went dark. The lights came up. The crowd let out a groan. Sort of an, "OHHHHHAAAAAAHHHHHHH." Costner jumped up and ran to the projection booth as did a half dozen Orion executives. Just as the projectionist warned, the brand-new projection bulb blew out. Replacing the now burnt-out bulb took delicacy and time because of the heat the bulb generates. Costner and the executives crowding into the booth only made things worse, increasing the projectionist's anxiety.

Fifteen or twenty minutes later, the lights went down and the audience went, "AAAAAHHHHH." Except, in his rush to get things going, the projectionist skipped a reel.

The story had advanced to an entirely different place. Once again, the lights came up, the screen went dark, and the audience went, "OOOOUUUUUHHHH." Another twenty minutes passed. I began to wonder if I would make it back for the 11:00pm News.

Finally, the right reel appeared and *Dances with Wolves* resumed. *Dances with Wolves* went on to sweep awards season, winning seven Oscars including Best Picture, and Best Director for Costner. He has enjoyed a long career since with lead roles in memorable films including *Silverado, The Untouchables, No Way Out, Bull Durham, Field of Dreams, Waterworld,* and *Tin Cup*, and character roles in recent years including the very popular series *Yellowstone*. Costner returned to the Uptown in 2006 for the premiere of *The Guardian* and good naturedly answered questions about the night the bulb blew out during the *Dances with Wolves* event, the worst premiere of the best movie.

Screenings at the Uptown always felt special. A generation of Washingtonians remember *Star Wars* at the Uptown, where it played from 1977 to 1978. I interviewed many celebrities on the red-carpet including Sir David Lean for the restored version of *Lawrence of Arabia* in 1989, Madonna and Warren Beatty for *Dick Tracy*[48] in 1990, and the cast of *Jurassic Park* in 1993, including Laura Dern, Jeff Goldblum, and Morgan Freeman. Russell Crowe and Director Michael Mann appeared to premiere *The Insider* in 1999.

I watched dozens of movies from the Uptown balcony, some of them great, others improved by the Uptown experience. I most fondly remember an anniversary screening of *The Wizard of Oz*, a timeless film in a timeless place.

34
Silence of the Lambs: 1991-1992

My News Director Kris Ostrowski stopped me in the hall. "Some movie company's going to shoot a couple of scenes with George Michael in the studio in the morning. Drop by and see what's happening." The next morning, a camera crew and I crowded into the control room and discovered Jonathan Demme directing a television appeal by an actress playing a U.S. Senator. In the scene she addresses the camera, pleading with a kidnapper to let her daughter go.

Demme set up a second scene on the Channel 4 News set. Two actors playing a male/female anchor team toss to George Michael, who uses the name Gene Castle in the segment. The three of them react to the Senator's appeal. George says something along the lines of, "if there's any justice, she'll get her little girl back."

I had no idea I was watching Jonathan Demme create two key moments for *The Silence of the Lambs*. Demme shot these in late November 1989. More than a year passed before *The Silence of the Lambs* opened in theaters. Based on Thomas Harris' novel, the film starred Jodie Foster as Clarice Starling, a young FBI trainee tracking a serial killer.

Washington, D.C.

Her boss recommends she interview Dr. Hannibal Lecter played by Anthony Hopkins, a brilliant psychiatrist imprisoned for serial killings and cannibalism. As an added irony, *The Silence of the Lambs* officially opened Valentine's Day in 1991.

My brush with movie making took place because Jonathan Demme liked George Michael's *Sports Machine*. By the 90s, George had a national reputation. His Sunday night half hour sports wrap up appeared on most of the NBC stations across the country. George's one size fits all sports show satisfied sports junkies in the decades before ESPN. Demme's proximity to George and need for a TV studio brought Hollywood and Channel 4 together. While in the D.C. area, Demme filmed scenes at the FBI training facility in Quantico, Virginia, and some other scenes in nearby Baltimore.

Movie marketers consider February a so-so month to open a film. *The Silence of the Lambs* disproved that theory. A year later, at the 1992 Academy Awards, the thriller received seven nominations and accomplished a highly unlikely sweep of Oscars major awards, including Best Picture, Best Director for Demme, Best Actress for Jodie Foster, Best Actor for Anthony Hopkins, and Best Adapted screenplay.

Demme generously allowed me to interview him. I think we mostly talked about why he wanted George in his film. I also remember Demme's kindness to our local director Jesse Vaughn, assigned to help him in the control room.

Jesse wanted to make films, entering several local short film contests. Our director shared his dream with Demme. Normally you might expect a successful filmmaker to nod his head and drop a word of encouragement or two. Instead, Demme gave Jesse some names to call. As a result

Jesse Vaughn worked several years in the film industry. He directed the comedy *Juwanna Mann* in 2002 as well as a season of *In Living Color,* thanks to introductions and contacts made through Jonathan Demme.

Other directors came through Channel 4, filming pseudo-news anchor segments. Ivan Reitman directed a scene for *Dave* in 1993 featuring the political panel of *The McLaughlin Group*. Reitman glared at me and my camera, making it clear he didn't like us hanging around, doing his best to encourage us to leave, even thought he was shooting on our Channel 4 turf.

Two of the nicest guys in Washington helped jump start the careers of Joel and Ethan Coen. The Coen brothers hit their stride in *Barton Fink* (1991). An intense John Turturro plays a deeply unhappy writer suffering writer's block on a less than brilliant screenplay. Washingtonians Ted and Jim Pedas owned the chain of Circle Theaters in Washington. They connected with the Coens, producing most of the Coen's early films, including *Blood Simple, Raising Arizona, Miller's Crossing,* and *Barton Fink*. Next time you search for a good movie, download *Barton Fink*.

The Crying Game (1992) opened at the Outer Circle Theater on a crisp fall Friday night. When I arrived, the box office sign read "sold out." The manager waved me in, saying if I couldn't find a seat, I could sit on the back steps. Spread out at the top step of the rear exit, I quickly grew interested in the story of a member of the IRA, played by Stephen Rea, who connects with a British soldier held prisoner played by Forest Whitaker. The IRA promise to execute the solider unless British authorities trade an IRA prisoner for him. Realizing he will die, Whitaker asks his captor to look after his lover, played by Jaye Davidson.

Rea and Davidson meet, connect, and fall in love, leading to a scene where they undress preparing for intimacy. Suddenly, the audience gasped. I rarely felt the mix of confusion and surprise that moment created in that crowd. When I remember *The Crying Game*, I remember the amazing reaction of an audience that could not quite believe what they were seeing. One of the great things about the twist in *The Crying Game* remains that most film fans keep the twist secret from those who haven't seen it. My lips are sealed.

35
JFK and the *Citizen Kane* Oscar

"Hey Arch, have you ever held an Oscar?" Patricia O'Brien, the novelist married to Washington D.C. icon Frank Mankiewicz, had a twinkle in her eye.

"This is the Oscar Frank's father won for writing the script of *Citizen Kane*."

AND THEN SHE HANDED IT TO ME.

The Oscar for *Citizen Kane*. I held it in my right hand. It was heavy in both weight and history. Herman Mankiewicz won it in February, 1942, after wrestling with Orson Wells for credit in a dispute ultimately settled by the Screen Writer's Guild. Both men received screenwriting credit with Mankiewicz' name listed first. It was the only Oscar *Citizen Kane* received, losing Best Picture to *How Green Was My Valley*. In the years since, critics regularly rate *Citizen Kane* the greatest film ever made.

The Oscar I held and the achievement it represented are examined in the 2020 film *Mank*, the story of brilliant, flawed, writer Herman Mankiewicz as he navigated Hollywood's golden age.

I wish I'd known Herman Mankiewicz. I received a dose of his wit in a few encounters with his son Frank, a Washington player in Democratic politics. History remembers Frank Mankiewicz as Robert Kennedy's press secretary —the grieving figure who announced RFK's death after his assassination in 1968. Frank Mankiewicz managed George McGovern's Presidential campaign in 1972, moving on to become President of National Public Radio and ultimately working as a public relations executive for the prestigious Hill and Knowlton firm.

Washington, D.C.

I met Frank in 1992. That year director Oliver Stone hired Hill and Knowlton and Frank Mankiewicz to help promote his controversial film *JFK*. Stone wanted Congress to release some of the files of the House Committee on Assassination's investigation of the death of President Kennedy. The files could create interest in *JFK*'s theories of the forces behind the President's death. When Stone arrived in Washington to lobby Congress, Frank Mankiewicz and his wife hosted an opinion leader's dinner, inviting local celebrities and film critics to share one course of a meal with Oliver Stone. They invited me because at the time, my movie reviews on WRC-TV carried some weight in town.

Oliver Stone brought his fabled intensity to the event. When he sat with us at our table, his aura was overwhelming. He talked a mile a minute with the zeal of a man who believed he and only he knew what happened to President Kennedy in 1963. The friend I brought said talking to Stone gave her a "brain ache." Me too. At least I got to hold the historic *Citizen Kane* Academy Award.

Congress released some of the assassination files, but none backed up the theories promoted in *JFK*. The day after the Oscars, MPAA President Jack Valenti (not incidentally a former LBJ aide and lifetime loyalist) denounced the film, a highly unusual condemnation of movie and moviemaker by the motion picture industry's chief lobbyist.

I encountered Frank a year later, on the twentieth anniversary of the Watergate break-in. In June, 1973, burglars, led by G. Gordon Liddy, entered the Democratic National Committee headquarters hoping to sabotage George McGovern's Presidential Campaign. Frank Mankiewicz, the guy who ran McGovern's campaign, naturally held a grudge. McGovern lost the 1972 election by a landslide, even as news of the Nixon White House involvement ultimately led to the President's resignation. Twenty years later, G. Gordon Liddy emerged as a celebrity, author of a best seller and host of a popular radio show.

To mark the Watergate anniversary, WJFK-Radio rented space in the Watergate Hotel for a remote broadcast of G. Gordon Liddy's show. Local media, including me, swarmed the event. Liddy interviewed a couple of authors who wrote about the break in. Liddy even invited some of the D.C. police who arrested him and his crew the night of the burglary.

Frank Mankiewicz joined the media crowd watching Liddy perform. I waved and went over with the camera crew to ask Frank what he thought of Liddy's celebrity and this anniversary show. Frank turned to my camera, took a deep breath, and snarled: "Despicable," staring straight into the lens to emphasize his succinct comment. I think I saw a hint of a smile, but I'm not sure.

Some months later the Newseum asked me to interview Frank about *Citizen Kane* and his father's role writing it, followed by a screening of the film. I prepared calling Frank a few days in advance for a phone interview. I remember Frank talking about Orson Wells and producer John Houseman breakfasting at his home. He reminded me the Hearst newspaper chain hounded his father after the film's release. *Citizen Kane* has long been considered a thinly veiled critical portrait of William Randolph Hearst. Of everything Frank and I discussed, what I most remember is how proud he was of his father's work. After our interview on stage before the screening, Frank stayed to watch the film and so did I.

A few years later I called Frank hoping to report a story on the most famous Oscar in film history sitting on his library shelf in Washington D.C. Frank informed me the family sold the statue. When we appeared at the Newseum, he refused to bring the Oscar because of insurance considerations. Some might find it shocking to sell this heirloom. Frank said, "my wife thinks she saw a picture of it in Steven Spielberg's living room. I'm glad it has a good home." And then he laughed. (Frank's son Ben says Spielberg didn't buy it. The owner of the Herman Mankiewicz Oscar remains a mystery. Ben told me someone in the family needed money and a family decision resulted in the sale.)

Frank Mankiewicz died in 2014. Mark Shields, the syndicated columnist and wit, told me Frank's funeral took place at the Washington Quaker meeting hall, also known as the Friends Temple. According to Mark, Frank's Rabbi began his homily noting that many were surprised a life-long religious Jew would select a Quaker temple for his funeral service. The rabbi paused, adding: "But then, some of my best Jews are Friends."

Father and son would love that line.

36
A Few Stories

(L-R) Me, Willem Dafoe, Barbara Harrison
Courtesy WRC-TV

During the 1989 Inauguration, Barbara Harrison, one of the most genteel women ever to work in television news, prepared a report on the history of inaugural balls. Standing outside the D.C. Convention Center, she delivered her introduction.

Meanwhile, back at the station, the tape machine jammed. The director screamed in her earpiece: "Fill! Fill! Keep talking." Looking like a deer in the headlights and wondering how long she needed to talk she began:

"We think of the balls at inauguration time, but did you know, the first three Presidents had no balls at all."

I met John Corcoran when he wrote an article on feature reporters in 1975 for *Washingtonian Magazine*. Cork jumped from magazine writing to TV news as an on-air movie reviewer and feature reporter for Channel 7. One of his reports featured an orchestra following him around

Washington, D.C.

for a day providing background for his adventures. At the end of the story, Cork walked into the studio trailed by a dozen performing musicians. His career took him to Los Angeles as the entertainment reporter for KABC-TV and later KCAL-TV.

Cork and I like each other, and often sat together at movie previews in the Motion Picture Producer's Association screening room. Occasionally I would leave a screening to hit the nearby men's room. During one screening, when I returned, Cork leaned over and whispered, "you missed the UFO landing." Cork often greeted me as "…the only critic in America who referred to the flying saucer in *Sophie's Choice*."

The events of September 11, 2001 severely curtailed the use of news helicopters in the Washington area. Since then, helicopters have been banned from flying within ten miles of the Washington Monument. Prior to that, local stations used helicopter services daily for aerial shots of traffic jams and other events. The pilots tended to be daredevils.

Our station needed some aerial shots of the city and assigned one of my favorite cameramen. Strapped in high above the city, legs dangling in the air, he reached back to change his camera battery. In those days a camera battery weighed twenty pounds and was about the size of a thick novel. As he reached back and unplugged his battery, the chopper hit a bump. He dropped the battery.

Imagine: a twenty-pound black box hurling thousands of feet to the ground somewhere over Washington. For days, managers searched the papers for news of a mysterious hole in someone's roof, or worse, an individual felled by an unidentified falling object. A few days later, a woman called NBC, saying she found a black box in her flowerbed with an NBC Peacock on it and did we know anything about it. Somebody from the engineering department went out and retrieved the dead battery saying as little as possible.

Old timers at Channel 7 have their own stories about their fearless helicopter service. In the days when 7's call letters were WMAL, they operated out of a remodeled ice rink on Connecticut Avenue. Occasionally the chopper would bring reporters back from the field, landing on top of a building across the street. Sometimes when a reporter cut a deadline close, the chopper would swing as low as possible over WMAL's roof. Four or five people would stretch out a blanket. The reporter on deadline would toss his film or video into the blanket to save precious minutes.

The late Jim Clarke, a well-respected senior Channel 7 reporter, gets unofficial credit for the tape drop idea. Clark also suffered the first casualty, watching from the air as his tape cassette missed the blanket and shattered into a thousand pieces. I heard a rumor Clark jumped from the chopper onto the blanket more than once to make a deadline.

One of Washington's most delightful characters, Helen VerStandig wise-cracked her way around town as Madame Wellington. She and her husband procured a patent on cubic zirconium aka fake diamonds, selling them as Wellington Jewels. Madam Wellington joked about playboys buying her merchandise for their mistresses. Helen smoked with a long cigarette holder. I got to know her covering The Great American Smoke-Out, an anti-smoking event she always attended, dramatically tossing an entire carton of cigarettes into a roaring fire. She always resumed smoking the next day.

She could drink any man under the table and often did. I ran into her at a neighborhood Greek restaurant late in her life. "Oh Madame Wellington, how are you?" I gushed. "Not bad," she rasped, "for an old bag."

She and her husband lived a feisty life, bordering on open-marriage.[49] One night at the bar of a black-tie event, a highly juiced man made a pass. She looked at him and said, "come on, fella, I'm taking you home." She poured him into her Cadillac and piloted up Wisconsin Avenue, pulling into the driveway of an imposing brick Georgian edifice. "This is my house," she said. "Give me time to put the car in the garage. Then knock on the door and I'll let you in." He got out. Madam Wellington drove off, leaving him standing at the entrance of Gawler's, the city's most prominent funeral home.[50]

Willard Scott remembered the night he went to Gawler's to pay his respects to Louie Allen, a longtime D.C. weatherman and Willard's competition on Channel 9. The Channel 9 Station Manager stood by the coffin and said hello to Willard. Then he said, "Louie was the best forecaster in Washington, wouldn't you agree?" Willard said yes. "No one can replace Louie." Willard nodded. The manager looked at Willard and said, "got a minute?"

Jerry Nachman charged through Washington midway of his colorful career in broadcasting and print. In the early 80s he ran WRC Radio, turning the station into a successful news talk station. Rewarded with the job of News Director at WNBC in New York, he returned to Washington as general manager of WRC TV. Unhappy in that position, he returned to New York as editor of *The New York Post*, inventing the outrageous headlines that made the paper famous, including 1990's "Best Sex I Ever Had," attributed to Marla Maples discussing Donald Trump. Nachman returned to MSNBC as an executive and program host.

Nachman took a job with the Walt Disney Company developing programs. One show, *The Investigators*, would follow the work of four *Sixty Minutes* style reporters as they assembled various investigative pieces. The program needed an assignment manager. Nachman remembered the great Jim Snyder, the genius behind the success of Channel 9 who became Vice President of Television News for *Post-Newsweek*. Nachman called him up, describing the show and telling Snyder he could make him a national star if he'd come to California and play the assignment manager. Snyder thought about it a minute and said, "you don't want me—you want Ed Asner." With that, Snyder slammed down the phone.

And I have a few stories to tell on myself. In 1989 the great director Sir. David Lean brought his restored *Lawrence of Arabia* to the American Film Institute. Our interview went well enough and when I finished asking him about the legendary film, it came time for my cameraman to tape a few shots of me listening. I went into the usual rote expla-

Washington, D.C.

nation, "now Sir David, the camera's going to swing around and take a few cutaways of me." With a twinkle in his eye, Sir David Lean exclaimed, "young man, I know what a cutaway is. I INVENTED the cutaway." And, of course, he probably did. All I can add is we both laughed long and loud at my stupid gaff.

The Washington developer Abe Pollin, earned the respect of a grateful city when he built the MCI Center in a previously blighted area of downtown Washington. Pollin wanted the Three Tenors to open his arena, but couldn't book them. Barry Manilow performed opening night December 10, 1997. Still, Abe had opera and class and the Three Tenors on his mind. In August of 1998, Luciano Pavarotti landed at the private airplane terminal of Reagan National Airport to do a few interviews about a possible concert at the MCI Center.

I arrived with Phil Jacobs, a fidgety skittish cameraman. Phil and I entered the room and sat in a corner while Pavarotti answered questions from the respected WETA-FM radio classical music host Nicole Lacroix. Phil, unable to sit still, began adjusting his light stand. Suddenly, the stand fell over with a crash. Pavarotti stopped talking. He jerked his massive head toward Phil and me. Eyes blazing, pointing directly at us, he screamed: "YOU. OUT!"

We got out of there faster than a couple of high school kids caught toilet papering a house. Well, that's it, I thought. I've just been thrown out of an interview with Pavarotti thanks to nervous Nelly, my cameraman. Even Phil looked stunned, as we beat it out of the room.

Fortunately, the great tenor, noticed my hat, a new straw Borsalino fedora. Luciano was wearing a similar hat, most likely a Borsalino. We both tipped our fedoras, then fingered the brims going, "Ahhhh." All was forgotten and forgiven, except for recently when I ran into Phil and reminded him of the day Pavarotti threw him and me out of the interview room.

I emceed the Silver Circle Award of the National Academy of Television Arts and Sciences for several years. The award honored longtime Washington television professionals with careers of twenty-five years or more. Honorees would tell stories about their career as they accepted the honor.

Charlie Stopak worked as a local television director in the beginning years of Channel 7. Programs went on the air live, including the children's show *Claire and Coco* starring a kindergarten teacher and her poodle Coco. One afternoon, the guest included a trained monkey. The animal and his handler came into the studio early to warm up the audience. The kids loved the monkey's antics as he danced around the set. Suddenly, the monkey stopped, rolled his eyes, and fell over—dead. The monkey's owner gasped, horrified. The kids started screaming and crying.

The stage manager began the count: "Five…Four…Three," and yelled into his headset, "Charlie, the monkey died, what do we do?"

Charlie screamed into his headset, "stick your hand up the monkey's ass—and work him like a puppet!" I believe the longest laugh I ever heard took place the night Charlie Stopak told his story of the monkey that died on the kid's show.

37
My Home Town

NBC promoted our News Director Bret Marcus to New York's WNBC-TV. Bret's departure opened the door for Kris Ostrowski, a newsroom veteran. She worked as Assistant News Director for the previous two bosses.

I loved standing around shooting the breeze with Kris. When news of Bret's departure went public, Kris casually mentioned, "I think I'm gonna apply. What do you think?" I said, "do it." Stepping up to News Director, Kris brought institutional memory of the moves that turned our newsroom into a winning team. Kris talked straight, loved Washington football, and chased ambulances for fun. She beefed up hard news and kept a balance with sports and features.

Kris possessed great story sense. When Lucille Ball died in 1989, she put me on the top of the newscast, and filled that hour with the wonderful scenes from *I Love Lucy*, such as the grape stomping segment, the candy factory work, and the Vitameatavegemen commercial. When Johnny Carson announced his retirement, she brain-stormed running something on Carson every night during his last week. Our ratings soared during those special events.

For the fall of 1992, Kris proposed, more or less off the top of her head, a series on home towns. At that time, TV stations produced series to run Monday through Friday. Vance, Doreen, Bob, George and I would visit the place where we grew up for "My Home Town."

The idea struck a chord with me. I love my home town of San Antonio, Texas. I returned every year to visit my mother and drive by places important to me, including my high school, and old houses where relatives lived. Kris sent Byron York, a great producer and friend, and cameraman Jim Forest with me.

Getting ready for the shoot, I mapped out a packed schedule. We started at the Alamo and the Riverwalk downtown, then on to my high school where I arranged to interview my drama and speech teacher Jean Longwith. In 1964, she put me on stage as emcee of the school talent show

Miss Longwith pointed me toward a broadcasting career. In our interview, she described me as an 18-year-old wise ass.

I showed pictures of my father, a local golf champion, and a film of him at the driving range which I cut in with pictures of me. I mentioned his death 23 years earlier. Then I interviewed my mother in the house where I grew up.

My mother possessed a thick Southern accent and a wicked sense of humor. We stood in the kitchen. I began by saying, "I always thought this house was huge when I was growing up, but now I wonder how the four of us fit in here."

"Well," she said with a sly grin, "you were smaller then." I could hear the cameraman stifling a laugh while struggling to keep the camera steady.

The story featured local landmarks, my high school, my mother, my father, death and loss, and a picture of the Texas Hill Country, noting that most native Texans hoped to return some day. To close my story, I took viewers to Inspiration Hill overlooking the city. In high school we parked on this hill, hoping to get lucky with a girl. Now the city lights twinkled as I said, "coming here I've shown you people and places, what I can't show you are feelings, that are as bright to me as the stars on a Texas night."

I came on the air when the video ended and started to talk. To my surprise, I got a catch in my throat. Nothing came out. An unexpected well of emotion rose inside me. The piece stunned the floor crew and the other anchors. I walked out of the studio to a hush. That spring I won a local Emmy for "My Home Town."

"My Home Town" renewed my love of television feature reporting. I believe Kris Ostrowski's idea to show the personal side of the anchor team deepened our relationship with each other and with the audience.

Doreen showed home movies and talked to one of her elementary school teachers. Vance showcased the trusted aunt who helped raise him. George remembered his mother making it possible for him to attend a baseball game in St. Louis, where he grew up. Bob Ryan visited his home town near Boston, talking about his parents and missing them.

The other night I watched *Ladybird*, Greta Gerwig's 2017 film about a rocky mother/daughter relationship portrayed by Laurie Metcalf and Saoirse Ronan. When the daughter leaves for college, she barely speaks to her mother. Away from home, after an especially hard night, she leaves a message on her mother's answering machine, reaching out to remember driving around her home town and the appreciation they both shared for the beauty of local landmarks. I have that same feeling—a love and longing for my home town of San Antonio, Texas.

"My Home Town" aired during one of my hardest personal times. My marriage to Sheila ended earlier that year. Our mutual ambition had kept us together. Sheila moved from television to advertising. After several successful years as an Account Manager, she opened a thriving advertising agency with two partners. Things progressed until 1990, when the economy turned sour. The loss of a big account ended the business. I doubt I offered the emotional support she needed. We separated in 1991. I think grief over my broken marriage spilled into "My Home Town."

38
Spielberg's Sister

Out of the blue I received a call from Steven Spielberg's sister. She wondered if I would help a fundraiser for the Noyes Children's Library in Kensington, Maryland. I offered to take two people to a movie premiere, a fund raising gimmick I often donated. Soon, I met Susan Spielberg Pasternak and liked her. Spielberg's sister lived in Silver Spring. Her husband worked for the county government. Susan lived the life of a Silver Spring mom, except a mom with a nice bit of celebrity sibling status. After we met, Susan and I crossed paths at movie previews, especially movies directed by her brother. At a Spielberg preview, I usually managed to include a sound bite or two from Sue.

In 1993, Susan's brother received Academy Award nominations for both Best Picture and Best Director for *Schindler's List*. I called Sue to ask if she and her husband planned to attend. During our conversation I blurted out, "what are you going to wear?" She offered to show me her choices, all paid for by Steven. A camera crew and I spent an afternoon taping Sue trying on various outfits.

Schindler's List won seven Oscars, including Best Picture and Best Director honors for Steven. It remains a masterpiece, one of the definitive Holocaust films. Spielberg based the story on the novel *Schindler's Ark*. Liam Neeson starred as Otto Schindler, a German industrialist who saved almost a thousand Polish-Jewish refugees by employing them in his factories.

Schindler's List premiered in Washington November 30, 1993—a benefit in cooperation with the newly opened

United States Holocaust Memorial Museum. Spielberg attended and so did his sister. During an interview, I told Steven about Susan and her outfits and watched as he muffled a giggle.

In 1993, *The Fugitive* reminded me of the night I wandered into *Indiana Jones and the Temple of Doom*. Once again Harrison Ford, in this story a doctor wrongly convicted of murdering his wife, escapes deputies escorting him to prison after a horrific railroad crash. The opening of *The Fugitive* rivals the rolling boulder in Indiana Jones. When the crash finished, the audience let out a collective, "whooooah" and started applauding. Tommy Lee Jones won the Best Supporting Actor Academy Award for his relentless portrait of U.S. Marshall Girard, determined to bring the escaped man to justice.

What's Love Got to Do With It? recreates the career and abusive marriage of Ike and Tina Turner. Many of the scenes of Laurence Fishburne as Ike berating and beating Angela Bassett are hard to watch. During the screening, a guy behind me said out loud, "what's wrong with him?" I interviewed Fishburne and quoted the comment, turning the question to him, "what was wrong with Ike Turner?" The question threw both of us, and I think I remember Fishburne answering, "It's hard to put in words." A recent documentary on Tina Turner included her appearance at a press conference stating emphatically she had not seen the movie and did not intend to.

I came out of the screening of *Groundhog Day* thinking, "gee, that was really good." *Groundhog Day* achieved classic status in the years that followed on cable and streaming. It won Bill Murray a new level of respect as an actor.

The *Groundhog Day* producers somehow talked the eccentric Murray into giving a few satellite interviews. At that time, actors would sit in a studio, look into a camera, and respond to questions they could only hear in an earpiece. Murray agreed as long as the stations provided reverse video. He wanted to see the person talking to him. We agreed, and set it up technically. When my time with Bill Murray began, I called over several people in the newsroom to look in my camera and say hello to him, which I think tickled him a little. At least we tried to do something different.

39
Carson and Leno and Letterman

Courtesy WRC-TV

JAY LENO MADE ONE OF HIS FIRST VISITS TO WRC in 1986. He launched a schmooze tour that year as part of his campaign to inherit *The Tonight Show*. Jay happily agreed to an interview for *The Arch Campbell Show*. I taped an interview backstage where the station kept flats and backgrounds. Going with my show's barebones look, we hauled in the old moth-eaten couch used on the show. Leno liked it because it gave him something to make fun of.

We talked about his life as a stand-up comic. He remembered working flea bag clubs, including one simply called NUDE. I liked Leno and he liked me. Over the next twenty years, whenever I saw him, he mentioned the moth-eaten couch, the backstage interview, and called me the lead in to Station Sign Off. Leno's put-downs included, "stay tuned for Arch followed by 'Lamp unto my Feet.'"

David Letterman didn't visit affiliates or give many interviews. He agreed to one series of satellite interviews with several affiliates. I asked him about Stupid Pet Tricks and mentioned a rabbit I owned saying the bunny could lift weights (OK, I exaggerated just a little). Letterman started calling me "Bunny Boy" and "Bunny Rabbit Boy."

When GE acquired NBC in 1986, Letterman brought a tape crew to GE headquarters bringing along a fruit basket, allegedly as a welcome gift. The Security People did not get the joke. GE Security gave Letterman a hard time, at one point shoving the camera and camera operator. Letterman gleefully showed the footage on *Late Night*. That comedy bit shined a light on an inconvenient truth. General Electric, a multinational bottom-line corporation, possessed little affinity for show business. They bought NBC to turn a profit.

I loved Letterman and watched his 12:30am *Late Night* whenever I could. I rarely watched *The Tonight Show* with Johnny Carson. As for Leno, I found him too eager to please. Letterman had a dangerous quality I loved.

"Mr. Nice Guy" Leno hired a tough agent named Helen Kushnick. At some point she negotiated a contract with a secret clause giving Jay Leno *The Tonight Show* host job when Carson retired. In the spring of 1991 various publications floated rumors NBC wanted Carson to retire. The stories pissed Carson off. At the May 1991 affiliate meeting Carson shocked the company with the surprise announcement he would retire in a year. Privately, Carson accused Leno's agent of planting the stories urging him to leave. NBC announced Jay Leno would take over after Johnny Carson.

I interviewed Leno a few months before his start date, May 25, 1992, asking if his plans for the show included an announcer. I think I cupped my hand over my ear in the style of a 1930s radio voice. With a twinkle in his eye, Leno said, "I'm looking for an older man, possibly with a mustache and a deep voice." Laughing, I told Leno I fit the bill. *Washingtonian Magazine* printed a half serious rumor that *The Tonight Show* was considering me to replace Ed McMahon. I called my agent. Of course, Leno had no plans for me. For a few weeks, the rumor spread that I would leave for Hollywood. I even produced a mock audition tape, inserting outrageous laughs at Leno's jokes and a few other gags.

Carson's final shows attracted record audiences, especially his last show on May 22, 1992. The 11:00pm News ratings jumped during "Johnny Carson Week."

Letterman represented the creative choice to replace Carson. Leno represented the safe choice. General Electric, the bottom-line corporation, took the safe choice. Letterman expected that his years in the slot following Carson gave him the right to move up. Losing *Tonight* to Leno pissed him off. Letterman had another year on his contract. He announced when the year completed, he would leave NBC.

Leno's ratings immediately sagged. Faced with losing Letterman, NBC secretly offered Leno's job to Letterman. Letterman refused and left for CBS. Beginning September 13, 1993, *The Late Show with David Letterman* on CBS cut deep into Leno's ratings.

It took almost two years for Leno to turn things around. In July, 1995, actor Hugh Grant booked an appearance to plug his new movie *Nine Months*. A few days before his appearance, police arrested Grant with a prostitute in his car. Hugh Grant agreed to honor his commitment and appear on *The Tonight Show*. Leno opened with, "what the hell were you thinking?" which got a huge laugh. Interest in the segment and publicity about the interview helped boost Leno back into first place.

Leno had a built-in advantage. NBC enjoyed the strongest affiliate line up of the major networks, going back to the beginning days of television. At CBS some of the affiliates delayed Letterman in favor of more lucrative reruns or movies.

With all the NBC stations airing Leno at 11:30pm and some of the CBS stations airing Letterman after midnight or even later, Leno emerged on top.

Our feisty News Director Kris Ostrowski left suddenly in the fall of 1992. Gossips whispered about a profanity laden blow up between our boss and the General Manager. Her replacement, Dick Reingold, arrived with a long history in local news and many creative ideas. He also came to carry out the General Manager's wishes.

GE's corporate culture gradually impacted entertainment coverage. GE pushed stations to conduct satellite interviews with celebrities in NBC shows.

I made many trips to L.A. as Leno struggled to gain his footing. One story line the new boss encouraged was "Jay Leno's Secret Plan to overcome David Letterman." I produced a behind the scenes story on *The Tonight Show*. I stood to the side watching Leno perform his own warm up, which included questions and answers from the audience. One audience member stood up and said, "what's Arch Campbell doing standing over there?" Leno laughed and said I was there to report a fabulous story on him that would make all the difference in his career. Then Leno shot me a withering look.

We'll never know if Letterman might have attracted an even larger and more lucrative audience than Leno on NBC. Every night when I got home, I watched Letterman on CBS. I never watched Leno.

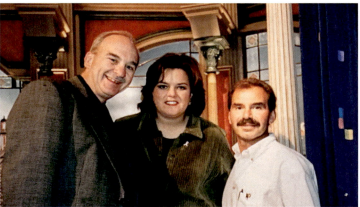

Top: Cheri Oteri, Saturday Night Live
Middle: Rosie O'Donell
Bottom: Whoopi Goldberg
Courtesy NBC4 Cameraman Chester Panzer

40
Change

WHEN SHE FIRST BECAME NEWS DIRECTOR, Kris Ostrowski casually mentioned something that would change television news forever. "In the future, news will be story oriented, not segment oriented." In other words, instead of waiting for the sports segment or my entertainment segment, viewers would stay glued to a story as it developed in real time. Kris' prediction came true on June 17, 1994.

That week L.A. police found O.J. Simpson's wife, Nicole Brown Simpson, and a friend Ron Goldman, brutally murdered outside her Los Angeles condo. Police charged the well-known celebrity O.J. Simpson with double murder. He arranged to turn himself in to authorities a few days later at 11:00am Pacific time June 17th. Simpson didn't show up. Police started hunting for him.

Someone spotted O.J. in the back of a White Ford Bronco on an L.A. freeway. Police followed the Bronco. They didn't pull it over because O.J.'s driver Al Cowlings called saying O.J. was in the back seat holding a gun to his head. The white Bronco with dozens of police cruisers following crept along the highway at about 35 miles an hour.

Local L.A. television pioneered the use of helicopters, mainly for traffic coverage, then for police chases. This day, the choppers started following the odd procession. A little after 9:00pm on the east coast, the networks began breaking into prime time, reporting Simpson had a gun to his head in the back seat of the Bronco.

NBC was broadcasting the NBA finals. As the other networks broke into their programming, NBC put Tom Brokow on the air and squeezed the basketball game in a box in the bottom quarter of the screen. The slow-moving procession mesmerized the country.

This breaking news offered the ultimate hook. Viewers thought they might watch O.J. kill himself on live TV. The chase extended until almost 11:00pm eastern time. Finally, Simpson went home. Once inside, coverage continued. Networks didn't dare break away with the possibility that O.J. might commit suicide once inside his house. Long after midnight, east coast time, O.J. surrendered and was taken into custody.

The O.J. chase ushered in the era of breaking news. From now on, viewers would watch something unedited, live.

New technology contributed. In the 1980s Channel 4 operated one or two live trucks. My live shots from the Oscars required reserving expensive AT&T phone lines. New satellite technology made live shots easier. One phone call to a technician set up the shot. WRC and the network purchased dozens of live trucks. Instead of coming on set, reporters worked on location, live in the field. When a reporter couldn't get to the scene of a story, he or she stood outside nearby, giving the appearance of immediacy.

Corporate ownership, consultants, and technology changed priorities. GE Corporate pinched pennies where possible. My lucky timing in contracts in 1984 and 1987 ran out in 1990. Instead of a big raise, I traded a small salary cut for a longer contract.

I traveled to Los Angeles at least four times a year, for on set visits to NBC series including *L.A. Law* and *E.R.* An NBC travel agent made our travel arrangements. We flew budget, staying in hotels with corporate rates and discounts. The days of John Rohrbeck casually saying, "get a room at the Bel Air Hotel, you'll love it," changed to lessons in filling out expense reports sent to New York for approval.

Washington, D.C.

Jerry Nachman, the creative genius who ran WRC Radio and then WNBC TV News, arrived in the late 80s to run WRC-TV. An old school creative, he kept my show on the air because he liked it, even when the network moved it from 1:00am to 2:00am clearing the way for all the NBC owned stations to air the syndicated *Showtime at the Apollo*.

Nachman wanted to buy expensive syndicated programming as lead ins to the afternoon news. GE corporate refused. Nachman resigned, and returned to New York as editor of *The New York Post,* ushering in an era with his brand of outrageous journalism, and screaming headlines such as "Headless Body in Topless Bar."

The Arch Campbell Show died when a guest agreed to travel from New York to D.C. to stage a dog fashion show. We promised she would finish in time to catch the 9:00pm shuttle back to New York. Of course, the taping ran late. The angry guest hired a limo to drive her back to New York City and sent the bill to WRC. The new General Manager took one look, refused to pay the bill, and canceled my show.

Satellite technology replaced the NBC syndicated news service. Satellites made uploading and sharing tape from all the affiliates possible 24 hours a day. *The NBC News Channel* feed replaced the one-hour "A" news feed. Pictures of an airplane landing on a highway or a car smashing into a store replaced polished reporter packages. *News Channel* dropped my movie reviews, once aired on as many as 50 stations around the country. Now, they provided film clips, and behind the scenes footage, available for free. Stations snapped up the video for expanded newscasts in the early afternoon and early morning.

Somehow, WRC's 11:00pm News remained intact. Jim Vance and Doreen Gentzler emerged as the city's most popular and respected news anchors. Bob Ryan's weather topped all others. George Michael became the prime television sports source in Washington.

I held on to one of the most unique positions in local news. Few stations handed a movie reviewer/feature reporter a regular Monday through Friday late news slot. Working on the 11:00pm news, I could attend a preview, come back, do an instant review, and insert freshness and excitement into the newscast. The 11:00pm arrangement set up perfect program flow: News into weather into sports into entertainment into Carson. Every now and then, a consultant would try to tinker with the format. One night they switched me and George. We both hated it, complained, and our News Director switched us back. We did not need fixing.

WRC possessed one other benefit: luck. New owners at Channel 9 cut costs. In 1987, Channel 9 dismissed Davey Marlin Jones, my competition and the city's most unusual movie reviewer. Davey's departure made me the only game in town. I did not celebrate. More cutbacks came to Channel 9, where executives fired personalities and demoralized staff. Maureen Bunyan, one of Washington's first Black female anchors, disappeared from the air after 22 years of success.

On January 14, 1992, Glenn Brenner, one of the greatest local news talents in the country, died of a brain tumor. Brenner combined sports with outrageous humor and stunts. He found a feisty nun to pick NFL football games. She ended the season with a better winning percentage than the "experts." Brenner drove the Oscar Meyer Weinermobile around Washington for a segment. Upon receiving a parking ticket, Brenner said, "you're giving me a ticket because my wiener's too big?" Management brought Warner Wolfe back to replace Brenner, only to discover Wolfe had lost a step. Channel 9 dismissed Warner Wolfe in 1995.

Channel 9's ultimate tone-deaf decision severed Gordon Peterson, the equal of Jim Vance, as dean of local anchors. Channel 7 hired both Bunyan and Peterson, immediately cutting into 9's ratings. Channel 7 also hired away Channel 9's weatherman Doug Hill. Each departing familiar face from the once unbeatable Channel 9 raised our ratings at Channel 4, as well as the ratings of both Channels 7 and 5.

Channel 7's delight in hiring well known Washington faces kept salaries high. Jim Vance taped an audition with Maureen Bunyan at Channel 7 during one contentious negotiation with NBC Corporate. When news of the audition leaked, the GE accountants agreed to Vance's terms. Management appeared to take Channel 9's demise to heart, thinking twice before pushing out their best-known people.

41
Second Chance

My wife Sheila Campbell achieved great success in the advertising business, forming her own agency in Bethesda, Maryland. We encouraged each other's ambition, possibly to the detriment of a well-rounded marriage. After nineteen years, our partnership unraveled. When we agreed to divorce, I took off a week and returned to my home town. I slept in my old room in the house where I grew up, opening the windows to hear dogs barking, a rooster crowing and the bells of the Shrine of the Little Flower church nearby. One night, my mother Martha said, "don't worry, Archie, you'll be OK." And I was, living on my own for the next few years.

    I made an unexpected connection with an old friend. Paul Hanson graduated a year ahead of me at Jefferson High School, an outstanding student and athlete. His mother Evelyn Hanson taught English at the school. Paul grew up a block from our house. He received an appointment to the U.S. Air Force Academy, an extraordinary honor for our neighborhood. Twenty-five years later, he moved to D.C. to work in the satellite industry. Mrs. Hanson and my mother insisted we get in touch. I invited Paul to play golf. To our mutual surprise, we both had a great time and started playing regularly.

    One spring, Paul and I decided to fly to San Antonio to visit our mothers, and play golf. That weekend, Mrs. Hanson asked me and my mother to join her and Paul for Sunday services at Laurel Heights United Methodist Church. I noticed a woman named Gina Gilland listed as Associate Minister. I expected an older matron. I did not expect the curly haired beauty who led the liturgy. Afterwards, at lunch, I said, "who was that woman? I'd like to get spiritual with her." We all laughed. I forgot about it.

Mrs. Hanson remembered. She pulled out a folder of articles about me my mother had given her and brought them to Reverend Gilland, saying, "this man wants to meet you." As it turned out, Gina was single, divorced after a few years of marriage. She rolled her eyes, said OK and gave Mrs. Hansen her phone number.

One night, Martha called coyly saying, "I have a present for you. Here is the phone number of that minister you liked." I laughed and wrote down the number. I also barked, "what am I gonna do with the phone number of a woman sixteen hundred miles away?" Then I forgot about the whole thing.

Memorial Day weekend, 1993, George Michael, revealed he would film scenes in the upcoming feature film *Eight Seconds* in San Antonio. *Eight Seconds* told the story of rodeo rider Lane Frost, a performer George featured on his network *Sports Machine* over the years. The station sent me down to produce a story on George and the movie. I offered to stay at my mother's house. As I made my arrangements, I called Gina. She actually took my call, telling me she was scheduled to perform a wedding, and I could come along. When the ceremony ended, she said her good byes and got out of there almost as quick as I exited a screening on deadline.

The wedding completed, Gina and I drove downtown to the Little Rhein Steak House on the San Antonio River. After dinner, we stopped at the Liberty Bar on Josephine Street, an old building locally famous for leaning like the tower of Pisa. Between the summer night and a couple of Shiner Bock draft beers, lightning struck. Back in Washington, she and I burned up the long-distance lines, flying back and forth between D.C. and San Antonio until neither of us could stand it anymore. Seven months after our first date, we married in Laurel Heights Methodist Church, New Year's Day of 1994.

The church was filled with people important to both me and Gina. My entire life seemed to gather in Laurel Heights that day. Mrs. Hanson, who drove me to kindergarten forty years earlier, sat up front with my mother and sister. My mother's best friend Smitty found me before the service proclaiming, "what a beautiful day for Archie to get married."

Gina Gilland and I married January 1st, 1994

Most of her congregation turned out for our service. Cousins from Alabama and San Antonio attended, as well as childhood and family friends, and teachers from Jefferson. Jean Longwith read scripture. Revelations 21 verses 1 through 4, "then I saw a new heaven and a new earth." Five hundred people filled the sanctuary, a communion of saints witnessing our second chance.

I told Gina it felt like the scene where the nuns give away Maria in *The Sound of Music*. The whole thing happened because George Michael had a cameo in a not very successful movie.[51]

42
Movies: 1994-1997

1994: REMEMBER "THE WORLD'S WORST FILM Festival" in 1980? The festival honored director Ed Wood, whose low budget films included *Plan 9 from Outer Space* and *Bride of the Monster.* The reassessment of Ed Wood inspired director Tim Burton to tell Ed Wood's story fourteen years later in the comic biopic *Ed Wood*. Martin Landau won the Academy Award for Best Supporting Actor as Bela Lugosi, the one time horror star reduced to working in Wood's shoe-string projects. Johnny Depp caught just the right touch of dreaminess portraying Ed Wood. I have a fondness for *Ed Wood* because I had so much fun at the original festival that re-discovered him.

With John Turturro at the AFI

John Turturro excels at playing hotheads. *In Quiz Show*, he plays Herb Stempel, furious at the producers of 1950's television quiz *21* for pushing him off the program in favor of the more handsome and scholarly Charles Van Doren. Stemple's complaints resulted in a congressional investigation, ruining the reputation of those involved including the scholarly Van Doren. I watch *Quiz Show* every few years and find it as great as ever. Writer Doris Kearns Goodwin references her husband Richard Goodwin's investigation in her recent memoir of their marriage *An Unfinished Love Story*.

The Shawshank Redemption opened to limited success in 1994. Over the years fans discovered the story on cable and streaming. Tim Robbins plays a man wrongfully convicted of murder. Morgan Freeman befriends Robbins in prison, narrating the story. I met and interviewed Morgan Freeman on several occasions. He brightened up talking about *The Shawshank Redemption*, saying he received more response to that film than any other. *The Shawshank Redemption* remains hard to resist.

Speed made Sandra Bullock a star. The movie succeeded because of a simple thriller premise. Bullock plays a passenger on a bus wired to explode if the bus travels at less than 50 miles an hour. Keanu Reeves plays a bomb expert who happens to be on board and tries to diffuse the explosive. The scenes of the bus racing through L.A. mixed comedy and terror leading to a delightful Hollywood ending.

Sandra Bullock grew up in Arlington, Virginia, just outside D.C., and attended Washington-Lee High School. I immediately obtained Bullock's high school annual photo and spoke with some of her teachers who, of course, remembered her fondly. Sandra Bullock has returned to Washington to raise funds for Cancer research in honor of her late mother Helga and to support the American Red Cross.

Tom Clancy took a vacation and missed the world premiere of *Clear and Present Danger*. Harrison Ford missed it as well because of bad weather. My story centered on my fellow reporter Barbara Harrison, who played a reporter in the film. *Clear and Present Danger* seemed great at the time. Maybe now, not so much.

In 1995 NBC produced a four-part miniseries based on a script by Tom Clancy. The network pressured Clancy to submit to an interview about the project. To my surprise, Clancy told the network he would talk to me. I knew

Washington, D.C.

Clancy lived in the area. I learned he owned several acres on the Chesapeake Bay in a modern home built on the site of a former summer camp. Clancy would not provide written instructions to his compound. Instead, the crew and I agreed to meet Clancy's friend in a close-in D.C. suburb, and follow him to Clancy's place. We drove for more than an hour, arriving at a heavily fortified estate. A tank stood by the entrance. During our interview, Tom Clancy barked some of his answers but also revealed a charming side. Walking around the property, we stopped as the *Queen Elizabeth 2 (QE2)* sailed up the Chesapeake to the Baltimore Harbor. Pretty neat watching an ocean liner float past your backyard.

I could feel the excitement on premiere night for *Pulp Fiction* at the Embassy Theater on Florida Avenue. Quentin Tarantino hit a home run in a series of set pieces. Exposure on rental and cable and now streaming have made this gem even better over time. When I surf my smart TV and find *Pulp Fiction*, I pop in, if only to see Travolta dance with Uma Thurman. On preview night, when Travolta and Uma took to the dance floor, the crowd let out a collective, "Ahhhhhhhh."

Michael Douglas, and Annette Benning attended the D.C. preview screening of *The American President*. I remember they came to the Avalon Theater, near my house. I also remember the night because the cameraman's sound went out about half way through the interview. I had quite a time piecing something together for the late news.

Aaron Sorkin wrote *The American President* for Rob Reiner to direct. *The American President* most certainly inspired the long running NBC series *The West Wing*. In fact, the TV series used the movie's sets. Sorkin and company traveled to Washington several times a year starting with season one in 1999. I stood on the sidelines of many outdoor shoots with an NBC publicist and enjoyed a friendly relationship with Martin Sheen, Alison Janney, and Bradley Whitford.

Babe reminded me of my story on Spot the Pig in 1975. In the film, Babe avoids his intended role as Christmas dinner by learning to herd sheep. *Babe* was the first time I noticed James Cromwell, who went on to a long busy career playing older alpha males. I would like to tell you my pig Spot avoided his intended role. Alas, life doesn't always turn out like a good movie script.

I walked into a showing of *The Usual Suspects* cold—no idea what to expect. I love film noir and this old school story combined crime and a mystery and a great cast including Gabriel Byrne, Stephen Baldwin, Benicio del Toro, Kevin Pollak, Chazz Palminteri, Pete Postlehwaite, and Kevin Spacey, who steals the show. The audience let out a sigh at the ending, one of the great movie finales.

1996: I count *Big Night* among my favorite movies—a delicious story of food, brotherhood, passion, and heartbreak. Tony Shalhoub plays a frustrated chef. Stanley Tucci, his brother, runs the business side of their restaurant as it struggles to stay afloat. A rumored visit by bandleader Louie Prima sparks a last-ditch cooking marathon in preparation for the great musician. I love *Big Night* for the ending—a silent reconciliation between brothers resulting in another one of those sighs I love when a movie leaves the audience welling with emotion.

I've watched *Fargo* at least a dozen times and never get tired of it. Writer/directors Joel and Ethan Coen, achieved an amazing balance between crime, violence, and comedy, with Frances McDormand providing a ray of goodness at the center as a pregnant Police Detective unfazed by anything.

Every weatherman in town attended the preview

screening of *Twister*. Of course, I brought Bob Ryan with me to review *Twister* that night on the news. Ryan liked it although both of us thought the grand finale where Helen Hunt and Bill Paxton jump out of their truck and into the middle of an F5 tornado went a couple of bridges too far. The weather people in the audiences hooted and hollered at the finale, I suspect secretly wishing they could experience an F-5 tornado, instead of watching it on a big screen. Hollywood tried again with a remake in 2024. Recently Bob Ryan went to the cineplex to see the sequel, *Twisters*; he gives it a thumbs down.

1997: A handful of people settled into the small Tenley Circle Theater for the evening show of *Eve's Bayou*. Actress Kasi Lemmons wrote and directed the story of a woman's childhood memory of her father and his infidelity. Set in rural Louisiana, *Eve's Bayou* touches on superstition, fortune telling, and voodoo curses. Critics praised *Eve's Bayou* as written by a woman for women, long before the MeToo movement.

A few minutes into the screening, an entourage arrived into the theater—a giant man, surrounded by other men with a small woman by his side. They looked around and picked seats on a side aisle apart from the others watching. I heard somebody whisper, "that's Mike Tyson." The woman with Tyson was his second wife, a local (Potomac, Maryland) physician named Monia Turner.

Eve's Bayou opened in November, 1997, not that long after the infamous Tyson versus Evander Holyfield boxing match which officials stopped when Tyson bit off part of Holyfield's ear. I could feel a chill in the auditorium when Tyson and his group entered.

I'm pretty certain Mike Tyson's wife wanted to see *Eve's Bayou* because of the subject matter. I noticed the men surrounding the couple shifting in their seats. Thirty minutes after they arrived, the group left. Dr. Turner divorced Tyson a few years later.

43
Diana and Michael

Now some bragging. I–ahem–met Princess Diana. I actually shook hands with her. Not long after the Princess announced her divorce, *Vanity Fair* maven Anna Wintour lured Diana to Washington for a fashion benefit in September 1996 for the Nina Hyde fund for breast Cancer research.

I hustled to the National Building Museum to interview Anna Wintour. The Princess stood right next to her. Someone said, "Arch, may I present the Princess of Wales." Diana turned to me and flashed those eyes. Suddenly a million watts of star power looked my way. She extended her hand and I gently shook it. Touching her hand practically made me explode. After that, I think I blacked out, except I can tell you Webster's Dictionary must have created the word "charisma" in Diana's honor.

Back at the station, waiting to go on the air during the commercials, George Michael asked, "did you really meet her?" I answered, "yes." For some reason I added, "I could make that woman happy." The laughter at that remark continued as I came on the air.

My home phone rang early Sunday morning, August 31, 1997. Princess Diana died in a car crash in Paris. Our ambitious News Director Dave Lougee wanted a one-hour special that morning. I rushed to the station, pulled footage of the charity event where I met the Princess, and talked about her other Washington visits and star power.

Washington developer Alan Kay earned a place in D.C. society in the 1980s when he bought Merrywood, the storied home of Jackie Auchincloss aka Jackie Kennedy aka Jackie O. In 1990, Michael Jackson arrived at Merrywood for a fundraiser for the Capitol Children's Museum, hosted by Dianne and Alan Kay. The Press registered in the mansion's garage. Alan Kay recognized me and waved me in with my cameraman.

Walking around, I noticed the grand level of decoration. Standing on the back balcony, overlooking the Potomac with the lights of the mall and U.S. Capitol in the distance, I said hello to another of my favorite Washington characters, Victor Shargai. Victor got around. He operated as a behind-the-scenes power at the Kennedy Center and with the Helen Hayes Theater awards. Victor also worked as a decorator, giving him entrée into most of the city's grandest homes. Looking around at statues and ornaments and pieces representing Washington's new gilded age, I said, "good God Victor, who decorated this place?"

Victor shot back, "I did, you idiot." And we both doubled over with laughter.

As did Princess Diana, Michael Jackson stood in a corner surrounded by fans. Someone recognized me and said, "Arch, come meet Michael Jackson." He extended his hand and I took it. It was cold as a fish exhibiting no strength or grip. But there it was. I shook hands with Michael Jackson.

That night I opened my report saying, "not since Elvis came to the White House has there been so much excitement in Washington." MJ's people went nuts over that remark. Michael loved Elvis and loved comparisons to "The King." Michael Jackson's people immediately called wanting a tape, which I sent. I imagine that tape now sits buried somewhere in Michael's memorabilia.

44
Wright Says Wrong!

"This is Bob Wright's office. Do you know who that is?" And then the voice paused to let it sink in. "He wants you to call him as soon as you get this message."

I knew who Bob Wright was—President and CEO of NBC. I could not imagine why he wanted to talk to me. I punched in the number provided.

"Oh yes," the woman from the original message said with the same hint of menace, "he wants to talk to you."

Mr. Wright came on the phone and didn't waste any time with formalities.

"Why did you get in touch with Evelyn Y. Davis?"

Evelyn Y. Davis made her name at stockholder meetings. Buying shares in multiple corporations, she attended annual meetings asking uncomfortable questions such as, "why do you pay your CEO so much money?" She once nominated Ralph Nader to the board of General Motors. She dreamed up outrageous costumes. At a meeting of Alcoa Steel, she wore an aluminum dress. Evelyn published a newsletter *Highlights and Lowlights* which qualified her for a White House press pass. She instinctively knew how to get under the skin of corporate types, who in turn bought her off with attention and subscribing to her newsletter.

Our News Director, Dick Reingold, thought it would be fun to produce a series about unusual places in Washington. I proposed a feature on Evelyn's gravesite in Rock Creek Cemetery. Located near the entrance to the historic graveyard, a large stone several feet high features her name, birth date, and entire resume. Evelyn Y. Davis constructed a monument to herself.

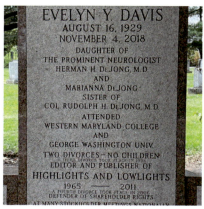
Rock Creek Cemetery, Washington, D.C.

Daughter of the Prominent Neurologist Herman H. DeJong, M.D. and Marianna DeJong. Sister of Col. Rudolph H. DeJong, M.D. Attended Western Maryland College and George Washington Univ. Two Divorces. No children. Editor and Publisher of Highlights and Lowlights—1965. Defender of shareholder rights at many stockholder meetings nationally.

She married a third time and divorced. She directed a stone mason to carve in small letters under her previous information:

A third divorce took place in 1994.

Two smaller stones flank the central piece, one with the inscription:

Recognized at White House Press Conferences by several Presidents since 1975.

The other stone features the words she lived by:

Power is Greater than Love, and I did not get where I am by standing in line nor by being shy.

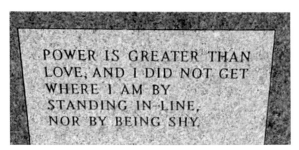

Rock Creek Cemetery, Washington, D.C.

On a chilly February afternoon in 1996, I met Evelyn at her grave. She lived another 22 years—which gave her plenty of time to enjoy her monument.

At the grave site, Evelyn proudly read her motto, "Power is Greater than Love. And I did not get where I am by standing in line or being shy." The two of us sat on a bench she erected to view the gravesite. Toward the end of the interview, Evelyn laughed, adding in her thick eastern European accent, "here I am with a handsome young man sitting on my bench on a cold winter's day."

Washington Post writer John Kelly disclosed more of Evelyn's story in a follow-up feature in 2021. Davis was born in Amsterdam into a wealthy family that was part-Jewish. As a youngster, she was put in a concentration camp with her mother and brother. She saw a lot of people being abused and sent to Auschwitz and other extermination camps. She saw that those people were forgotten. And she decided she would not be forgotten.[52]

I think Evelyn called Bob Wright to brag that Channel 4 was going to do a feature story on her and he should pay more attention to her because she was important, and Arch Campbell wanted to put her on television…or something.

Back on the phone with Mr. Wright, I quickly explained the story and her gravesite and our series. He cut me off, completely unamused.

The Accidental Critic

"You have stepped in it," Wright said, "wherever you go, whatever you do, she will hound you."

I stammered something about canceling the story.

"Oh no, no, it's too late for that." I don't remember much else about the conversation because I think Wright ended the call.

Mr. Wright didn't say cancel the story, so it ran. I don't think our News Director Dick Reingold knew about the call. If he did, he might have had a nervous breakdown.

General Electric Corporation considers Bob Wright one of their greatest executives. He made a lot of money for GE and GE stockholders, adding networks including MSNBC and CNBC. He did not care about humorous news stories on disruptive corporate gadflies with outrageous gravestones.

Me and Mr Wright
Photo courtesy Marty LaVor

I only heard from Evelyn one other time. She insisted I cover the delivery of her new Chrysler. In typical fashion, she insisted Chrysler's CEO present the car to her. Warren Brown, the late automobile reporter for *The Washington*

Post stood next to me. We giggled, as Warren whispered, "she does this every time she buys a new car."

I shudder remembering Bob Wright's phone call. On the other hand, I gotta say my visit with Evelyn Y. Davis at her wacky grave resulted in a pretty good story.

45
Movies: 1998-2001

1998: I liked *Shakespeare in Love*, except count me among movie lovers who believe *Saving Private Ryan* deserved the Best Picture Oscar for 1998. In case you've forgotten, *Saving Private Ryan* lost Best Picture to *Shakespeare in Love,* although Steven Spielberg won Best Director. The years haven't been kind to that decision, nor should they. I was standing with a microphone outside the K B Cinema after the first show of *Saving Private Ryan*. The veterans who attended that first show came out shaken. As I started my interview, the cameraman's pager buzzed. Police reported a shooting at the Capitol. My piece never aired, but I still remember the look on the faces of the WWII veterans I met after that first *Saving Private Ryan* screening.

1999: I didn't expect much when I settled into the first showing of *The Sixth Sense* in August of 1999. The whispery audio and slow story gave the screening a heavy feel. And then, Wham!…the twist at the end. The audience gasped. Most of the movies I love come with the kind of jolt I got in *The Sixth Sense.*

The crowd did more than gasp at *The Blair Witch Project.* Everybody was buzzing about *The Blair Witch* that summer. Three student filmmakers hike into the woods near Burkittsville, Maryland and disappear. The movie shows their "found footage," possibly explaining the witch did something to them. In a triumph of marketing and forward thinking, producers used the internet to spread the legend of the Blair Witch, insisting on the truth of the story. I went over to the Outer Circle Theater with a crew for a Friday showing and interviewed kids standing in line.

Everybody loves a good ghost story and this one turned into the viral hit of the summer.

The director came to town and I sat up an interview. I walked into a room and saw Eduardo Sanchez, a young nice-looking guy. Eduardo smiled and said:

Eduardo Sanchez wisely ignored my advice

"Do you remember me Arch?" I blanked, wondering what I'd done this time. Eduardo went on to explain a few years earlier he interviewed me for the Montgomery College school newspaper.

"After the interview I told you I wanted to go to film school. Should I go to USC or the University of Central Florida? You said 'USC.' I went to Florida and now I've got a hit movie."

I could only laugh. Eduardo met Daniel Myrick in Florida. Together, they developed a screenplay. In the process, *The Blair Witch Project* invented the "found footage" genre—widely copied in the years that followed. Eduardo and Daniel Myrick received the Independent Spirit John Cassavetes Award in 1999. Edwardo has since enjoyed a thriving career in film and television. I've seen him dozens of times since that first interview. We always laugh about my advice.

2000: when I think of *Almost Famous*, I think of Tim Russert, whom I saw at the preview screening at the fancy new Mazza Theater. Russert loved movies. Whenever I saw him at NBC, he asked what I liked at the time. One of the friendliest men ever to work in network news, Tim Russert died of a heart attack June 13, 2008 while recording voice tracks at NBC, a hard-to-accept sudden death.

The Russert family held Tim's wake at St. Alban's, the private school on the grounds of the National Cathedral. The line of people wanting to pay respects to the family stretched around the block. I spotted a familiar face. I told Phil Donahue NBC had a special line for employees. Phil told me he didn't work for NBC and didn't want to take the place from someone more deserving. Phil Donahue stood in line for more than an hour.

2001: one character dominated movies in 2001: Harry Potter. The film of the first of J.K.'s Rowling's blockbuster novels, *Harry Potter and the Sorcerer's Stone*, earned nearly a billion dollars worldwide in 2001. *Harry Potter and the Sorcerer's Stone* led to eight movies in the series, expanding the idea of a franchise. Before *Harry Potter*, film series generally stopped at three. And if you notice today, movie series such as *Fast and Furious* continue well past seven, to infinite chapters.

46
Bob Long, Hot Tears of Despair

With Bob Long
Courtesy Carol Joynt—Q and A Cafe

I DID MY BEST WORK FOR THE BEST BOSSES— the creative ones who burst into a room spewing ideas. Every morning at WFAA-TV in Dallas, Marty Haag charged in shouting assignments. Marty kept his office door open, available to anyone who wanted to brainstorm.

Dave Nuell possessed the same kind of energy at WRC. Nuell delighted in standing on top of a desk barking orders, waving his arms, even dropping his pants. Jim Van Messel, who followed Nuell, spoke softly, nevertheless spinning dozens of ideas and concepts just to see what stuck. Kris Ostrowski charged through the newsroom like a quarterback. Her great ideas, such as "Johnny Carson Week" and the "My Home Town" series, gave me a creative jolt. Ostrowski, like my friend Jim Snyder, had a sharp eye for talent. Two of the anchors she identified and helped hire, Doreen Gentzler and Jim Handley, worked decades at WRC. Handley continues working as I write this.

Things changed in television news as big corporations bought stations and watched the bottom line. Instead of delighting in ideas, a new breed of news manager emerged who excelled at budgets and marketing. Consultants determined many of the stories. In the new corporate atmosphere, Washington sometimes became a stepping stone to New York or L.A., rather than a destination.

One guy broke the mold: Bob Long. His deep voice (he sounded like William Conrad) and wicked sense of humor won over the newsroom immediately when he arrived in December 1999. I crossed paths with him in the parking lot the day he started. "Hi, Arch, I'm the new guy."

Bob Long grew up in Washington. During high school he worked in radio news at WWDC AM. A stint in the Marines turned him into a combat correspondent. He jumped from stations in New York to Los Angeles. He produced documentaries in Zaire. Returning to L.A. he worked in entertainment, including programs *In Search of with Leonard Nimoy* and *Real People*. Then he returned to the Middle East with financing to build a film studio. The Gulf War changed those plans, so he returned to KNBC TV in Los Angeles as managing editor.

Linda Sullivan, our new General Manager, appeared reserved and strictly business. She surprised the newsroom choosing Bob instead of the usual corporate candidates. Bob, with his broad experience, knew the pressure of reporting and producing. As it turned out, the combination of Ms. Sullivan and Bob Long created another golden age.

Long wore bow ties, drank martinis, and instilled confidence. He ran the newsroom with the mantra: "you're doing a great job so just keep doing what you do." Bob started and concluded every rating period with a brilliant series of emails known as the "Hot Tears of Despair" letters. For example, at the end of the November rating book in 2000, he wrote:

The Days Dwindle Down…

…to a precious few, and I smell napalm on the crisp autumn air. We all know what the smell of napalm means.

Grand slams are becoming a habit with us and this November Sweep looks to be as decisive and invigorating as the presidential race was turgid and enervating.

I will mark the end of the book by repairing to Clyde's Chevy Chase this Wednesday night. If we still had parties, I would invite you to join me…But this really isn't a party. It's more like an obligation. So perhaps I will see some people like you and offer them a mug of something exotic that this news organization has once again harvested from Wisconsin Avenue (location of Channel 9) and Tilden Street (location of Channel 7)—hot tears of despair.

Bob never made us swallow the management bullshit. Previous News Directors would threaten and bribe talent to attend station money making events such as the News 4 Health Fair. Instead of telling us to attend or else, Bob sent out this memo:

The Health and Fitness expo brings in enough money to cover a significant piece of our talent payroll and it represents one of the few opportunities viewers have to get close to the people they so loyally welcome into their homes. For both reasons I know you will want to give the event and the community the respect they deserve. Nanette will be around to sign you up. Thanks.

I attended happily, after several years of grudgingly showing up.

A few days after 9/11, a GE official addressed the network newsroom. Word got around that instead of thanking everyone for their hard work, the official complained that GE insured the airplanes that crashed that day, and the event would harm the corporate bottom line. When asked about the comment, Long rasped: "the man is a cipher."

Thanks to Bob Long's "do what you do best" philosophy, I took a few chances. Bob Rutledge, an editor who hid his talent as a cameraman because he didn't want to cover wrecks and fires, brainstormed with me. We produced stories on aloha shirts, unusual bars, Mt. Airy, North Carolina where they celebrate Andy Griffith Days, and an entire segment on the return of hats. As my hair thinned, I discovered I looked good in a fedora. I spoke to some hat sellers and found old footage of men wearing hats, ending the piece with a shot of me on the street throwing my hat into the air. The hat falls in front of a bus which promptly moves forward, smashing my hat into something looking like a misshapen dinner plate.

I ended the piece wearing the flattened fedora with the line, "I'm Arch Campbell, and I think I need a new hat."

A few days later, Bob Long suggested he and I go hat shopping. I picked him up and we drove to Andrea's on Georgia Avenue and followed with a visit to the Parkway Deli near the neighborhood where Bob grew up in Silver Spring.

Bob Long's health showed many red flags. Word raced through the newsroom of Bob's Cancer diagnosis. Doctors removed his kidney, but he returned in good spirits. "Oh, it's nothing, I just drink a beaker of medicine every now and then to keep the beast at bay."

Washington, D.C.

The golden age of Bob Long suddenly ended. A new General Manager arrived, anxious to make his mark and win promotion to New York. In July 2003, Bob Long announced the company was transferring him to L.A. to run the KNBC-TV newsroom. We gathered in the newsroom as Bob told us good-bye. He burst into tears in the middle of it, recovered, made a joke, and moved forward. Most of us teared up as well.

Here is Bob Long's last memo to his adoring employees:

I am going to Los Angeles because I believe it is the right thing for me to do and because I believe you will continue to be an extraordinarily fine and successful newsroom without me. This has all come about quite suddenly, and the details are still being worked out. I do know that at almost 59, I am gratified to still be considered able to mount a charge and swing a claymore. Having been summoned, I will go. It is the process that brought me here for one of the great times of my life. Baltimore got my kidney, but you claimed my heart.

My friend and fellow reporter Tom Sherwood assembled Bob's memos in a volume called *The Book of Bob*. Tom explained it as, "a collection of company emails saved by Tom Sherwood for just such a horrible occasion as the departure of Bob Long, NBC4 News Director."

Bob Long ran the KNBC Newsroom six years. In 2009 he decamped to Istanbul to teach journalism ethics. Bob returned to D.C. often during those years, throwing himself a party at the bar at Matisse on Wisconsin Avenue or Clyde's in Northwest D.C. He moved back to D.C., taking a job as a program analyst for Voice of America. His legendary get togethers reunited those of us who loved him. We gathered for the last time in the fall of 2016 to say goodbye at Arlington National Cemetery, where Bob, the Marine veteran, received burial with full military honors.

47
The Best Interview I Ever Did: 2003

Courtesy WRC-TV

John Travolta loves airplanes. He owns several, including a 727. He also owns a pilot's uniform and cap, which he wears when he flies his airplanes. In 2003, the Smithsonian officially opened a grand new museum, the Steven F. Udvar-Hazy Center, a dazzling display of aviation and space artifacts. Two large hangars display hundreds of airplanes, including the supersonic Concord, and the space shuttle Discovery. Travolta arrived for opening day in December, 2003.

Travolta agreed to sit for satellite interviews to promote the new museum. The Smithsonian offered a spot to Channel 4. Fortunately for me, Charlie Bragale, the crack assignment manager, got the call and said, "we'll send Arch over to talk to Travolta when he finishes."

Washington, D.C.

Ushered into the giant hall, we found Travolta perched on a stool with an earpiece giving the same answers over and over. When he finished, the Smithsonian crew snapped off the lights. As he stepped down, I said, "hey John, we want to put a portable mike on you, follow you around, and let you show us what you like in here."

His eyes lit up. Off we went. We gave an airplane geek the chance to wander around a giant hanger full of planes: new planes, old planes, supersonic planes, space planes. I think Travolta had his pilot suit and cap on. I remember I only needed to say, "so what do you like?" He and I and the camera crew roamed the museum for almost an hour.

At one point, Travolta asked me to name my favorite airplane. I told him about producing a story in the 70s, when the supersonic Concord landed daily at Dulles Airport. People would drive out on the little-used Dulles access road, pull over, get out of their cars, and watch the Concord descend. Those thrilling landings reminded me of watching passenger trains with my father.

In the 80s, film companies began pushing movie junket interviews. They would pay for a plane ticket and hotel room to New York or L.A. for a dozen or more reporters. Stars of the films involved would settle into a professionally lit space as a publicist ushered in one reporter after another. A second camera recorded the reporter asking questions. The arrangement implied a favorable report on the film. I know of several reporters who attended a junket every weekend.

I succumbed several times, sometimes when I was already in L.A. or New York for other events. Rarely did any of these interviews yield much of interest. One time I made Madonna laugh, but I can't remember the wisecrack that did it.

John Travolta walking around the Udvar-Hazy Museum broke the mold. He wasn't plugging a movie or himself. He was sharing his love of airplanes and showing a side of himself rarely seen.

Years later, I crossed paths with Travolta on a red carpet. To my delight John Travolta said, "I remember you, Arch. That was the best interview I ever did."

48
Synergy

WHEN I WORKED IN DALLAS, MY BOSS MARTY Haag had given me the mantra: "Cover the Arts." When GE bought NBC, their mantra became: "Cover our Shows."

I spent many hours on the sets of NBC series, including *Homicide, Law & Order, Law & Order: SVU,* and *West Wing.*

Homicide: 1993–1999

Homicide filmed in an abandoned Harbor Police building in Baltimore, about thirty miles from D.C. Almost every wannabe actor in Washington landed some kind of role on *Homicide*, usually one or two lines as a bystander. D.C. actors joked that you only mentioned *Homicide* on your resume if you HADN'T appeared on it. A couple of times when I arrived with a cameraman, the director pressed us into service, placing us in a shot as if we were covering a news briefing or crime scene.

Writer David Simon based *Homicide* on his years covering crime for the *Baltimore Sun*. Simon went on to create several other important dramas including *The Wire*. I watched occasional episodes of *The Wire* when it first aired on HBO. A few years after *The Wire*'s finale, I watched the episodes in order on DVD. Then, I got the brilliance of it. Simon created an overview of a gritty American city: crime, drugs, politics, education, and journalism. He created a new form, the sixty-hour movie, leading to our streaming revolution.

Stand-up comic/actor Richard Belzer created Detective John Munch for *Homicide*. Belzer as Munch grew into one of the most memorable characters in television. During one of my first interviews I wore sunglasses, not knowing Belzer and/or Munch always wore sunglasses. After that, whenever I interviewed him, Belzer insisted I put on my sunglasses. He always wore his, even at night.

Over the years Belzer and Detective Munch morphed into the same person. Belzer and his character believed various conspiracy theories, starting with the Kennedy assassination. Belzer and Munch appeared as hard-shell cynics protecting a sentimental heart. After *Homicide*, the character transferred to *Law & Order: SVU*, keeping Detective Munch on national television for 23 years. He also popped up on several different networks and shows beyond the *Law & Order* franchises, including *The Wire, 30 Rock, the X-Files,* and *Unbreakable Kimmy Schmidt.*

I arranged a feature on Belzer when the Improv Comedy Club booked his stand-up act. He possessed the ability to rant. Standing on stage, the six-foot-plus Belzer stopped his set to scream about the club's low ceiling. Just looking at his head brushing the ceiling made me laugh, and I roared when he yelled, "can this ceiling be any f***ing lower?"

Law & Order: 1990–Current

I visited *Law & Order* in New York many times, although rarely did I visit an actual set. *Law & Order* used New York City locations extensively, such as the city court house, the bus depot, and crime scenes often set in various real parks and neighborhoods.

Many actors don't like reporters and cameras around when they work. Others gladly take time to say hello. One of the nicest was Jerry Orbach, an under-appreciated Broadway legend. Orbach starred in the original production of *The Fantasticks*, introducing the song "Try to Remember." He played the lead in the long running Broadway shows

Chicago, 42nd Street, and *Promises, Promises.* Later, he voiced the singing candelabra Lumiere in Disney's *Beauty and the Beast*, and played the father in the beloved film *Dirty Dancing.*

As Detective Lennie Briscoe, Orbach worked steadily from 1992 to 2004, playing to a generation who by and large knew little of his earlier success. One evening, Orbach appeared for a Q&A session hosted by Smithsonian Associates at the Smithsonian Museum of American History. He told wonderful stories, including dodging a pass from Broadway legend Ethel Merman. I would always mention Ethel Merman to him when we talked. He, in turn, would smile and deftly evade my question. I felt deep sadness when Jerry Orbach passed away from prostate Cancer in 2004.

Sam Waterston, the Yale educated actor with a stellar resume, dreaded talking to press. Most of the times I visited the *Law & Order* set, Waterston refused interviews. On one visit to the courtroom set, the press person convinced him to talk to me. We set up, and the camera started rolling. At that moment, the director called him back to the set. Waterston gave me a little smile, probably of relief, and hurried back to work.

In 1994, NBC Press called, requesting I interview S. Epatha Merkerson, who played Lt. Anita Van Buren on *Law & Order*. Epatha recently married a guy who worked for the District's Parks and Recreation Department. Her new husband had a long-time friend who worked as cameramen at Channel 4. I interviewed the newlyweds at their home in the Washington suburbs. Epatha and I bonded as we were both newlyweds.

I would catch up with Epatha whenever she came to Washington as well as on the *Law & Order* set in New York. For many years, Epatha emceed the local D.C. theater

Helen Hayes Awards. One summer she spent part of her hiatus starring in a production of *The Old Settler* for the Studio Theater. I'm sorry to write Epatha's marriage didn't work out, ending her D.C. connection. She completed 17 seasons of *Law & Order* in 2010. She has starred on the NBC medical drama *Chicago Med* since 2015. I saw her briefly a few years ago when I was working at WJLA-TV. Her eyes lit up when I shouted out, "Epatha!"

Law & Order: SVU: 1999–Current

Something sparked between me and Mariska Hargitay. In 1997, Mariska landed a recurring role on *ER*, NBC's Thursday night powerhouse drama. She played a comically inept desk clerk who begins a relationship with the doctor played by Anthony Edwards. NBC Press set up satellite interviews with about ten stations. Mine came last. Something about my voice (she couldn't see me but I could see her) or my questions really appealed to Mariska. I think possibly she hoped the attention on *ER* would lead to her big break, and I provided some of that attention.

Mariska's big break occurred when she won the lead in the new *Law & Order* spinoff *Law & Order: SVU*. On my first visit to the set, as I walked into the most unglamorous Secaucus, New Jersey warehouse location, I heard a voice saying, "oh boy, Arch Campbell's coming today. I can't wait to meet him." With that, I saw a tall beauty with flashing eyes, striding toward me, arms outstretched, catching me in a bear hug. I could hardly breathe. As I said, I think she connected me with the time before her big break. I received a similar greeting on several other visits.

Mariska has showbusiness in her DNA. Her mother, Jane Mansfield, rated with Marilyn Monroe on the list of 1950s sex symbols. Mariska's father, Mickey Hargitay, won the title Mr. Universe in 1955, as well as multiple other body building awards. Together Mansfield and Hargitay

Washington, D.C.

appeared in several movies including *Will Success Spoil Rock Hunter?* (1957), *Promises! Promises!* (1963), and *Primitive Love* (1964). Jane Mansfield won notoriety for her nude layouts in *Playboy Magazine* and for her nude scenes in *Promises! Promises!*

Mariska rarely speaks about the tragedy of her mother's death. In 1967, a car carrying Jane Mansfield, with her third husband, her lawyer, and her three children, crashed into the rear of a tractor-trailer. The crash sheared off the top of the car, killing the three adults in the front seat instantly. Mariska survived, asleep in the back seat. Occasionally Mariska refers to the pain of growing up without her mother. On one visit, we set up an interview at the desk of her character Detective Olivia Benson. I noticed Mariska keeps a small picture of Jane Mansfield on that desk.

Mariska's co-star Christopher Meloni grew up in D.C, attending St. Stephen's & St. Agnes School in Alexandria, Virginia, where he played quarterback on the football team. Alumni still remember a big game Meloni won in high school. Always happy to find a local angle, I called the NBC press department, asking if Christopher was planning any visits home. He told them he wasn't coming for a while, but suggested I go over and interview his mother.

One Friday night Mrs. Meloni and I sat in her living room and watched an episode of *Law & Order: SVU*. She was a polite, gentle, fun-loving good sport, even as I pushed her about watching her son in harsh situations and his role on *Oz*, an HBO prison drama that pushed the limits of gritty TV.

The next time I visited the *SVU* set, Christopher charged toward me with a big grin and told me how much his mother enjoyed the visit and her TV spot. I have fond memories of *Law & Order: SVU* as I enjoyed two professional friendships, plus celebrity kisses and bear hugs.

The West Wing: 1999-2006

The NBC Press office called and asked me to tape some actors as they filmed a scene in front of the U.S. Capitol. When I arrived, Bradley Whitford and Dule Hill walked and talked until a director yelled, "cut," and then returned to their original position to do it again. When they finished, I asked them about the new show, *The West Wing*, which they described as being about working behind the scenes for the President of the United States.

Martin Sheen, whom I remembered from so many great movies in the 1970's including *Apocalypse Now* and *Badlands*, played the President. *The West Wing* caught on almost immediately. The producers, wanting a Washington presence, began coming to D.C. at least four times a year. I spent many hours watching cast members film inside D.C. schools, outside the Executive Office building, in and around various government buildings. When Sheen arrived at the airport, people shouted, "President Bartlett" or just, "Mr. President." Sometimes people actually thought Sheen WAS President. He got a kick out of that. Martin Sheen loved to talk and visit, an easy affable, friendly actor.

SYNERGY

Going behind the scenes often didn't yield much more than, "here I am, behind the scenes." NBC wanted tie-ins to their prime-time programs and I did the best I could under the circumstances. My fondest tie in took place the night *Homicide* debuted.

Kris Ostrowski wanted something to tie in following *Homicide's* debut show, which followed the Superbowl that year on NBC. A couple of newsroom characters knew an editor at Channel 7 named Joe Hansard. As it turned out, Joe, who filled his time with acting jobs, landed a role in the first *Homicide*. He played a witness to a crime. Joe has a dry laconic way of talking and more than a little attitude. In his scene, a detective presses him for details. Hansard answers: "I was drinking, I don't remember."

We set up live to interview Joe on the big night. Once on the air, I gushed about the new show and showed the clip featuring Joe, then we came back live to me and Joe. I asked about his experience on set. Joe looked at me deadpan and said: "I was drinking, I don't remember."

I still laugh at the memory. As it turned out, later in my career, I worked with Joe on a cable TV comedy/entertainment show. Some of our bits survive on YouTube. You can look them up under *The Arch Campbell Show.*

49
Donald Trump and a Few *Apprentice*s

WHEN I FIRST HEARD ABOUT NBC'S ATTEMPT at a reality series, *The Apprentice*, I figured it might last a few weeks and fade into obscurity. Instead, *The Apprentice* made Donald Trump nationally famous and ultimately helped elect him President of the United States. At the time, Donald Trump had the reputation of a tabloid huckster, a guy who built condos in Manhattan and owned some casinos that went bust in Atlantic City. *The Apprentice* changed that, starting in January 2004.

Mark Burnett, who produced the ultra-successful *Survival*, came up with the idea. Sixteen contestants would participate in assignments designed to impress businessman Donald Trump. One contestant would face elimination every week. The winner would receive an executive position with the Trump Organization paying $250,000 a year.

The first task began with the contestants divided into two teams, eight men versus eight women. Each team received $250 seed money to buy supplies to sell lemonade on the streets of New York. The women picked a great location in Midtown and quadrupled their money. The men picked a poor location and only doubled their money.

Trump took a particular dislike to contestant Sam Solovey, a local guy from suburban Potomac, Maryland. At the conclusion of the first episode in his conference room, Trump lasered in on Sam and spat out the words, "you're fired!" Sam glared at Trump and refused to leave. This extra drama gave the first hint that *The Apprentice* might turn into a hit. The next day comics and wise acres everywhere repeated, "you're fired!" A cartoon showed Donald Trump in an argument with a chicken. Trump looks at the chicken and says, "you're fried!," a twist on "you're fired!" (Trump later tried to trademark "you're fired!" but the patent office vetoed his request.)

I met Sam Solovey at an *Apprentice* premiere party. The contestants couldn't speak until they had been fired, so Sam mimed an interview. I used him miming things like zipping up his mouth, locking it and throwing away the key. The morning after the first show, Sam appeared on *The Today Show*. NBC established *Today* would interview the discarded contestants the morning after their dismissal. Sam brought his fiancé Lori Levin to the studio. After Katie Couric interviewed him, Sam got down on one knee and asked Lori to marry him. Katie giggled and rolled her eyes and the crew roared with laughter. Sam made an impact, and made *The Apprentice* even more interesting.

A few weeks later I went with a cameraman to Sam's apartment in the Willard Condominium in Friendship Heights. I planned to watch an episode with him and get his comments about the show. Sam's fiancé Lori, a teacher at Somerset Elementary School, surprised the cameraman and me with a beautiful dinner. She treated us as honored guests. The hospitality of the soon-to-be married couple was lovely.

Sam returned to *The Apprentice* a couple of episodes later, always as comic relief. He made a hilarious promo with Trump. When season one ended Sam went into the real estate business. He's one of the most successful agents in Washington, D.C. I've run into him over the years at movies and shopping malls. We laugh about his brush with fame.

In 2016, more than a few reporters tracked Sam down wanting his take on the man who fired him. By this time, Sam had distanced himself from Trump and *The Apprentice*. Instead of an easy Trump put-down, Sam gave reporters some thoughtful analysis. Sam told One American News: "I think I have a very good grasp of why Trump was successful in his Presidential campaign. He has a very powerful personality. He draws you in. He owns the room. He is always the center. His 'politician' is not an act. One thing I noticed very early on is that he is a very patriotic person and is very proud of America. The biggest mistake the media makes is that they see Trump's flaws as his weaknesses. But there is a naturalness to him and his flaws are part of his appeal."

I traveled to New York several times during the first two seasons of *The Apprentice* for behind-the-scene coverage. The network provided a crew to grab pictures of contestants on various assignments. Those trips included interviews with "The Donald" himself in the iconic Trump Tower conference room. Trump always entered the room a little gruffly, clasping his hands saying, "OK, let's go."

On my first visit, I stepped back and watched while two

Washington, D.C.

other reporters talked with him. Then Trump looked my way and said, "let me spend a little time with my friend." I gave him a fist bump knowing he hates to shake hands. Trump calling me "my friend" either meant he'd seen me on the news when he came to D.C., or (and this is the version I believe) he confused me with my fellow reporter, Pat Collins.

Sometime in the early 90s, Trump and his then girlfriend Marla Maples arrived at the Four Seasons Hotel in Georgetown. As they entered the lobby, they continued a loud public argument. Witnesses told *The Washington Post* Marla took off her huge engagement ring and threw it at him, causing Trump to get down on his hands and knees looking for the expensive ring while whimpering for Marla to forgive him.

Pat Collins, who possesses a wicked sense of humor, went to the Four Seasons the next day and recreated the scene. Collins demonstrated a ring throw and got down on all fours to replicate Trump crawling on the floor. I think Trump thought I was Collins. If so, it appears Trump has a sense of humor. During my interviews he always got right down to business, doing whatever he needed to promote *The Apprentice.*

The first season of *The Apprentice* made a star of another Washingtonian, Omarosa Manigault-Stallworth, now best known by the one-word moniker, Omarosa. An Ohio native, Omarosa came to town to earn a Masters and PhD in communications from Howard University. She had worked in the office of then-vice President Al Gore. By 2003 she was an instructor at Howard.

I got her number from an NBC publicist and called her up. Omarosa loved appearing on television. She knew how to give a great interview without giving anything away. She became the show's backstabbing high drama villain. Trump

The Accidental Critic

fired her on episode nine saying she was difficult to work with and made too many excuses for her shortcomings.

I can assure you the whole thing was an act. Omarosa was smart, charming, funny, and a pleasure to be with. The night Trump fired her she drove to the station with her mother for a segment on the 11:00pm News. I called her mother: Mama-rosa. Both women loved the nickname.

Omarosa moved to Beverly Hills, and turned her notoriety into a reality show career. Donald Trump's company produced a dating show with her: *The Ultimate Merger*. For a while she was engaged to the actor Michael Clark Duncan, remembered as the supernatural prisoner in *The Green Mile*. Omarosa was with Duncan when he suffered a heart attack in 2012. He died in the ICU at Cedars-Sinai Hospital in L.A..

I ran into her on a red-carpet years after the show. Omarosa told me she knew I'd been sick, and had been praying for me. By this time, she had become an ordained Baptist preacher.

She stayed on Trump's good side. She campaigned for Trump in 2016 as director of African-American Outreach. She served on the president-elect's transition team executive committee.

Omarosa became an assistant to the President and Director of Communications for the Office of Public Liaison in January 2017. White House Chief of Staff John Kelly fired Omarosa December 13, 2017, citing, "money and integrity issues." She turned the experience into a tell all book *Unhinged*. The next year she competed on *Celebrity Big Brother* and later *Big Brother Australia*.

Few people remember the name of the winner of the first season of *The Apprentice*. Everybody knows Omarosa. And everybody knows Donald Trump.[53]

50
Movies: 2002–2006

2002: Nia Vardalos' *My Big Fat Greek Wedding* turned into the surprise hit of 2002. Her story about a Greek woman looking for love as well as someone who could fit into her outrageous family, struck a nerve with audiences. I especially liked her father's dependance on Windex, which he used on everything including small cuts and insect bites. I have personally saved several CDs with the aid of Windex, and used it successfully on insect bites.

2003: Robert McNamara made a rare in person appearance at the E Street Theater January 6, 2004 to discuss *The Fog of War*; the Errol Morris documentary on the military industrial complex and the steps that led America into the Vietnam War. McNamara was in his late 80s at the time and appeared frail. Occasionally an angry Vietnam vet would get up and shout at him. McNamara kept his cool, during an extraordinary appearance. He would refer the angry vets back to the movie, a thoughtful discussion of the forces that cause wars.

2004: *Sideways* previewed at the Arlington Drafthouse Cinema, a fun venue for a delightful mismatched buddy road trip comedy. Paul Giamatti plays a down on his luck divorced teacher and wannabe writer. His pal Thomas Hayden Church, an over-the-hill actor, will soon marry an attractive woman whose father plans to bring him into a successful real estate business. Giamatti suggests the boys make a one-week road trip to wine country. Along the way, they meet two waitresses played by Virginia Madsen and Sandra Oh. Their connection leads to emotional disaster and a broken nose. I watched *Sideways* on a streaming service recently and it remains as fun and satisfying as that night at the Arlington Drafthouse. Director/screenwriter Alexander Payne and writer Jim Taylor won the best screenplay Oscar for *Sideways* at the *77th Academy Awards* in 2005.

2005: *Good Night, and Good Luck*—I remember watching Edward R. Murrow host *Person to Person*, interviewing celebrities in a cloud of smoke on a two way hook up. Murrow's commanding voice and formal manner impressed me, even though I watched these shows at the age of eight or nine. George Clooney, by now a powerful entertainment presence, used his power to green light the story of Murrow taking on U.S. Senator Joseph McCarthy, whose unfounded accusations of Communist anti-American activity ruined careers and lives. Clooney played Fred Friendly, Murrow's producer and later President of CBS News. Just writing these sentences makes me want to watch *Good Night, and Good Luck* again.

2006: *Borat: Cultural Learnings of America for Make Benefit Glorious National of Kazakhstan*—I knew Pat Haggerty from the Columbia golf course. Haggerty's friends started buzzing when he showed up in the trailer for *Borat: Cultural Learnings of America for Make Benefit Glorious*

Nation of Kazakhstan. Comic actor Sasha Baron Cohen created Borat as an Eastern-European fish out of water. Filmed in ad lib situations, he aimed to coax his subjects into embarrassing situations and prompting them to make embarrassing statements.

Haggerty worked as a professional speaker and media trainer. He received a contact from a documentary company explaining a foreign reporter was traveling the country trying to understand our culture. The traveler wanted help understanding American humor. Haggerty signed a release and received a $400 fee. In the session, he teaches or tries to teach Borat how to tell a "not" joke, in which a speaker makes a statement, pauses, and adds the word "not" turning the statement upside down. Haggerty's pupil studiously avoids learning the skill. Unlike other unsuspecting participants in the movie, my friend Pat managed to avoid embarrassing himself. Pat relished talking about the experience, while contributing a lesson on graciousness and the ability to take a joke, especially when the joke's on you.

51
The Big C

I SCHEDULED A WEEK OFF IN AUGUST 2005 TO take care of a bunch of medical things. I made appointments with my dentist and my dermatologist and scheduled the office visit necessary for a colonoscopy. Ten years earlier, my family doctor told me to arrange for the test. I shrugged it off. A few years later, my annual physical included the name of a doctor who performed colonoscopies. I called and discovered it took two appointments, one a pre-check and a second for the procedure. Work kept me busy, so I delayed again. By this time Katie Couric's husband had died from colon Cancer. Katie advocated for colon Cancer screening. She created a leap in acceptance in March 2000 when she underwent the procedure live on *The Today Show*.

Five years after Katie's demonstration, I knew I needed to check the procedure off my must-do list. My friend Pat Collins, son of a long time D.C. doctor, knew his way around the local medical community. Collins told me to call Dr. Michael Keegan. I scheduled the office appointment, dealt with Keegan's grumpy staff, and got ready for the big day.

The unpleasant preparation began with no solid food the day before the test. I swallowed a gallon of foul-tasting stuff that left nothing remaining in my system. The morning of the event, Gina and I checked into to a surgical center. Oh yeah, you had to bring someone to drive home.

The technician administered twilight anesthesia, putting me in a dreamy half-awake state. I heard muffled voices, and the scope coming out and going back in and then something about marking something. At one point, I felt the instrument poking something inside me. It hurt a little and I groaned. The procedure finished. When I dressed, I was told to see Dr. Keegan in his office. I thought this was standard procedure. I can't tell you exactly what Dr. Keegan said. In my defense, I was still coming out of anesthesia. Dr. Keegan said something about calling another doctor and finding something and I said, "oh, some polyps?" and he said, "no, a tumor."

Leaving the building, still groggy, I told Gina, "don't get upset." I went right into denial. She glared at me. As we left, I glimpsed the writer Larry L. King, author of *The Best Little Whorehouse in Texas* in the lobby. I mentioned him to Gina and started to go over to say something. She grabbed my arm and marched me to our car.

I called the surgeon Dr. Keegan recommended, Dr. Martin Paul. His office said he didn't have any appointments for a few weeks. I said, "oh, ok." A few minutes later, Paul's office called back and arranged an appointment the next day. When I met Dr. Paul, the truth began to dawn. The friendly good-looking surgeon smiled and said, "oh yeah, you've got Cancer."

Back at work, I needed to inform my boss. Vickie Burns replaced Bob Long as News Director. A Chicago native, she worked for several stations in her home town and earned a reputation as an excellent producer at NBC owned WMAQ-TV. Her promotion to Washington and first job as a News Director put her on the corporate escalator. Vicki and I had a pleasant enough relationship, although I'm not sure she appreciated WRC's unique culture or my place in it.

I walked into Vickie Burns' office. She was on the phone and waved for me to leave. I went back to my office and sent her an email. "I have Cancer." A few minutes later, she came into my office and hugged me. "Take all the time you need." Over the next few days, I scheduled follow-up appointments and waited for September 13, the date of my surgery. The date arrived soon enough.

Fortunately, medicine had by then progressed to laparoscopic surgery. Doctors no longer needed to cut a patient open like a filleted fish. Instead, a small instrument made a tiny insert, went in, cut out the tumor and part of my colon, and fished the bad part out. The new technique significantly reduced the cut and stitches necessary. I'm guessing at this as I'm no medical professional. When I woke up, I felt sore but nothing like if I'd been cut wide open.

My good pal Bob Ryan showed up with roses from his front yard. We laughed about old times. One night after the 6:00pm news, Vance and Doreen arrived, causing much excitement among the nurses. Friends and relatives visited.

My good friend Bobby Abbo, who owned The Roma Restaurant across from the Uptown Theater, brought a can of beans. He knew colon surgery patients could not leave the hospital until they pass gas. During Bobby's visit, I achieved that milestone. Farting was such sweet sorrow.

The appearance of so many friends made me so happy I failed to notice that neither the WRC TV General Manager Michael Jack, nor News Director Vickie Burns came to the hospital. Bob Long, or Kris Ostrowski, or John Rohrbach would have been there the first day.

In recovery at home, I began every morning taking a walk, extending my distance daily. It took a month to regain my strength. I returned to work in mid-October, 2005. Cancer had more in store for me.

In the hospital, both Dr. Paul and Dr. Keegan informed me I would need six months of chemotherapy. They delivered me to the care of Dr. Fred Smith, one of the leading oncologists in Washington. Dr. Smith showed me around his "Chemo Lounge," a large open room with recliners for patients and chairs for family. Before treatment began, I returned to the operating room. Dr. Smith recommended a port inserted in my chest. I thought of the port as a sort of human wall plug. Once in, nurses could plug an IV of medicine directly into the port and into my system.

The chemo required two or three hours of IV drips. I would leave with a portable pump carried on my shoulder like a purse or carry-on bag. The pump delivered medicine over a three-day period. I asked to have infusions Friday mornings. I would wear the pump over the weekend. Gina figured out how to uncouple the device after 36 hours. With this schedule, I would only miss the early newscast every other Friday and still appear on the 11:00pm News.

I didn't notice too much after the first treatment. Carrying the pump around for a couple of days didn't bother me. Some side effects eased in after the second treatment. I developed a touch of neuropathy, a numbness in my feet and the tips of my fingers. My taste buds changed. Cold food gave my mouth a burning sensation. All food began to taste bland.

The medicine included a big dose of steroids. At first, I felt a little high, or at least full of energy. One Friday I came home completely wound up. I turned on TCM and stayed up until 3:00am watching the 1941 version of *The Wolf Man*. Over the weekend the drugs wore off and I slowed down to a crawl. I lost my appetite. My weight dropped. By the end of the six months, I dropped fifty pounds. For a while I enjoyed watching my weight go down because I wanted to lose weight. However, I do not recommend chemotherapy for weight reduction.

I hardly remember working. I know I reported entertainment news and reviewed a bunch of movies. I interviewed celebrities on the red carpet at the *Kennedy Center Honors*. NBC broadcast the Winter Olympics. The broadcast preempted the 4:00pm News, pushing the late

News past midnight. Vickie Burns assigned me to anchor a prepackaged program of Olympic highlights called *The Olympic Zone* or *The O-Zone* Monday through Friday evenings at 7:30pm. I don't follow sports and never cared about the Olympics but I was glad to host this because it gave me a role.

I remember interviewing Dame Edna, who was in town in February 2006 with her one woman show *Dame Edna: Back with a Vengeance*. Australian comic Barry Humphries, dressed as a zoftig purple haired matron, delighted in asking interviewers personal questions about lifestyle and clothing choices. "Where did you get that suit? What did you pay for it? Why?" I laughed and laughed, forgetting that I looked ghastly. Every now and then I caught a whiff of sympathy, either from the comic and/or Dame Edna.

One Sunday morning, I went on location with *The West Wing*. Martin Sheen gave me a hug. One of the local crew members working told me he and his church were praying for me. I happily accepted all prayers.

Fifty pounds lighter, I wandered the station looking haggard. The head of Human Resources strongly suggested I take medical leave. The Friday of my final treatment, Dr. Smith looked at me and said, "I think you've had enough. We'll skip this treatment. Sometimes, you don't really need all twelve." I returned to the HR head. She told me to go home and not worry about coming back. I stayed home a month.

And then the medication started to wear off. Food started tasting good again. I returned in early April. A few weeks later, I walked through the news room. Vickie Burns called out across the newsroom, "hey Arch, you look good."

When I received the diagnosis, I looked around the NBC building, wondering if I would ever see it again. At home I wondered if I would never see Gina again. I emailed

Bob Long in L.A. He reminded me that he'd been living with kidney Cancer several years. Dr. Smith suggested a mentor program. He paired me with a former patient named Scott Faley. His colon Cancer treatment concluded a year earlier. During my treatment, Scott called and visited, reminding me to eat, even taking me out to dinner several times to make sure. When I finished treatment, Dr. Smith asked me to mentor other patients. Telling others, they could survive and providing my presence to someone else helped me survive.

In the chemo lounge I watched drama and received inspiration. We patients bonded. I could see fellow members improving, as well as others getting worse. I watched a high school principal return to the lounge after learning medicine could do nothing further for her. During my treatment, I watched life and death, hope and dismay, every other Friday for six months.

I don't like language about fighting or beating Cancer. I prefer survive. I survived.

52
Blindsided

Arch Campbell
Arts & Entertainment

NEWS 4
WASHINGTON, D.C.

Life looked a little better by November 2006. I gained some weight and my energy started coming back. My contract kicked into another one-year cycle. If management fired me, they would have to pay the entire year plus 62 additional weeks of severance. I figured it would cost too much to dump me, at least until my contract ended.

The ax was falling. Wally Bruckner, George Michael's star reporter and weekend sports anchor, left at the end of summer. The weather department cut Clay Anderson. I.J. Hudson, the seasoned reporter who segued into reporting on the new technology in segments titled "The Digital Divide" announced he would depart at the end of the year, making clear this was not his choice. Most shocking, Susan

Kidd, an extraordinary anchor, told *The Washington Post* she'd been, "kicked to the curb." The General Manager pushing her out, Michael Jack, a proud Black man, headed the diversity initiative for the entire network. Susan Kidd was a strong African American presence and powerhouse of more than twenty years on WRC. November 17th, George Michael, the nationally known sportscaster, announced he would leave the daily newscast in March, when the sponsorship of *The George Michael Sports Machine* ended. George said he and General Manager Michael Jack couldn't come to an agreement.

I figured I would work the rest of my contract and retire, or change to part-time. I concentrated on staying active and generating unique feature stories. I traveled to Stephens City, Virginia to the Family Drive-In Theater, one of the few outdoor drive-in movies remaining. Classic car owners arrived early to show off their 50s and 60s treasures. Families turned out to watch their children on playground equipment. The snack bar hummed, sundown arrived and the feature began—Disney's *Cars*.

When talk of gentrifying H Street, NE stirred up controversary, I visited a prominent Black-owned barbershop. The barbers and the guys getting haircuts shouted out, "Arch," and beckoned me and the camera in. My white face fit in fine with the guys in the H Street barbershop. They loved the idea of the area improving. I returned a few weeks later for the return of the renovated Atlas Theater, closed after the 1968 riots, as a performing arts center.

During my absence, a new producer—half my age—took over the 11:00pm news. One night he responded to my story pitch with, "…that's OK, take the night off." I remembered Jim Vance and his demotion to the 5:00pm news years earlier and Vance's mantra: "be cool." Still, I felt vulnerable on the days I only appeared at 4:00pm, spouting

The Accidental Critic

entertainment news available anywhere. I doubled my efforts to go into the field and develop stories that could run at 4:00pm and 6:00pm.

One Thursday I arranged a story on Carol Joynt's Q and A Café, a monthly guest interview hosted by a former television producer at Nathan's Bar and Grill. Carol Joynt took over the Georgetown pub run by her husband after he died unexpectedly.

Q and A Café grew into a celebrated event, and generated some extra lunch business for Nathan's. The day I attended with my camera crew, Carol booked former Senator Fred Thompson, considering a run for President, as guest speaker. In my pre-interview Thompson said, "I see Arch Campbell's here, so I know this is an important occasion." I knew Fred from his various film roles and his stint on *Law and Order*. That afternoon I put the story together for the 4:00pm news. I pitched a longer different version for the 6:00pm News. The 6:00pm producer liked me and often ran my reworked stories.

"Oh, I've got a good story; this former TV producer owns Nathan's and hosts these live in-person celebrity interviews. Today she's got Fred Thompson. This is a great local story." He shook his head and looked away. "Sorry, Arch, I can't run it today."

I went on set for the 4:00pm news, and then came back to my office. The answering machine red light blinked on my phone. I punched in the numbers. Vickie Burn's voice came on. "Arch, you have an appointment in (General Manager) Michael Jack's office tonight at 6. You will need to steel yourself for this meeting."

And that's when I knew 32 years of success, heartbreak, hard work and fun was coming to an end.

53
Blindsided, Part 2

My favorite foursome - we worked together 27 years.
Courtesy Carol Joynt—Q and A Cafe

I CALLED MY AGENT, RICHARD LIEBNER, THE quintessential New York agent. Liebner kept several phones going at once. He picked my call up right away, as if expecting it. Maybe Vickie Burns tipped him off. Liebner told me to go to the meeting, to stay calm, and to not agree to anything.

A long hallway led to Michael Jack's office. His secretary looked down and waved me in. The General Manager, Michael Jack, the Human Resources Director Rachael Manning, and the News Director Vickie Burns, arranged themselves around a coffee table, with an empty chair left for me. My chair put me directly across from Michael Jack with the others on either side. Everything looked clearly arranged to give them an advantage, most likely recommended by some consultant.

Just to screw with them and break the silence I said, "but I don't want a contract extension." Nobody laughed or even acknowledged my comment. Michael Jack cleared his throat for his obviously rehearsed speech.

I'll spare you the details other than to say it followed the usual blather, basically, "you're great, but we're buying you out anyway." They gave me until the end of the year, about six weeks, to accept their terms. They would pay off the rest of my contract, about nine months. I would also receive the union-dictated severance of 62 weeks on top of the buyout. They would pay my eight weeks of vacation. It came close to two year's salary. If I didn't agree, they would pay me bi-weekly until the contract ended, keep me off the air, and prevent me from working at another station. I asked about staying part time. Michael Jack quickly said, "no."

What Michael Jack didn't know or bother to find out was that after working 32 years and a few months and having passed the age of 60, I qualified for full retirement, including a guaranteed pension. With their sour faces and squinty eyes, I had the feeling they wanted me to feel bad about what amounted to a golden parachute. I told them I'd talk with my agent and left.

I suppose I'm lucky they didn't tell me to get out that day. I imagine they feared an age discrimination suit. I also believe firing me the same year I had Cancer made the company vulnerable. A few months earlier, Michael Jack asked me to help his wife book celebrity guests for *The Kojo Nnamdi Show* on the Howard University PBS station where she worked. Should I bring that up? I didn't help her much and I wonder if that made this personal. I called Liebner, told him what they offered and he told me to let things sit.

Plenty of signs existed, including the rash of firings before mine. In 1990, 1995, and 2000, my agent negotiated five-year contracts. In 2005, GE began cutting the length of personal services contracts. My 2005 contract lasted two years, with an opt-out clause at the end of a year.

Despite Cancer, age discrimination, and the business with Michael Jack's wife, I didn't want to sue. I think it didn't occur to these people that, after 32 years, I felt loyal to WRC. I remembered the struggle of the 70s, the improvement during the 80s and assembling the team of Jim, Doreen, George, Bob, and me as the fifth wheel. I would have happily worked out something. The management preferred an ambush.

That meeting took place November 15th. Word immediately leaked. John Maynard, a reporter for *The Washington Post*, dropped an email titled: "Inquiry from *The Washington Post,*" a classy way of saying, "I hear you got fired." I put him off. After all, I hadn't agreed or signed anything. I thought about things for two weeks. The more I thought the more I realized I had to take their deal. It was too good financially.

I sent an email to Bob Long in L.A. subject line: "Storm clouds on the horizon."

Bob messaged back, "I do not like this news." I stopped in Tim Russert's office. I told him the company bought out my contract and that I wanted to tell him how highly I regarded him. "I can't believe what these people are doing," Russert said.

"I've gone up and complained, and they just don't get it."

On November 28, I sent an e-mail to the staff confirming my departure. I sent a copy to John Maynard at *The Washington Post*. As soon as I hit send, I heard groans in the newsroom. My email quoted *The Godfather*: "they made me an offer I couldn't refuse." I also said, "good actors know when to make their exit. The time has come for mine."

The next day, my face appeared on the front page of *The Washington Post* style section. The headline read: "WRC Cuts Change Face of Local News," with a secondary line, "Competitors May Benefit from Loss of Popular Team."

Washington Post media reporter Paul Farhi wrote:

The roster of personalities whose contracts have not been renewed or were bought out early includes 5:00pm anchor Susan Kidd, sports anchors George Michael and Wally Bruckner, technology reporter I.J. Hudson and weekend weatherman Clay Anderson. Including Campbell, who has been on News4 since 1974, the departing news people have collectively appeared on WRC newscasts for more than 115 years.

The man supervising the station's overhaul, WRC President, and General Manager Michael Jack, declined to discuss future cost-saving measures, although he noted that NBC's streamlining initiative will run through 2008.

Jack expects the station to maintain its dominant role because, he said, viewers won't see much that is different about its newscasts. 'Our ratings are based on our long-standing image in the community,' he said. 'It's the product, it's the presentation, it's viewer loyalty.'

Later in the article Farhi added:

Since TV news-watching is often the product of habit, local stations make even small changes to their newscasts—their most profitable programs—at their peril. WRC's competitors see parallels between the station's downsizing and a similar campaign by

WUSA several years ago. In a bid to lower overall costs and attract younger viewers, Channel 9 parted ways with several familiar veterans, including sportscaster Frank Herzog, anchor-reporter Mike Buchannan, weatherman Doug Hill and anchor Gordon Peterson, the dean of local news personalities, who joined Hill at WJLA (Channel 7). WUSA, once Washington's news leader, has yet to recover fully.[54]"

A second article, "Arch Campbell to Leave WRC by Year's End," accompanied the longer story. In that article Maynard quoted me saying, "they gave me a choice between retirement and retirement, so I took retirement."[55]

Vickie Burns passed me in the newsroom and spit my line back at me, "they gave me a choice between retirement and retirement, so I took retirement." She sounded furious. I looked back at her with a blank expression.

54
Changing Channels

My agent Richard Liebner pitched me to the other stations in town. Channel 5 had mushroomed from an also-ran independent to a Fox-owned powerhouse. Channel 5's 10:00pm News received the highest news ratings in town. They added local competing newscasts at 5:00pm and 6:00pm. Channel 5's local morning News often surpassed NBC's *Today Show*. My friend Tony Perkins made a personal pitch on my behalf. Channel 5 said no.

Channels 7 and 9 wanted to meet. Both offered part-time daily fee work. Channel 9 broadcast from a beautiful facility about a block from Channel 4. If I joined Channel 9, my commute wouldn't change. However, Channel 9, the station that once dominated Washington television, now struggled to find an audience.

Channel 7 collected talent. They caused a stir when they hired Maureen Bunyan in 1999, four years after her unhappy departure from Channel 9. Channel 7's ratings began to rise. In 2003, Channel 7 hired CNN anchor Leon Harris. He joined Channel 9's former lead weatherman Doug Hill and ABC sportscaster Tim Brant in a revamped anchor team. A year later, Gordon Peterson, the powerhouse anchor of Channel 9 News, joined 7, teaming with his former partner Maureen Bunyan for the 6:00pm News. The hour between 6 and 7 with Peterson and Bunyon and ABC News produced stiff competition for Channel 4. Gordon Peterson's wife suggested Channel 7's new slogan: "All your Favorite People on the Same Station."

Bill Lord ran the Channel 7 newsroom. I knew his reputation from his years as News Director of KNBC.

Washington, D.C.

We met in a Starbucks in Roslyn, across Key Bridge from Georgetown. I spotted Lord and said, "I want to see what a good manager looks like." He smiled and sat down. We talked about NBC. He worked as a network reporter in the Middle East and worked for John Rohrbeck in L.A.. Lord offered two days a week; Mondays with entertainment news, Thursdays with movie reviews and weekend events. I told Lord I wanted an office and he agreed. Liebner negotiated a very generous daily fee. Channel 7 was on the rise creating real competition for Channel 4. Word might have filtered back to Channel 4. One afternoon Vickie Burns said, "New York says you can come back part time in August" (9 months hence). A real offer would have come through my agent. I smiled and said, "oh, that's nice."

I tried to put the best face I could on my final weeks at Channel 4. Sometimes I would walk into the newsroom and yell, "dead man walking." That either got a laugh or a wince. Not long before the end of December, I went to Human Resources and signed a non-disclosure agreement. They gave me a separation contract spelling out the money they owed me, or shall I say the blood money I would receive.

My last week at Channel 4, Diane Rehm invited me to talk about broadcasting for an hour on her national NPR show. I told her off-mic that I was going to Channel 7, and she didn't seem bothered because we both knew that ending a 32-year association was the point. Things were changing in broadcasting.

Thursday, December 21, 2006 marked my final day on the air. I worked on my farewell story for several days. A few minutes before 7:00pm, I sat next to Vance and introduced a career retrospective: my start in Dallas, the story of me and the turkeys, the feature on Spot the Pig, the *Star Trek* premiere, and my movie reviewing career. I found old footage of Roseanne Barr, Martin Lawrence, and Ray Romano on my late-night show. I showcased the story on "My Home Town," my scenes in Madonna's documentary *Truth or Dare,* and playing golf with Tip O'Neill, Sam Snead, and Bob Hope. I mentioned my Cancer and the value of colonoscopies and all the great names I worked with including Willard Scott, Jim Hartz, Dave Marash, Katie Couric, and Vance. The story ended with a shot of me walking through the newsroom with a cardboard box full of keepsakes. In voice over I said:

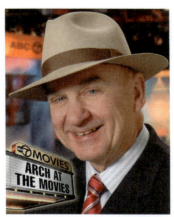

"I've packed up my office, I'm taking my memories with me. Bring on the Future."

Before it aired, Vickie Burns and her assistant Margie Ruttenberg watched and blanched. First Margie came to my office saying they wanted some edits. I gave her a withering look and said, "I can't do that." Vickie Burns walked into my office. "This is going to reflect badly on our newsroom." I answered, "what do you want me and Vance to do, sit out there and cry?" Invoking Vance shut her up. To her credit she didn't stop me from airing the piece. Of course, it reflected badly on Channel 4. I think it unnerved management that I was leaving with a smile on my face—looking to the future, rather than feeling bad.

My final story aired toward the end of the 6:00pm News. I came back on the air.

Washington, D.C.

George Michael, Bob Ryan, and Vance gathered around me. The three of us had worked together since 1980, about 27 years. I thanked everyone for watching adding, "I won't say goodbye, I'll only say 'next.'" Then the four of us joked and laughed and my time ended. I left the studio. After the commercial Vance came back on the air, looked at the camera and said, "this has been a terrible day, but we will endure."

Doreen previously scheduled vacation the week I left. I'm sorry she wasn't on set for my send off. Some weeks earlier I stopped in her office to tell her about my departure, before it went public. Doreen got up, ashen-faced, hugged me, and slumped in her chair. George Michael worked a few more weeks until his contract ended. After George's departure, Doreen hosted me and George and Vance and Bob and our wives for a small dinner party. I remember that night as low key and quiet.

Doreen's dinner was the last time the five of us would gather. Not long after his departure, doctors diagnosed George Michael with leukemia. He and I kept in touch, comparing his treatment for blood Cancer to mine for colon Cancer. Gina and I visited George in Sibley Hospital shortly before he passed away Christmas Eve 2009. Seeing my friend in a coma shocked me. George's family arranged for his funeral at the Washington National Cathedral. Gina was working in the clergy and music departments at the Cathedral. The clergy staff asked her to deliver the homily, which Gina titled: "George lived life large."

A few days after Christmas, the newsroom organized a farewell party for me, Susan Kidd, and I. J. Hudson at Guapo's, a Tex-Mex restaurant on Wisconsin Avenue. My friend Michael Flynn made the arrangements. His fifth-grade teacher, Melinda Matson, and I knew each other in junior high and high school. She told him as a student in

Fairfax that she knew me and maybe he would grow up to become a television reporter. Michael told me the story when he came to work at Channel 4 and we immediately bonded.

I phoned, emailed, and invited dozens of names from Channel 4's past: Jim Hartz, Dave Marash, Lea Thompson, Stan Bernard, Kelly Burke, and several others. Their presence turned my going away party into a broadcasting reunion.

With a smile and a straight face, I personally invited Michael Jack and Vickie Burns. Michael Jack said, "oh, I'm taking my family to the islands for Christmas." Burns quietly said she would be out of town.

John Maynard put me back in *The Washington Post* January 9, 2007 in: "Arch Campbell, Part II: Critic Joins WJLA." He quoted Bill Lord on Channel 7 and their collection of talent, Maureen Bunyan, Gordon Peterson, Doug Hill, and reporter Mike Buchanan.

"You have to look at each one of these individuals. Each one of these individuals really are people that we want on our team. Which one would you turn down? Would you say no to a Gordon Peterson or an Arch Campbell or a Mike Buchanan?"

Maynard quoted me saying there's at least one advantage to no longer working at the NBC station.

"Let's just say I'm breathing a sigh of relief that I never have to watch *'The Apprentice'* again."

MSNBC talk show host Chris Matthews lived next door to me in Chevy Chase, Maryland. I always liked Chris, especially his snarky attitude. We often bellowed at each other from our front yards. When my move to Channel 7 made the paper, he saw me and yelled, "Channel 7: where the dinosaurs go to die." Funny—just true enough to be funny. Matthews' wife Kathleen worked for Channel 7

News almost 30 years. As I arrived, she left the station to take a corporate role with the Marriott Corporation.

I made my first story for Channel 7 purposely playful. The station featured a Jumbotron on the front of the Rosslyn, Virginia office tower where they broadcast at 1100 Wilson Boulevard. For my first day they featured my picture with giant words: "Welcome Arch Campbell." I took footage and showed a few other things around the station including my new office. On the wall behind my desk, I hung a photo of Davey Marlin Jones. Appearing to talk to Davey, I said, "watch over me, O Great One." Off screen, a voice yelled, "stop talking to the pictures Arch and get to work."

Friends at Channel 4 told me when I came on Channel 7 for the first time, every TV in the Channel 4 newsroom was turned on full volume. People in the newsroom could see Vickie Burns in her office behind the glass wall glowering. When I finished, the Channel 4 newsroom burst into applause.

Cheers or not, the truth remains—I didn't want to leave Channel 4. I would have happily stayed-part time for less money. I believe different management could have finessed a better outcome. I worked for Channel 7 and News Channel 8 for the next eight years. My thirty-two years at Channel 4 define my career.

*Reunion at my Channel 4 Sendoff
(L-R) Bob Ryan, Me, Trish Burke, Stan Bernard, Vance, Lea
Thompson, Joe Krebs, Kelly Burke, Jim Hartz*

Courtesy Ray East

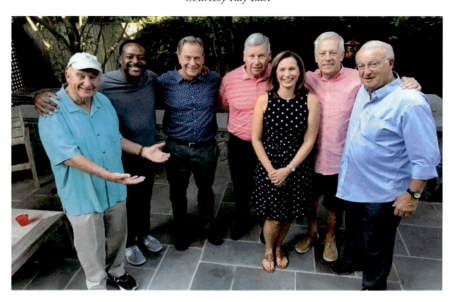

*Channel 7 team in Alison Starling's backyard
(L-R) Me, Leon Harris, Bill Lord, Tom Brant,
Alison Starling, Doug Hill, Gordon Peterson*

55
A New Start

Gordon Peterson gave me a hug. Maureen Bunyan kissed me. Doug Hill and Tim Brant slapped me on the back. Leon Harris and Allison Starling offered more hugs. Everywhere I went in the Channel 7 Newsroom, I received a gracious word of welcome. Bill Lord, as promised, arranged a very nice private office with my own printer and television monitor. The promotion department took photos, printed up business cards. People smiled when I came into view.

Channel 7 didn't require much. I reported entertainment news on Mondays, and reviewed movies on Thursday. I appeared at 5:35pm on Channel 7. The station operated a separate cable channel—News Channel 8. When I finished my appearance on Channel 7, I walked over to the News Channel 8 studio and introduced the same segment with a different anchor team a few minutes before 6:00pm.

Not long after I arrived, Bill Lord caught me by surprise. "We want you to cover the Oscars." Channel 4 had stopped sending me to the Oscars ten years earlier. Unlike my NBC years, I would work with ABC, the network that carried the show. Channel 7 went all out. A second reporter/anchor Leslie Cook, joined me on the trip with our own cameraman Marty Doan, a station veteran. I would report for the evening news and Leslie for the morning news. Nominated films that year included Martin Scorsese's crime drama *The Departed*, as well as *Babel, Letters from Iwo Jima, Little Miss Sunshine,* and *The Queen*. Leading up to the ceremony, I produced a story titled: "Wouldn't it be great if *Little Miss Sunshine* won Best Picture?" *The Departed* won, but *Little Miss Sunshine* represented the kind of easy to like film I favor.

The Accidental Critic

On one of my first days, I met Kyle Osborne, a fellow entertainment reporter working for News Channel 8. I immediately told him I had not come to compete with or interfere with any of his work. Kyle forecast the weather, and hosted an entertainment show *Entertainment Forecast*. A few days after I started, Kyle invited me on his show, asking about my career, and about my bout with Cancer. Kyle and I became friends rather than competitors.

The Retirement Living Channel, a new organization programming for seniors, reached out. The network had started a daily newscast, and wanted my movie reviews.

I worked with some well-known names from the early days of CNN, including Mary Alice Williams, Felicia Taylor (daughter of actor Rod Taylor) and Fred Grandy (Gopher on *The Love Boat*).

My agent negotiated another generous daily rate. I continued to appear every Friday morning on WASH-FM, recording segments for the weekend. With the Channel 7 job, and the Retirement Living work, and WASH-FM, plus my NBC retirement check, I was making more money than when I worked full time.

Houston businessman Joel L. Allbritton owned Channel 7 and cable channel News Channel 8. The Allbrittons gave the station the flavor of a family business. Everyone knew to sit up straight when Mrs. Allbritton, a lively Southern belle named Barby, walked through the newsroom. She often dished out a wise crack or word of hello. When we crossed paths, she would greet me with, "what's new at the picture show, Archie?" Bill Lord told me Mrs. Allbritton sometimes wore white gloves to check the tops of desks and tables for dust. She wanted the station as clean as her homes in Wesley Heights, D.C. and River Oaks, Texas. Compared to Channel 4, Channel 7 sparkled with modern furnishings and updated facilities.

Washington, D.C.

My new friends whispered a few in-house *no-nos*. According to rumor, Barby disliked double breasted suits on men. I put mine in the back of my closet. Young women wearing clothes too revealing heard about it. Gossips reported one young woman was fired for wearing something that looked like a slip on the air.

The most delightful gossip, probably apocryphal, concerned an interview with Prince Charles. At that time, the Allbritton family controlled the Riggs Bank. As bankers, they enjoyed a connection to the Bank of England and the royal family. During an interview with Prince Charles, a Channel 7 cameraman took a behind-the-shoulder cut away, revealing the royal bald spot. Leon Harris told me much later the reporter was given instructions not to ask the Prince about Princess Diana, who had just divorced him. Of course, the reporter led with the Diana question. At any rate, the transgressions got the poor scribe fired, and the story has grown exponentially ever since. Channel 7's quirkiness reminded me of my early days at WFAA in Dallas, when the prominent Dealey family ran *The Dallas Morning News* and WFAA-TV as their personal fiefdom.

The Allbrittons moved from Houston to Washington in the 1970s when Joel brought controlling interest in the Riggs National Bank. In 1977, Allbritton acquired Channel 7 when he bought *The Washington Star* newspaper and its assets. The FCC gave Allbritton three years to break apart the newspaper/broadcasting concentration. Allbritton proved himself a sharp operator. He sold *The Washington Star* to Time-Life, keeping Channel 7 as well as a couple of other small stations owned by the company. Time-Life couldn't make a go of *The Star* and closed the beloved paper in 1981. The television stations Allbritton kept continued to make juicy profits. Mr. Allbritton changed the call letters from WMAL-TV to WJLA-TV—his initials, Joel A. Allbritton.

When I arrived in 2007, the senior Mr. Allbritton was handing the reigns to his son Robert. As heir apparent, Robert recruited a group of *Washington Post* reporters to create the internet news site *Politico*. The new website grew into one of the leading online news sites. Robert had good reason to take pride in his success. He walked the halls proudly, friendly, and accessibly.

Rounding out the management team, tall, handsome Fred Ryan ran the station as General Manager. Fred's resume included years with President Reagan as a White House assistant. Ryan also served as Chairman of the Ronald Reagan Presidential Library. He put his movie star looks to good use, lubricating clients and coordinating the needs of the family with the needs of the station.

Politico assembled a huge group of reporters and interesting people, including Mike Allen, known for his scoops and reporting, as well as his eccentricities. Mike's quirks included a six-foot pile of clippings and papers spilling out from the corner of his cubicle into the hallway. Mike loved movies. He always had a good word and several inquiring questions for me.

I met and enjoyed many conversations with Andy Glass, who once worked for the legendary *New York Herald Tribune*. I prompted Andy for stories about his fellow writers Tom Wolfe, Judith Crist, and Jimmy Breslin. Andy and I also debated and shared our favorite new movies and series. *Politico* teemed with creative energy. For a while, *Politico* published in newspaper form. They asked me to contribute movie reviews, making me a print journalist, at least for a little while.

Robert Allbritton pursued another idea, a fusion between cable News Channel 8 and the internet. The new organization hunted for a web domain name without much success. As with *Politico*, it was a cable/web fusion filled with talented people. Eric Wemple came from *The Washington Post* to oversee editorial. He began to label his work TBD: "to be determined." The name took hold.

The lure of TBD brought my friend Bob Ryan from Channel 4 to Channel 7. Robert Allbritton, Fred Ryan, and Bill Lord all trumpeted Bob's arrival, practically throwing rose pedals at his feet in an all-staff meeting. Bob's departure put another dent in the WRC dream team. I enjoyed having my old friend within reach again, although we didn't quite have the fun of our salad days at Channel 4.

As part of TBD, the bosses wanted Kyle Osborne and me to host a two-man movie review show, a local version of Siskel and Ebert. Just as we began brainstorming, Kyle left the station, following a frustrating argument with another employee.

I learned about Kyle's departure when his show producer, LaTanya Horne, rushed into my office. "Arch, you've gotta host Kyle's show tomorrow. He's not here anymore." The show *Entertainment Forecast* showcased satellite interviews, movie reviews and coming attractions on stage. I gamely sat in, reading a very talky script. I wasn't very good on that first show.

Nobody cared about my rocky debut because the D.C. Lottery sponsored *Entertainment Forecast*. The show needed to run no matter who anchored it. Thanks to the lottery, I inherited a new gig. TBD hired Steve Chaggaris, from CBS News, to oversee programming. Steve began to drop into my office and encourage me to liven things up. He beamed when I asked to change the title to *The Arch Campbell Show*. I owe much of the success of that show to Steve's encouragement.

I recruited a cast of supporting characters for the revamped *Arch Campbell Show*. I ran into Joe Hansard working as an editor in the Channel 7 Sports Department.

Joe broke me up years earlier in his live interview after the premiere of *Homicide*. I created a role for him: "guest announcer." I alternated Joe with another friend, Sonya Gavankar, once Miss D.C. and now a host on News Channel 8 as well as at the Newseum.

Both Joe and Sonya displayed a wicked sense of humor, Sonya mugging for the camera, and rolling her eyes at my remarks. Joe produced comedy segments on his iPhone. An amateur actor, Joe hilariously plugged his appearance in straight to DVD movies or his cameos as a bad guy on *America's Most Wanted*. I invited various cable and Channel 7 anchors as guests. As a gag, I started a segment I named, "Ask Arch," after the feature I once hosted on Channel 4. This time, my guests or side-kicks read bogus letters I wrote using fake names to set up what's now known as "dad jokes." The segments gave my guests something to do. I used friends' names as authors of the mail, including Angus LaMonde, Elizabeth Maloney, and Doctor Tom Havell.

Our studio session lasted exactly one hour. The program aired with no editing, giving a live effect. Working with the director Kristie Maryott, I encouraged her to simplify. The program began with me at a desk, and the announcer in a corner of the studio framed by ladders, old lights, a stuffed rat, and a neon sign reading "Arch." The main guest, usually an actress or actor promoting a play or movie, stood in front of a green screen with a humorous background. I conducted the interview in a double box. I talked in one square to the guest in a square next to mine. The double box eliminated the need for complicated close-up shots or camera changes. Kristie could cut from a double box to a single shot and back.

Speaking of the double box, humorist Dave Barry complained during his interview about not being seated next to me. I got out from behind my desk, walked out of frame over to his spot. Spontaneously, Barry moved from the green screen to my desk. We changed places and continued the interview. Unplanned, the switch received a gigantic laugh. On every show, I made sure three or four interns in the studio laughed and clapped and provided an off-screen laugh track. Pretty soon, people in the newsroom came in to watch.

Frequent guests included my old friend Dick Dyzsel, who played Count Gore on Channel 20's *Creature Feature*. When the station canceled the show, Dick took a breather, then reinvented the program online. Count Gore would arrive in full costume, walking around the building, dropping into the adjacent CVS drugstore where he would bite the neck of anyone who recognized him. My pal Bob Ryan often appeared, sometimes as, "The Anonymous Weatherman," wearing a Groucho Marx set of glasses and mustache. The Channel 7 Head of Engineering appeared as, "The Anonymous Engineer," wearing a paper bag over his head.

"Bare bones," describes the News Channel 8 version of *The Arch Campbell Show*.

The version I hosted 20 years earlier on Channel 4 used multiple cameras, a lighting director, two stage managers, an in-studio audience of 50 or more, and unlimited producing, directing, and editing. *The Arch Campbell Show* on News Channel 8 possessed none of these advantages. The little cable show LaTanya Horne, Kristie Marriott, and I cobbled together far surpassed the big budget one I did on Channel 4.

Top: Dave Barry
Middle: Count Gore aka Dick Dysel
Bottom: Bob Ryan as the Anonymous Weatherman

Top: Sonya Govankar
Middle: Joe Hansard
Bottom: Kristie Marriott (Director), LaTanya Horne (Producer),

56
Patton and Me

A GUY NAMED JAMES WHO WORKED ON THE Channel 7 floor crew often dropped in my office. He liked movies and new things, and I liked talking with him. One day he contributed to my knowledge of a comic actor named Patton Oswalt.

"Have you heard of this guy Patton Oswalt? He does stand up and he's really funny. He roasts you in his act. Have you heard about this? Man, he CREAMS you."

Well, no, I hadn't heard that. I kind of remembered Patton from *Ratatouille*, the Pixar comedy about the rat who wanted to work as a chef. Oswalt voiced the rat. I remember liking the movie. I had a lot going on that day, so I just shrugged at James and forgot about it.

Then I heard from my father-in-law. When Gina's father retired as a Methodist minister, he bought a new car with Sirius radio. My father-in-law discovered the Comedy Channel, and heard Patton's bit on me. With great amusement, even a little bit of glee, Gina's father told me he listens to a comic who makes fun of me and what did I think of that?

I started looking into Patton Oswalt.

It turns out Patton grew up outside D.C. in Sterling, Virginia, graduating from Broad Run High School in 1987. He enrolled at William and Mary where he discovered a talent for comedy. After college he moved to L.A. and worked as a character actor and comic. His big break came when he joined the cast of *King of Queens*—a sitcom I never watched. He got an even bigger break as the voice of Remy the Rat in *Ratatouille*, the Pixar animated movie I liked and recommended.

Washington, D.C.

The internet helped me find Patton's 2007 stand up album *Vampires and Lollipops*.

During his set he talks about growing up in the D.C. suburbs in the 1980s and trying to be cool or even rebellious while living in a family that demanded order. Patton's father was a Marine Corps officer. He named his son after World War II General George Patton. Ironic, eh?

Patton attended Broad Run High School about the time I hit my stride reviewing movies on Channel 4. Nobody ever told me exactly how to review movies, but I wanted to differentiate myself from Davey Marlin Jones on Channel 9. Davey took an artsy approach that sometime left viewers wondering what he thought. I made my reviews as broad and approachable as possible. I used humor and gave a clear star rating. My approach kept me going for a generation. However, my middlebrow reviews didn't agree with young Patton Oswalt.

In *Vampires and Lollipops* Patton talks about growing up so close to sophisticated Washington, D.C. but having to live in the planned community of Sterling. He goes on to say Sterling was part of a "test" to see if you were willing to settle for a bland safe life or try for something more exciting. That's where I enter Patton's act:

> *And the person who administers your test year after year until you can't take it and you leave is the movie critic on the local news. That's the guy whose job it is to keep everything relevant and cool and important away from you so you have to get off your ass and find it on your own initiative and the guy we had—I owe this guy a dinner because he made me the pissy little world traveler I am today—ARCH CAMPBELL, on the local news outside of D.C. Oh my God, this guy—he would review movies. He would really say*

stuff like, 'uh there's this new movie from Australia—so right there whatever—called The Road Warrior. Now lemme get this straight. It's the future. There's no gasoline but everyone's driving around in cars. I don't get it. No stars—doesn't make sense.

But all is not bleak at the multiplex, there's a wonderful new movie out—not for the under 17's—it's a little surreal, but otherwise four stars all the way for Three Men and a Baby. Oh my goodness! Brilliant concept! It's three guys and there's this baby and they don't know what they're doing. The title makes me laugh.'

Patton goes on to say people like me on TV made him leave the safety of Sterling and move to L.A.. Patton's rant made the internet. I admit it hurt a little. I knew I couldn't do anything about it and time would pass and people would forget.

Fate intervened.

In 2011, Patton won a starring role in *Young Adult* with Charlize Theron and Patrick Wilson. In *Young Adult*, Patton's character suffers a beating in high school by a group of jocks who think he's gay. Now in his thirties he has a damaged organ and a permanent limp. He connects with Charlize Theron who returns to her home town in search of the man she once loved. During her visit, she has a meltdown. *Young Adult* is pretty good and so is Patton; in fact, he's the heart of the movie.

Allied Advertising, the company that promotes movies in Washington, sent me an email. Patton Oswalt was coming to Washington to promote *Young Adult*. Would I like to schedule an interview? Oh yes, I would.

There was a time I couldn't have parked my ego and played Patton's barbs for laughs. Early on, criticism stung me hard. However, over the years people started telling me how much they liked my work and knowing I probably didn't deserve the compliments, I starting taking the knocks in stride. They sort of off-set each other. So, I wasn't looking for revenge. I just wanted to see what would happen when we met.

I waited for Patton in Channel 7's lobby. The station had big glass doors. I could see him in the distance walking toward me, with his assistant and the movie publicist. I stood up. The publicist said, "Arch, this is Patton Oswalt." I smiled and shook his hand. He grinned and shook mine. We both knew our meeting was a momentous occasion.

"Come on up to the make-up room Patton. We're all set up and we'll be finished in time for you to appear on *Let's Talk Live*."[56] We went upstairs and I told Patton to sit in the make-up chair. He's short and a little dumpy. He looked like a little boy getting his first haircut. Patton put on his microphone.

I took the cameraman down the hall and told him to follow me as we walked in. Here's most of what happened. You can see the entire exchange on YouTube under *Arch Campbell meets Patton Oswalt*.

I walk in saying: "Patton. Patton Oswalt."

Patton obviously sensing what's going on looks at me with a devilish grin and says:

"Oh, I've been waiting very long to meet you."

I look at Patton and laugh. Then I say:

"This guy came into my office and said you were cracking on me. What have I ever done to you?"

Patton: "You made my childhood very difficult because every movie I wanted to see you gave it a horrible review and my parents would go, 'See, Arch Campbell hates it.' And I go, 'He doesn't understand.' You gave *Blade Runner* two stars."

I gave *Blade Runner* four stars. So, I said:

"I gave it four stars."

And Patton quickly rejoins: "Not when it came out."

I protest: "What?"

Patton says: "Show me the video tape."

And then I say something about how the tape is so old it's in the Smithsonian and why did he blame me for his rotten childhood.

Patton: "It's that weird memory of wanting the cool stuff to come in, but you were the arbitrator or it as far as my parents were concerned."

And then we laughed and kidded around and I read to him what he says in his stand-up act and we laughed some more and finally came to sort of a truce.

Patton: "You kept the gate closed so I had to climb over it. You know what? You were Mr. Miyagi[57] making me sand the floor. Arch, you weren't my enemy, you were the Arch on my bridge to my destiny."

Saying that, Patton leaned into the camera and mugged.

I finished the interview with a few questions about his movie. I think we actually liked each other. I led Patton to the cable studio for the talk show. I watched Patton's segment on the monitor in my office. He walked past my door on his way out, so I came out to tell him goodbye.

"Patton this was great—so nice to meet you."

He grinned and said: "Back at you buddy."

And then I looked him right in the eye and said: "By the way Patton, F**K YOU."

He roared. I roared. Friendship sealed.

Patton and Me, Part 2

Friends?

"Mr. Oswalt will see you now."

Patton wasn't finished with me. He returned to his home town of Sterling in December, 2013 to visit his parents. As part of the visit, he agreed to host a screening of Ben Stiller's remake of *The Secret Life of Walter Mitty*. Patton had a small part in the movie. He also liked the new Alamo Drafthouse in Sterling, often saying he wished the theater existed when he was growing up.

The Theater called and asked me to come out and

conduct a Q&A session after the screening. I told them I couldn't make it. Sterling was miles from D.C. and would have been a nightmare in traffic. The manager called back and said Patton requested me personally. A good friend, Owen Davis, offered to drive. Patton's parents came and I sat and watched the movie with them.

Patton and I had a great time on stage together. During the session I used the line I used years ago on Channel 4 about *Mad Max*.

"It's the future, there's no gas, and everybody's driving around in cars. I don't get it! "

Patton and the crowd screamed. He mimicked strangling me.

Later I saw Patton at his appearance at the 6th and I Speakers Series promoting his book about loving movies *Silver Screen Fiend*. I saw myself in his stories about lining up to watch classics at the New Beverly Theater in L.A. in the 90's. It reminded me of my days going to the AFI Theater and Circle theaters. Patton saw me, jumped down from the stage and gave me a hug.

Patton shows up at the Alamo Drafthouse in Sterling whenever he comes to visit his folks. I returned to introduce and moderate a session with him following a screening of *Sorry to Bother You* in 2018.

Patton suffered the death of his wife Michelle McNamara in 2016. A noted true crime author and researcher, Michelle pushed herself beyond healthy limits as she researched the Golden State Killer, a California serial rapist and murderer active during the 1970s and 1980s. After Michelle's death, Patton finished his wife's book *I'll Be Gone in the Dark*. He helped turn the manuscript into an acclaimed HBO true crime series. The project led to the capture and arrest of 72-year-old Joseph James DeAngelo. He confessed to multiple murder and rapes, and now serves a life prison term without the possibility of parole.[58]

Washington, D.C.

That night while the audience watched the film, Patton nursed a gin and tonic at a table in the bar. When I joined him, I began by stammering my sympathy acknowledging the death of his wife. He graciously accepted my acknowledgement that I knew he'd experienced a tragedy.

Once we went into the theater, the fun returned. Patton didn't really need me for much other than to introduce him. He maintains a huge following on Twitter (now X). One tweet filled the theater. The publicist who drove me to that screening said she'd never seen a crowd have that much fun.

I later told Ann Hornaday and Tony Kornheiser's producer Marc Stern about the evening. Ann, Mark, and I worked on a weekly movie review podcast. I had settled into the auditorium to watch the movie. Halfway through, an usher came with the message: "Mr. Oswalt will see you now." For weeks, they greeted me with, "Mr. Oswalt will see you now."

57
Whatever Happened to the Accidental Critic?

Washington Post front page August 28, 2014

I WAS JOKING AROUND IN THE CHANNEL 7 newsroom with Doug McKelway, an old friend who worked with me at Channel 4 and also jumped to Channel 7. My jaw started pounding. I heard a banging noise. My left eye clamped shut. Somebody said, "why are you wincing?" My eye released, the pounding stopped and our newsroom chatter continued. After a while, my left eye began to droop, especially when I spoke—not a good look on TV. Doctors diagnosed a malfunction of the seventh facial cranial nerve. A scan confirmed a vein in my neck pressing against my facial nerve. Physicians call it hemifacial paralysis.

A neurologist told me my options boiled down to brain surgery or botox injections. A surgeon said he couldn't guarantee brain surgery would fix it. I found Dr. Jodie

Barth, a physical therapist who worked mostly with Bell's Palsy patients. She sent me to a plastic surgeon for botox. The injections just above my eye, along my jaw, and in my neck froze the left side of my face and helped keep my eye open. Each treatment cost $1500 and lasted about three months. My health insurance did not cover the treatments.

I began to think about the end of my days on television, even though the Channel 7 management didn't seem concerned, or even notice my eye problem, and happily agreed when I asked to pre-tape my intro.

Channel 7 gave me eight delightful years. I felt loose and creative reviewing movies and producing an occasional feature story on an easy schedule. The years between 2007 and 2014 included some fine films: *No Country for Old Men* and *There Will Be Blood, Benjamin Button, The Silver Linings Playbook, The Hurt Locker, The Social Network, The Descendants, Bridesmaids, Argo, The Master, American Hustle, Boyhood,* and *Whiplash*. The weekly show I inherited delivered more fun and satisfaction than anything I ever did.

Allbritton Communications owner Joel L. Allbritton died in December 2012. Local television was changing. Stations groups were consolidating. The law that once limited ownership to five VHS stations now allowed groups to own dozens, even hundreds of stations. Robert Allbritton made his mark forming *Politico*. When the senior Allbritton died, the family naturally decided to take advantage of tax laws and sell the company, including Channel 7, while keeping *Politico*.

Potential buyers included ABC Television, as well as A.H. Belo, my former employer at WFAA in Dallas. Hearst Broadcasting showed interest. Sinclair Broadcasting, headquartered in nearby Baltimore, had expanded into one of the largest station groups in the country. Sinclair made the

The Accidental Critic

most generous offer of almost a billion dollars. The Allbritton's accepted.

Because of Sinclair's size, the Federal Communications Commission took more than a year to approve. They gave the go ahead in July 2014. On news of the approval of the ownership change, our boss Bill Lord posted a sign outside his office: "Keep Calm and Carry On," referencing Winston Churchill's advice to London residents during the World War II blitz. The first week they took possession, Sinclair fired Bill Lord.

When Sinclair took charge, I didn't have a contract. It expired a few months earlier. My television news career covered 43 years, 40 of them in D.C. My radio days expanded my broadcasting career to 50 years. I remembered the showbiz rule: "don't stay on the stage too long." I told Bill Lord, working during his last transition days, that I wanted to take a break, not retire, but take a break. I phrased it that way in case something I really wanted to do came my way.

My last week at Channel 7, I noticed Scott Livingston, Sinclair's Vice President of News, standing next to the staff mail boxes. I introduced myself and mentioned the irony of departing as Sinclair arrived. I told him I was taking a break for personal reasons. Of course, the personal reasons were that I didn't want to give Sinclair the opportunity to fire me. Livingston said he knew my work and that Sinclair would love for me to stay. He was being nice, and I was being nice, but the truth is my TV days were ending. My drooping eye wasn't getting better. I doubt Sinclair would pay the generous rate I received from the Allbritton's. An ownership change often signals a good time to depart.

The Washington Post called. They wanted to write a profile. I met with one of their top reporters, Manuel Roig-Franzia, to talk about my life and times. We had coffee at the American City Diner on Connecticut Avenue, a 1950s style diner, and spoke for an hour or two in a booth under a mural of Marilyn Monroe. The story ran on the front page of the August 28, 2014 *Washington Post*.

Manuel Roig-Franzia wrote a very kind article including this passage:

In the Insta-celebrity era of television news, the 68-year-old Campbell represents a slowly vanishing breed of broadcasters who've done it all and do it all—in the same market, a throwback to a time when versatility was everything.

The story captured the essence of my career. I stumbled into television news, struggled until finding my place reporting the kind of light feature stories once considered essential as the final story of a well-balanced television newscast. I anchored the news, reported the weather, covered wrecks and fires and elections, interviewed hundreds of celebrities, and began reviewing movies because I raised my hand when the boss screamed, "I want a movie reviewer. Who wants to do it?"

I never dreamed I would last this long or that my high school speech teacher's comment, "you have the gift of gab," would lead to a lifetime career.

Washingtonian Magazine sent a letter with a big surprise. They would include me among 2014's honorees as Washingtonians of the Year. I thought it was a joke, maybe Bob Ryan sending a variation on, "please return the towels!" Then an editor for the magazine called to set up a photograph. At the luncheon, held January 15, 2015, I spoke about living in D.C. since 1974 and the explosion of theater and the arts since the 1970s. I fondly remembered nights discovering creative performances in small independent theaters. In my speech I said something interesting happens somewhere every night in Washington. Of every honor I've ever received, I am most proud of my selection as a Washingtonian of the Year.

One of the Washingtonians of the Year, 2014

MY HOMETOWN

58
The Texas Eagle

I AM RIDING AMTRAK'S *TEXAS EAGLE* FROM Chicago to San Antonio, Texas, my home town. The guy across the table in the dining car asks about my trip. I start telling stories.

"A guy invented Fritos in San Antonio by accident. He was making tortillas and spilled some of the dough into a pan of hot oil. He fished it out and voila! Fritos. A little-known fact from my home town." I gain momentum and keep talking.

"When I was in college, you could walk into the Pearl Brewery and act like you just finished a tour. They'd give you two free beers, and wouldn't even check your ID. Lone Star brewed beer on the other side of town. I'd go over there and score two more free beers. Four free beers in an afternoon, how about that—underage too!" The guy in the dining car smiles. We look out the window as Amtrak passes a junk yard.

My Home Town

Amtrak doesn't hurry. *The Eagle* leaves Chicago at 1:45pm, rolling south to St. Louis by 7:30pm, on into the night to Little Rock, entering Texas at sunrise. From Texarkana, the train slouches toward Dallas-Fort Worth where it makes a slow meander south. The final 80 miles from Austin to San Antonio require three and a half hours. *The Eagle* takes a day and a half to cover the distance that an airplane makes in three hours.

My friends tease me. "Why don't you fly?" They know. I like trains.

In my childhood, Santa brought me electric trains at Christmas. My Lionel Santa Fe engine ran like a rabbit. My father and I nailed down tracks on a four by eight plywood board. We turned off the lights and watched the engine and cars race in the darkness.

The year I turned 7, my family and I boarded the Missouri Pacific *Texas Eagle* at San Antonio's suburban Monte Vista Station. The railroad built the little station on West Hollywood Street in the 1920s to serve the elite north side. My father wore a suit, tie, and hat. My mother selected one of her nicest outfits. She juggled my infant sister Marti in her arms. Our Pullman was the last car of the streamliner. The roomy cabin included a chair and sofa. On that trip, the dining car attendant walked the train ringing hand held chimes.

"BONG BONG BONG BONG. FIRST CALL FOR DINNER! BONG BONG BONG BONG. FIRST CALL FOR DINNER IN THE DINING CAR!"

He improvised a series of jazzy notes after the opening bars, adding merriment to the announcement.

My family made those train trips from San Antonio to Decatur, Alabama in 1953 and 1954. Sitting down for dinner, the steward noticed my 1½ year old sister. With a twinkle in his eye, he rolled up four cloth napkins, knotted them together and formed an elegant seat belt. "She won't fall out during dinner, even though we're doing 90 miles an hour."

The diner smelled of bacon and coffee and diesel fuel and cigarettes and the best food in the world. The waiters laid out china and silver on starched white tablecloths. Fresh flowers filled the vases on the tables.

The train carried a glamorous Vista Dome, with an observation lounge elevated above the car roof. I looked out at backyards and small towns and rolling countryside. The attendant tuned the dome's radio and picked up music. Eddie Fisher sang "Wish You Were Here."

That was then.

Amtrak covers dining car tables with paper. The microwaved food tastes lousy. It arrives on a plastic throwaway plate.

My Amtrak "roomette" barely has room for my shoes when I close the door. I have to walk down the hall when I need the bathroom. I toss and turn, and wake up groggy. No matter, I love the train anyway—the view, the motion, the transition to a far-away place.

Night falls and I spot the outskirts of my home town. I see the airport, then the Quarry, which we called "Cementville" because that's what they made there. We cross McCullough Avenue and a house my parents considered buying when I was a boy. I longed to live there because I loved trains, but my mother didn't want a home next to the tracks. We cross San Pedro on the railroad bridge and Hildebrand a few miles from Jefferson High School. The train glides past West Hollywood Street where the Monte Vista Station once stood.

Growing up, my father and I hung around this station watching the evening train. As the 8:15pm departed, my father reminisced:

My Home Town

"I brought your Mother to this station in 1943, so she could return to her home in Alabama and attend all the parties and showers that came with a wedding in a little town. I wrote her a letter every day until I drove out there to meet her. During the war, the government rationed gas, so our friends gave me their gas coupons to make the trip."

He looked wistful as he told the story.

The railroad closed Monte Vista in 1961 and tore the station down a couple of years later. Only the concrete slab remains. Weeds cover the property.

As Amtrak crawls into town, I recognize the streets of my childhood: Gramercy and Summit and Mulberry and my home street, West Mistletoe. We cross Woodlawn and Ashby and pass over the downtown expressway. The tracks lead to the once grand Missouri Pacific San Antonio depot.

Missouri Pacific closed the main depot in 1970 when they stopped operating passenger trains. A towering brass Indian stood on the highest point of the roof. Some brave soul climbed up and stole the Indian when the railroad abandoned the building. In the late 1980s a credit union renovated the space. The Indian mysteriously reappeared. When the credit union moved, the city turned the station into an urban bus center. Renovated to his former glory and back on his perch, the brass Indian looks over the roughest part of downtown. The city jail sits just across the tracks. A storage facility next to the station offers shelter to the homeless.

We roll on. Somewhere among mysterious warehouses Amtrak switches off the Missouri Pacific mainline to a little used Southern Pacific track. We go south, turn east, and then loop around and head north. The train moves so slow I swear I could jump off and jump back on. We cross Cevallos Street. I smile at the sight of "La Tuna," an outdoor cantina. Kids and bikers and old people sit under strings of colored lights sipping cold beer and eating tacos. The name has nothing to do with the fish. In Spanish, "La Tuna" stands for the flowers of a cactus plant.

I see the Alamo Dome and the tiny Amtrak depot. We don't stop—which seems strange. We head past the Southern Pacific's grand Sunset Station. A developer turned it into a music and club venue. It's seldom busy. *The Eagle* creeps into the Southern Pacific yard and halts. The engineer backs onto another track.

We lurch backward, retracing our steps past Sunset Station and back to the little Amtrak depot. The train stops. The conductor announces we have arrived.

Home.

59
The Ghost of West Mistletoe

"I AM THE GHOST OF WEST MISTLETOE," I SAY as I walk toward the front gate of a place I love on West Mistletoe Street in San Antonio. The owner, Kevin, laughs. I grew up in the house he and his wife Adriana bought from my mother in 1996. The family noticed my mother's obit and wrote a kind note. I mailed a Christmas card with photos from the 1950s. They replied: "Next time you are in town, please drop by and say hello."

I wonder if they saw me, all the times I slowly drove by, craning my neck for a glimpse of my childhood home? I love the line in the third act of *Our Town* when Emily returns from the grave to witness an ordinary day from her childhood. She realizes she can't stay, but hesitates and says, "one more look." Then she exclaims her love of life's ordinary joys.

The owner smiles as he opens the gate. "Come in, come in." He immediately takes me to a pair of footprints in the driveway next to the porch. "Who do these belong to?" I think he knew.

"They're mine. I made them when I was six." I still remember. "My mother loved Hollywood's Chinese theater. We had vacationed in California the year before workmen poured a new driveway. That morning in 1952, she took me by the hand and giggled as she helped me dip my feet into the wet cement."

My host's eyes sparkle. "Our children used to put their feet in those footprints, wondering about the kid who made them."

The wife eased out of the house and greeted me. She's quiet and reserved, married to a Boston Irish guy who wound up in San Antonio when the military stationed his father here. I looked like a hologram to them. "Can I go in the garage?" I blurt out.

"Well, it's full of boxes and stuff, but sure." They shove a few things around allowing me access to a spot on the wall where my father marked the growth of my sister and me. I see, "Archie, July 1959," in faint ball point.

"We came out here every few months so my dad could mark our height. See, I shot up a foot between 1959 and 1960."

A sturdy wooden fence encloses the back yard replacing the chain link fence of my childhood. The husband says our decades old chain link was so solid the construction crew used the anchor poles to reinforce their new fence.

"My parents installed the fence so I could have a dog," I recalled. "My mother thought a dog would help me adjust to the arrival of my baby sister Marti."

My mind drifted to the parade of dogs we owned: Claudia, a mixed terrier who immediately produced a litter of four pups: Prince, Claudia's offspring given away because he snapped at Marti; Ginger, the Cocker Spaniel who wandered into the yard without a collar and stayed until she bit little Joe Hammer from down the street; and Mutt, the leader of the neighborhood pack who chased cars until the unlucky day a driver ran over him.

The wife breaks my silence. "Do you remember the fig tree?" I nodded. "We cut it down because it attracted birds and made a mess. I miss it."

The fig tree: our neighbor Mrs. Hill canned those figs for us, as well as pears from a tree in the back corner. A stand of banana trees grew by the kitchen door. My mother tossed coffee grounds on the banana roots. One mild winter, a stalk emerged producing a single banana. I think the coffee grounds did it.

Bananas grow in Central America, not San Antonio. A crowd from the neighborhood assembled in our back yard to view the unusual sight. Our eccentric neighbor Helen pulled the banana off the tree, peeled it, and took a big bite. She offered some to my sister and me. My mother warned us Helen attended the Christian Science Church and didn't believe in germs. We didn't want her germs, and politely replied, "no, thanks." That winter, a "blue norther" blasted an ice storm into town and killed the banana tree. My mother planted day lilies in its place.

I turned to the wife. "I notice the house next door is for sale. Mrs. Hill lived there and was like a grandmother to us."

"Everyone who moves into that house gets divorced," she says. "I think there's a curse on it."

"Mrs. Hill's kitchen window looked out on our driveway. We often visited through her open window. She called my mother Mrs. Campbell; my mother called her Mrs. Hill. She lived with a profound hearing problem and wore a bulky hearing aid that hung around her neck with a wire attached to an earpiece. Her deafness made her shy and self-conscious. The Hills adopted a daughter. Mrs. Hill said her husband brought the baby girl home as a surprise. My mother noticed when the daughter grew up, she looked exactly like Mr. Hill."

"Oh my," my hosts exclaim.

"We had our share of excitement on this street." I laughed, "a guy at the end of the block ran one of the biggest gambling dens in town. The players hid their cars in his backyard. The cops raided the joint in the early 1960s. *The San Antonio Evening News* gossip columnist Paul Thompson put the raid in his front-page column, making West Mistletoe Street notorious."

"Across the street, police discovered a mechanic taking stolen cars apart and sending the parts to Mexico. *The San Antonio Light* headlined 'Chop Shop found on Silk Stocking North Side.'" Adriana and Kevin gasped. "My mother was friends with him. She gave the paper a quote. I think she said 'I know Juan wouldn't do anything wrong.'"

We chuckled and moved into the living room. The house filled with light thanks to removing my mother's heavy curtains and Venetian blinds from the 1950s. A big screen TV hangs above the mantle, surrounded by comfortable chairs. I brought my parent's mortgage papers, and a couple of other documents from 1951 when they bought this house.

"My Mother bought this house in 1951 for $23,500, with $9500 down and payments of $121 a month. She put the title in her name. Sometimes those payments stretched the budget, but she never missed one. For the rest of his life, my father complained my mother paid too much. She'd shut him up with a curt, 'I LOVE this house,' and shoot him a look as if to say, 'that's enough out of you.'"

My friends called our house "Tara" because it looks like a miniature version of the mansion in *Gone with the Wind*. Built in 1938, in Mount Vernon style, the front features a two-story porch set off by four columns. The porch creates a grand façade for an otherwise ordinary center hall colonial with three bedrooms, one bathroom, and a half bath under the stairs.

I asked to go upstairs. We walked into their daughter's bedroom on the southeast front corner. As we stepped into the room I said, "my father loved this room. He believed the Gulf breeze gusted up from Galveston right into these windows. I could almost hear him proclaiming, "this is the coolest room in the house! The southeast breeze, that's what does it."

We had to believe in the southeast breeze in the days before air conditioning.

Summer nights, with the windows open, I would sink into a pool of sweat. My father bought a gigantic Westinghouse fan. He wheeled the machine into the hall, turning it on full blast. Hot wind whipped through the rooms. Wooden blinds smacked the window frames. The open windows let in the neighborhood sounds. Dogs barked and howled at the moon. The bells of the nearby Shrine of the Little Flower announced the morning. A rooster crowed. A few blocks away, Peacock Military Academy roused the cadets with "Reveille." Over the years, we installed window air conditioners one room at a time. They muffled those wonderful sounds, but they also cooled the bedrooms making it possible to sleep on a hot summer night.

My sister and I shared this room until I turned 12. My parents allowed me to move to the back bedroom. My mother kept her books in this room. I loved reading about the Algonquin Round Table and the wisecracks of Dorothy Parker including my mother's favorite: "men seldom make passes at girls who wear glasses." I read Bennett Cerf's humor books and the novels of Sinclair Lewis, pretending I lived in the 1920's.

The neighborhood changed as my sister and I grew up. Families moved north to new houses with multiple bathrooms and central air conditioning. Baby boomers, including my sister and me, left for college and didn't return.

Death touched the street. Helen, the Christian Scientist who didn't believe in germs, lost her mother and then her husband. Mrs. Hill's husband died. Little Joe, bitten by the lost cocker spaniel in our back yard, endured the loss of his older sister.

One morning in 1969, my father, just 62 years old, died of a heart attack sitting in a rocking chair that belonged to his grandmother. I still own that rocking chair. A few days later, my mother and I sat in the living room. She jumped and said, "did you see that? Your father was standing there watching us."

His ghost didn't bother my mother. She lived in this house another twenty-seven years. I visited every year and slept in my old room. Some nights, after midnight, I thought I heard my father rummaging around downstairs.

My mother sounded odd on a phone call in 1995. Her doctor diagnosed a stroke, and hospitalized her for a week. I flew home. Mother told me to expect the arrival that week of Gloria, a maid who came every week, yet another in a series of unique characters our house seemed to attract. Gloria possessed a bubbly personality and a beehive hairdo. When I told her about my mother's stroke, Gloria wept.

The owners looked unsure about telling a story but went ahead. "You know, a woman named Gloria knocked on our door a few years ago. She told us she worked for your mother. We invited her in and she asked to see the bathroom because she loved the blue paint. We repainted the bathroom white, but she seemed ok with it."

We laughed and talked some more. After an hour, it felt like time to go. I thanked the couple for their kindness.

The day my mother moved to a graduated care facility she slowly made her way into every room as if to memorize it. This kind family has lived here ever since.

Their children, like my sister and I, grew up in this house. In recent years, San Antonio designated the neighborhood historic. Young families moved back and renovated. I love this neighborhood and love seeing others love it.

I didn't tell the story about my father's ghost. I didn't want to scare them.

It's OK. He's a gentle spirit. He's not the only ghost. The people I knew and the friends I loved, and the ghost of my younger self, they're all here. My mother's here too. She's not in the kitchen. She didn't like to cook. She floats above the roof.

I walked to the curb, turned around, and took one more look, like Emily in *Our Town*.

60
Martha's Vacation: 1942

"I CAME TO SAN ANTONIO on vacation, and I liked it so much, I stayed." My mother told this story all her life. Certainly, there was more to it, but I love her story anyway. Why not fall in love with San Antonio, Texas?

Martha Hightower boarded the train in Nashville, Tennessee, for San Antonio, in 1942. Her roommate Ruth, a chestnut-haired beauty, came to town a few months earlier, intent on marrying a handsome charmer named Smitty. Ruth turned down his proposal in Nashville. Later, she accepted and moved to San Antonio. Things changed, and they broke up. Ruth wrote my mother, telling her to come to San Antonio. Together they would find husbands. Wartime San Antonio brimmed with eligible men.

Late in her life I discovered the rest of Martha's story. It seems my mother came to Texas on the rebound. Her engagement to a Vanderbilt University graduate hit a bump when he introduced my mother to his mother. The old woman told her son he would never satisfy Martha. (My sister and I howled with laughter hearing this. "That was a smart woman.") A college friend visiting my mother let that information slip, knocking a little of the sheen off the tale of discovering a city so wonderful she couldn't leave. I asked my mother about her lost love. She coyly answered, "oh, we don't talk about that." She stuck to her story.

My mother used her lilting Southern accent to charm the world. She grew up the youngest of a well to do family in Athens, Alabama. In 1918, just before her fourth birthday, her mother (my grandmother) died in the Spanish flu epidemic.

With his wife gone, my grandfather brought his parents to live with the family. As the baby of this sad turn of events, raised by her grandmother, Martha received abundant attention. I think of her as a cross between a Tennessee Williams character depending on "the kindness of strangers," and Scarlett O'Hara happy to think about the hard things "tomorrow."

Smitty, the boy Ruth came to marry, joined the Army. Placed in procurement at Fort Sam Houston, Smitty caught on to the system in a flash. As World War II began, the Army hired a massive civilian workforce. Smitty easily found jobs for his friends, including his ex, Ruth. When Martha came to visit, Smitty and Ruth brought her to Fort Sam and signed her up. With a new job and Ruth for a roommate, Martha stayed.

Smitty provided something else. He introduced my mother to my father. Miller Campbell worked with his father managing cigar counters for the Finck Cigar Company. He traveled with his father to the small towns and crossroads of south Texas, hand lettering Travis Club Cigar signs and display cases. Showing me his paint box and brushes, he told stories of country bumpkins watching with awe as he lettered display cases. When his father died, Miller moved on, landing a civilian job at Fort Sam. Martha arrived in the same office. Smitty noticed that Miller noticed Martha and introduced them. Miller asked her out that day.

In 1942, my father was living with his mother in a little bungalow on Roseborough Street in South San Antonio. One Sunday afternoon Miller came home from a golf match. From a distance his mother appeared sleeping on the front porch. He drew close and discovered her slumped, dead of a heart attack. With both parents gone, my father feared loneliness. He pursued my mother with abandon. My parents shared the loss of their mothers.

Martha gleefully recounted her courtship to my sister and me. "Oh, he begged and begged me to marry him. I gave in because he was handsome and played the piano and would drive me anywhere I wanted to go." With a wicked smile, she added, "one time I made him drive me to the Southern Pacific station, so I could say goodbye to another boyfriend going off to war."

They married in the front parlor of Grandfather Hightower's Alabama home in January, 1944, sealing the unlikely union of my college-educated child-of-privilege mother, and my happy-go-lucky, not-quite solid citizen father.

61
Dangling from the Family Tree: 1946

(L-R) Mr. and Mrs. Bennett (hosts), my father Miller Campbell, my mother Martha Campbell, Great Aunt Mamie Dial

"Archie" my mother giggled "When you were born, the city threw a parade in your honor."

I arrived Thursday night, April 25, 1946, during San Antonio's gala Fiesta week. Like New Orleans' Mardi Gras, Fiesta celebrates spring with carnivals, pageants, and parades. Smiling, Martha added: "everybody in San Antonio came to visit you." The Friday Battle of Flowers parade marched by the Santa Rosa Hospital on East Houston Street, giving her visitors a prime view. It took years for me to realize her visitors came to watch the parade, not to see me.

I arrived as my mother discovered the collection of larger-than-life characters dangling from the Campbell family tree. The clan settled in San Antonio not long after the turn of the century when the Finck Cigar Company hired my grandfather, Archie Campbell, as sales manager and second in command. During the first third of the 20th century, Archie traveled the state writing contracts for hotels, stores, and restaurants to sell Finck's premiere brand, Travis Club Cigars. My grandfather and Mr. Finck made regular trips to Cuba to buy tobacco, traveling by boat from Galveston.

Late one night, riding home from mailing a letter downtown, my father told me his father's defining story. "He died of a heart attack in 1938. After the funeral, a woman came to the house, saying she was Archie's 'other wife.' She wanted to know if he left anything to her. We didn't know about her." Miller's mother slammed the door in a fury, and never spoke Archie's name again.

Daddy remembered his father, Archie, speaking respectfully about his thirty-year relationship with the Finck family, and his high paying job with the cigar company. My mother told me my Great Aunt asked why she named me for the family scoundrel. Martha answered she named me for my father, not my grandfather.

Archie's older brother, Zollie Campbell, worked as a cowboy on the Chisholm trail. A tough guy, Zollie joined the Texas Rangers and fought Poncho Villa in the Texas-Mexico border wars. He worked as a bodyguard for Texas Governor "Pa" Ferguson, the only Texas governor impeached by the legislature. "Pa" Ferguson's wife, now remembered as "Ma" Ferguson, won election to take Pa's place. In his later years, Zollie ran a ranch in Floresville, most likely owned by the Fergusons.

Uncle Zollie came to visit the first year my parents married. A grizzled cowboy in his 70s, Zollie clomped up the front steps in his boots and spurs wearing two six shooters, banging on the door with all his might. Miller and Martha weren't home. Zollie shouted, "where's Miller Campbell? I want to see him." That night the neighbor told Martha she thought the sheriff was looking for Miller.

I fondly remember my Great Aunt Georgia as a regal old woman living in a suite in the posh St. Anthony Hotel with her second husband, Harold Kayton, a wealthy businessman and entrepreneur. In photos from her youth, Georgia looks like a "Gibson Girl," with long hair piled on top of her head, clear complexion, and blazing eyes. Her beauty earned her a place in San Antonio society as the wife of a prominent dentist.

Family lore says Georgia's first husband reached for his gun while sitting in a dove blind. The gun fired and blew off his head. Everyone said it was an accident. An old saying goes: "what do you call suicide in Texas?" Answer: "a hunting accident." A little over a year later, Georgia married one of the richest men in San Antonio. Harold was 26, Georgia was 37. Do the math—11 years older than Harold.

My Great Grandmother, Mattie Goode, mother of Zollie, Archie, and Georgia, left Kentucky with her family for Texas after the Civil War. The group settled in Lancaster, south of Dallas. As a young woman, Mattie married George Washington Campbell, my Great Grandfather, in 1874. The newlyweds lived on a farm where Mattie gave birth to Zollie, Archie, and Georgia. Seven years after their marriage, George Campbell died. Mattie rented the farm, moved with her children to Ferris, Texas, and supported the family teaching school.

In 1890, everything changed. Mattie met Doctor James W. Russey, a dentist who talked Mattie into marriage and moving to a ranch in desolate Mitchell County, 275 miles west of Dallas. At forty years old, Mattie gave birth to my Great Aunt Mamie and two years later my Great Uncle Cecil.

Dr. Russey ruled the ranch with an iron hand. Zollie, Archie, and Georgia left as soon as they could. Mamie said Dr. Russey beat her and her brother. After a dozen hard years in Mitchell County, Mattie wrote her oldest sons, Zollie and Archie, to ask for help. The story goes Zollie and Archie showed up and, "ran the old bastard off the ranch."

A middle-aged woman with two small children, Mattie turned to Archie, who solved his mother's plight when he landed the big job with Finck Cigars.

The clan reassembled in San Antonio. Mattie bought a boarding house on Lewis Street near the present-day campus of San Antonio College. Archie and his wife and their two children lived with Mattie and her two children as well as one or two boarders. Mamie married one of Mattie's renters, a food broker named Preston Dial. With the backing of her mother and now prominent sister Georgia, Mamie climbed the rungs of San Antonio society.

Settling into a grand home in the new subdivision of Olmos Park, Mamie worked her way into leadership positions in numerous clubs and organizations. She and her mother set down roots in the socially prominent Travis Park Methodist Church. Undaunted by the sudden death of her husband in 1931, Mamie and her mother created "Miss Mamie's School for Little Children" in the quarters behind her house. A generation of wealthy San Antonio children ran and played in Mamie's backyard while she befriended their parents. Mamie put her boundless energy to work. She earned a living by day, worked a second job afternoons, and lived a society high life by night.

In 1939 Mamie organized the Pan American Council of International-Relations, under whose banner she traveled the world with the mission of, "exporting Texas friendliness to the world." *Life Magazine* profiled Mamie in a 1953 tongue-in-cheek article: "The Eyes, Ears, Nose, and Throat of Texas." Mamie and her council members met with government and royal family officials in far flung locations from New Delhi to Bogota to Beirut. The meetings included the presentation of a Texas Flag and a lusty chorus of "The Eyes of Texas Are Upon You." Mamie would christen bewildered foreign officials "honorary Texans."

Many of the sons of those honorary Texans came to San Antonio to train in the medical facilities on Fort Sam Houston Army base and Lackland Air Force base. Over the years princesses and princes called on and even stayed at Mamie's house. Mamie pulled the strings of her various clubs to entertain the dignitaries and set up future visits of her organization.

Life Magazine mentioned Mamie awarding University of Texas scholarships to foreign students during some of these ceremonies. The magazine's researchers discovered the "scholarship" amounted to a discount available to any foreign student. Like her older half-brother Archie, Mamie knew how to work a room, charm the uncharmable, and cast a spell.

My father considered Mamie a second mother. He grew up with her in the house on Lewis Street. When his mother died, he moved into Mamie's house in Olmos Park, paying a few dollars a week to share a room with Mamie's son and her younger brother Cecil, whom everyone called "Bubba." The household included Mamie's two daughters and at various times their husbands and children plus various guests and dignitaries. When I first watched *You Can't Take It with You*, I thought of Mamie and her house full of characters.

When my father convinced Martha to marry him, he brought her to Mamie's house for the full treatment. Mamie opened her arms, fussing over Martha, while mentally taking note that Martha came from a well-off family. Mamie's daughters pulled out the good china and served tea. "Welcome to the family," Mamie gushed. The visit sealed the deal.

62
The Woman Who Talked All Night

My parents on the San Antonio Riverwalk, 1943

MAMIE TOOK MY NEWLY-WED PARENTS under her wing. She invited them to her well-connected Sunday dinners, invitations that often included a request my mother bring the main dish, or as Martha put it: "Mamie will invite you to a ham dinner and tell you to bring the ham." Mamie's friends liked the young couple. My father was handsome and funny and played piano. Martha had her Southern charm and youth and beauty.

One evening Mamie announced a costume party. Miller came dressed as a woman, wearing one of my mother's skirts. He won the prize, described by my mother as a live chicken, looking old and sick as it squawked in a rickety crate. Martha turned up her nose and refused to take the animal home. The next Sunday, the main course at Mamie's was chicken. My parents remember saying, "oh Aunt Mamie, this chicken is delicious." And dropping their forks when Mamie told them it was the prize from the previous week.

When the war ended, Fort Sam Houston reduced the civilian work force, especially women. Martha stopped working when she got pregnant with me. Miller left a few months later. One of Mamie's friends connected Miller to the insurance business, arranging a job. After training and receiving his license, Miller sold a few policies, then joined a company selling to military recruits on the bases around San Antonio. Agents made pitches to new soldiers herded into meeting rooms. He sold dozens of policies, making enough to support a family and buy a new 1947 Studebaker.

Martha received income from stocks and farms in her mother's estate. In 1948, one of the farms sold, with the money divided between Martha and her brother and sister. Martha invested the nest egg in a duplex near St. Mary's University. The University Park neighborhood sprang up overnight after the War. Veterans and young families snapped up the duplexes.

Martha rented the other side of our duplex to her friend Smitty, who moved in with his wife and daughter. At night the families sat on the porch laughing and smoking while we children played in the front yard. One night, Smitty's wife asked Martha about Martha's Nashville friend who wanted to marry Smitty. The wives put us children to bed, then came back to the porch. My father planned to drive to Dallas on business early the next morning. He left for bed. Smitty, who now owned his own hardware store, turned in for the night. When my father rose early the next morning, Martha and Dorothy were still on the porch, talking. Smitty loved this story, saying it proved Martha could talk all night.

The Korean War made the insurance business even more lucrative. Miller sold insurance on military bases for multiple companies and started a group with agents working for him. Martha received another payment from her mother's estate. Smitty and his family found a new home on Beverly Drive near Jefferson High School. Martha wanted her own home as well. In 1951, a friend described, "the prettiest house in San Antonio, for sale on West Mistletoe Street." Martha took one look and had to have it. For the next forty-five years, everything in our family life; good and bad, joyful, and painful, revolved around the house on West Mistletoe.

63
The House on West Mistletoe

My mother's other favorite story, along with the one about coming to San Antonio and deciding to stay, narrated the first time she saw our house. "When we drove up West Mistletoe Street and stopped in front of this house, the real estate woman saw the look on my face and knew right then I would buy it."

Martha found her dream home during a seller's market, paying full price, $23,500, a striking sum for 1951. She had to have it. The house on West Mistletoe felt like a palace after living in our small duplex.

Saturday mornings, men cranked Briggs and Stratton gasoline powered lawn mowers, hoping to finish their weekly grass cutting before the hottest part of the day. The prettiest lawn on the block belonged to Helen Andrew, who lived two houses west of us. Helen fancied herself an artist. She gardened, created ceramics, painted, and sang, performing light opera for the ladies of the Eastern Star. Helen's voice blasted from the open windows up and down the street during her singing lessons. Dogs howled in harmony as Helen bellowed "He" and "The Lord's Prayer."

My father bought one of the first window air conditioners on the block. The giant Hotpoint machine hung out the window like a steamer trunk. An electrician ran a special 220-volt line to power it. The air conditioner barely fit into the dining room window. We closed the room, turned the machine on high, and huddled around it like Eskimos.

My first grade teacher told Martha she thought I couldn't see the blackboard. An ophthalmologist confirmed her hunch. My mother burst into tears. She wore glasses, often stumbling around without them in the name of vanity. The eye doctor diagnosed me as extremely near-sighted. I wore thick glasses from age six until I turned twenty-two when contact lenses became available.

My sister Marti arrived about the time Lucy delivered Little Ricky on *I Love Lucy*.

Martha named Marti "Martha" for her and "Frances" for her sister. Marti arrived six and a half years after me: a gap that separated us for some years, although Marti now enjoys introducing me as "her much older brother."

Toward the end of her life, I asked my mother to tell me about her favorite time. She remembered the year we moved to West Mistletoe Street. "I found the house I loved. You were here. Your sister was born. It was the happiest time of my life."

64
The Son of a Used Car Salesman

MY FATHER came home with exciting news. He and another insurance agent planned to go into the used car business. As partners, they would buy cars wholesale, sell them retail, and make loads of money. Daddy liked the idea of his own business. He persuaded my mother to sell her duplex, which she kept as a rental property. With that money, Daddy matched his friend's investment. They found a location on Quintana Road on the south side of San Antonio, and named the business Poor Boy Auto Sales.

My mother drove a one-year-old Ford and my father drove a recent model Plymouth. Both cars went on the lot for sale. Daddy would drive a car from their stock. He brought home a different car every night. I loved running to the driveway to see that night's model, sometimes a new Ford, or a two-year-old Oldsmobile or Cadillac. I would climb in, grab the steering wheel, and pretend to drive.

Some boys grow up playing catch with their father. I grew up running around '51 Bucks, '49 Lincolns, and fish-tailed Cadillacs. I loved the smell of gasoline, engine exhaust, and car wax. When a car needed a part, I rode along as Daddy combed junk yards on the worst side of town. I stood next to him during the wholesale car auction, watching old heaps, tailpipes smoking, hoods and trunks open, roll through a crowd of buyers, parade style. As an adult, watching a movie set in the 1940s, 50s, or 60s, I immediately identify the cars, and catch the mistake if a car's year doesn't match a story's time frame.[59]

To replace my mother's car, my father found a giant 1948 Oldsmobile sedan. One afternoon my mother piloted the Oldsmobile home from one of my eye appointments. The car stopped dead, right in the middle of Houston Street, the busiest street downtown. A man on the sidewalk offered to help. My mother got out. The stranger climbed in, started the Oldsmobile, and drove off with my sister Marti and me in the back seat. He drove around the block and returned to the spot where my mother stood, pleased he had helped this woman in distress. My mother got back in, furious, shaking at the thought my sister and I could have been kidnapped. That night, for the first time, I heard my parents exchange harsh words. My mother told my father in no uncertain terms to buy her a decent car. She added, "you'd better straighten this car business out, and quick."

I loved my father's car business, even though it ruined everything. He and his partner didn't get along, nor did they make enough money for both of them. His partner bought him out after the first year. Daddy opened his own car lot on Military Highway near Fort Sam Houston. He put up a sign, "Auto Sales Outlet" and parked twenty or so recent models under a string of lights. The business went well for about a year. When the lease ended, the owner of the property sold the land to a developer for an apartment building. My father had to scrounge around for a new location.

He transferred his cars to the front of a trailer park on the Austin Highway. His stock looked shabby with a bunch of house trailers in the background. Even as a ten-year old, I knew this place wouldn't make it.

The great Texas drought of the 1950s ended with four cloudbursts followed by a series of citywide floods in April and May of 1957. Walking home from school as rainstorms began, I crossed streets turning into rivers, spilling over the curb. West Mistletoe Street intersected with Kampmann Boulevard at the end of our block. Water rose from the intersection all the way to our front porch. Everything in the city stopped, as we endured one flood after another.

Then the sun appeared. The ground dried. My father's business stayed under water. The finance company that lent him the money for his inventory informed him he owed more than his cars were worth. Two men came to the trailer park and repossessed his stock. The business went bust. My parents lost everything except the house on West Mistletoe. Creditors couldn't take it for my father's debts because the deed was in my mother's name. My father never owned anything in his name again.

One night my mother's voice took an unusually hard edge. "I am NOT selling this house," she said. The next week she marched to the school board and applied for work as a substitute elementary school teacher. She used Aunt Mamie as a reference. At the dinner table in front of my sister and me, my mother said as if talking to herself, "the one thing I promised myself I would never do in life is teach school. And now I am." Martha wasn't laughing or joking. She taught first grade for the next twenty-five years.

She never forgave my father.

65
Woodlawn Elementary

Woodlawn Elementary teachers walked the halls in black-leather, square-heeled, lace up shoes, with stern expressions on heavily powdered faces smelling of lavender. Most of these women never married, devoting their lives to shaping young minds. Some started at Woodlawn when it first opened in the 1930s. One teacher arrived each morning in a black 1948 Packard sedan, driven by her father. Misbehaving children earned swift punishment. Elegant old ladies yanked little boys by our shoulders, shaking us into submission, detailing our failings through clenched teeth.

Woodlawn's un-airconditioned classrooms opened to a veranda; a long porch facing southeast to catch the illusive Gulf breeze. Afternoons, teachers opened classroom doors and windows hoping in vain for a cross breeze. Giant fans stirred the haze as the temperature soared.

Many of my classmates were Jewish, including my two best friends, Sheldon and Louie. The Temple Beth-El congregation met in a prominent domed building at Belknap and Ashby near my parent's first apartment. Agudas Achim congregation built a massive new temple at the corner of Donaldson and St. Cloud, just beyond Jefferson Village. The Agudas Achim history page describes the Jefferson neighborhood as the "center of Jewish life in the 1950s." I suspect the neighborhood lacked the deed restrictions of other areas. When my friends turned thirteen, I joined many other gentiles, attending the parties celebrating our friends' bar mitzvahs.

My Home Town

Jefferson Village, one of the first park and shop centers, gave our neighborhood additional glitz. "The Village" included Piggly Wiggly for groceries, Winn's Five and Dime, and Sommer's Drug Store with a soda fountain. Hamburgers cost a quarter. Sodas included the lime freeze: lime sherbet, chipped ice and fizzy water so cold it made your brain ache. Silvey's Record Store sold 45s for $0.89. You could ask for a record, go into a booth, and they would play it for you and you alone, even if you didn't buy it. I would ride my bike to "The Village" and stay for hours.

Near sighted and lousy at sports, I made my way cracking jokes and acting up—I brought a copy of *Life Magazine* to school with President Eisenhower's picture on the cover. I drew a bushy mustache and a monocle on Ike, turning him into Monopoly's money bags character. My teacher grabbed and shook me for disrespecting the President. She kept me out of recess for a week.

Boys discovered girls. Our fifth-grade teacher, Miss Maureen Messimer, suffered a melt-down, screaming at those of us who passed love notes to a girl named Ann. The girl's family moved to Houston, so we turned our focus to beautiful twin sisters Leigh and Lynn. Miss Messimer rewarded the boys in her class that year with low marks in "self-control."

In sixth grade, a local dance instructor organized ballroom classes. Spring filled with elementary school dances and graduation parties. With money she made teaching, my mother paid five dollars a month for my dance lessons. She overrode my father and gave the OK to invite my friends to a dance in our driveway for my 12th birthday. That night, about 9:00pm, my mother announced: "now, children, each boy may pick a girl and take a little walk around the block." Her walk around the block game certainly surprised me. Off we went, to do what sixth grade boys do when they get alone with sixth grade girls. Parents arrived at ten to pick up their daughters, only to discover many of them still out "walking." The event made elementary school history. My mother created the infamous highlight of the season.

The social triumph lifted my spirits after watching my mother's disappointment in my father's business failure. After that party, I determined I would do what I could to help. I took over the yard work, learning to operate the lawn mower and yard tools. Neighbors noticed and hired me for their lawns, even the neighborhood matriarch Helen beckoned me to cut and trim her meticulous garden. I didn't play sports. I cut grass. For the next several years I cared for multiple lawns on our block and stuffed twenty bucks or more a week into my piggy bank.

66
Life With Father

When his car business went bust, my father limped back into selling insurance, knocking on doors for $75 bucks a week. My mother's school teaching salary kept us afloat, and most important to her, covered the mortgage on her house on West Mistletoe. She landed a plum assignment teaching first grade at Ben Franklin Elementary, a ten-minute drive from home.

With my mother working, my father took up the slack. He rose early and made breakfast. He fixed our school lunches. Many nights he cooked. My sister Marti and I feasted on his "famous sandwiches," roast beef with bacon and dill pickle on toasted bread. He specialized in German potato salad—the kind with vinegar and oil and lots of onion instead of mayonnaise. A collection agency hounded Miller looking to settle his business debts. After a while they gave up, writing him off as a lost cause.

A new family moved into the duplex next door. The Caters bonded with my parents, while their children, Bob and Carol became constant companions for my sister Marti and me. We spent all summer together, sometimes in marathon croquet matches in their back yard. When the temperature reached 100, we burrowed inside for endless rounds of Clue, Monopoly, and Canasta. Mrs. Cater and my mother drove us to the Alamo Heights swimming pool. Other times we put on our swim trunks and turned the hose on each other.

A friend of Daddy's from the military insurance days sold new Lincolns at Turbeville Motors on Main Avenue. The friend said the dealership had an opening selling Mercury, Edsel, Rambler, and Jeep cars. Daddy got the job. Salesmen received their own demonstrator. His first day, Miller drove home in a new 1958 red four-door Mercury Monterrey. The shiny new car changed our fortunes overnight.

His used car debacle left my mother with a 1950 Nash, as ugly a car as Detroit ever produced. My father drove a 1948 Hudson in even worse shape. As we rode in back, my sister and I could see the street through a hole in the floor the size of a half dollar. A junk yard bought the Hudson for parts, paying Miller fifty bucks. My mother's teaching job enabled her to buy a not quite worn out 1953 Plymouth. The new Mercury made it possible to send the Nash to the junk yard. My sister and I stood in the front yard as Daddy drove it away, shouting, "goodbye doggy Nash. Goodbye."

Not only would Daddy sell Mercury cars for 1958, he would also sell Ford's imaginative new brand, the Edsel. Sometimes he drove home in a 1958 green and white Edsel Ranger. I loved the push button transmission in the center of the steering wheel, so modern and up to date.

Unfortunately, new car buyers didn't share my enthusiasm. The '58 Edsel and the '58 Mercury flopped. Miller complained about the required high-pressure sales techniques. The sales manager listened to negotiations captured by a hidden microphone. He criticized Daddy for not pushing his customers harder.

The commission on a car came to around $200 bucks. The goal was to sell five cars a month. He rarely sold two. One afternoon he came home early. The look on his face said it all. Fired. The fancy demonstrator went back to the dealer.

That week Miller took his troubles to our rich Aunt Georgia. She gave him $500 bucks, saying she was repaying a loan Miller's father made to her when she was young. He used the money to buy a low mileage '53 Ford for my mother. Miller took the worn-out Plymouth.

Riding around one night, my father and I drove past the dealership. A banner announced the arrival of the new 59s. A giant keyhole graphic covered the window at the end of the showroom, revealing a glimpse of the new model. We stopped and got out. As I gazed at the '59 Mercury, Daddy said ,"Someday, I'll come back and buy a new car from these people. That'll show 'em."

I knew we wouldn't. And we didn't.

My father soldiered on, staying busy and out of my mother's sight, excelling in the art of hanging out. Taking me with him, he would begin an errand to mail a letter, drop it by the post office, stop somewhere for a cup of five cent coffee, and ride through the city telling me stories about people and places and restaurants named Frenchy's Black Cat where they gave you a free meal if you walked in and they didn't have any other customers.

For a while he worked for an insurance company that required a sales report in their Dallas headquarters every Monday morning. The required report created the perfect excuse to visit the Missouri Kansas Texas (Katy) railroad depot on South Flores Street on Sunday night.

The Katy Flyer passenger train departed around 10:00pm. It carried a dozen baggage cars plus a couple of coaches and a Pullman. Most important, *The Katy Flyer* hauled a Railway Post Office car, a rolling railroad mail box. My father gave me the letter to hand to the mailman in the car. The railroad postman looked at the address and double checked, "Dallas?" before placing it in the Dallas mail sack set to arrive early the next morning.

As the train rumbled out, we jumped in our old Plymouth and gunned it up East Houston Street pulling into a vacant lot by the railroad crossing near the Joe Freeman Coliseum. Sitting in the dark, I could faintly hear the diesel horn. Then, a flash of light, as the railroad signal began to ring. The diesel horn blasted again, much louder, short-long-short-short. The ground began to shake as *The Katy Flyer* galloped across East Houston Street, racing into the night. Years later, watching the Air France Concorde land at Dulles Airport, I remembered the excitement of *The Katy Flyer* sprinting toward Dallas.

Picking me up after Boy Scout meetings or school events, Daddy and I stopped at little diners or drug store soda fountains. When he had a few extra bucks, we made our way to Main and Ashby and The Night Hawk, the hangout I loved best. A neon sign with a hawk flapping its wings marked the location. You entered through a side door to a long dark wooden counter with built in mahogany stools. Four booths lined the far wall under little stained-glass windows. My father's routine included a glance toward the booths and the sly aside, "I whispered sweet nothings in your mother's ear in those booths." The aptly named 1942 Edward Hopper painting *Nighthawks* reminds me of my father's San Antonio hangout.

One night we sat down and Daddy gave me a nudge. "Look!" he whispered. "There's Paul Thompson." Oh my God! Paul Thompson, San Antonio's most famous newsman sitting down the counter from us at the Night Hawk. He looked exactly like the drawing of his face that glared from the left side of the front page of *The San Antonio Evening News*: thick black frame glasses, bushy eyebrows, a wide brim fedora, and a snarl. Paul Thompson was San Antonio's version of Walter Winchell. The Night Hawk was his Stork Club.

Paul Thompson's column dished dirt on Baptist preachers running off with other men's wives, gambling dens and city graft, and young girls losing their swimsuit in the Alamo Heights pool—all items I read in his column and still remember.

During the week, after the news on KENS-TV, Paul Thompson grilled the city's most notorious citizens from 10:15pm to 10:30pm on *Paul Thompson's By-Line*. One night, Paul interviewed a stripper from the infamous Green Gate Club on St. Mary's Street. She told Paul she made $75 dollars a week and stripped so she could feed her children. The stripper started crying. Paul looked disgusted. Making no effort to hide his disgust, he snarled a few more questions, and then turned to the camera and hissed, "this is *Paul Thompson's By-Line*. Goodnight." And now he was snarling at the waitress at the counter of the Night Hawk. "Gimmie a piece of chocolate pie, and a cup of coffee."

My father and I froze. We couldn't speak. We certainly dared not speak to Paul Thompson. Just to see him gave my father and me a collective chill. We finished our food and left, thrilled by our glimpse of San Antonio's primo celebrity.

67
Success!

At last, Miller got a break. Yet another of his friends worked in sales for Ray Ellison Homes. The company constructed houses assembly-line-style in the Valley Hi subdivision next to Lackland Air Force Base. Soldiers paid $10,000 or less with no money down thanks to Veteran's benefits. The sales job paid $300 a month plus a commission of $40 a house. During one of his first months, Miller sold fifteen houses at $40 a house. His commission of $600, plus his salary of $300 totaled $900 in one month—a fortune, to us.

Ray Ellison built thousands of homes in San Antonio. I understand he lived a quiet simple life. I have a feeling he liked the musical *South Pacific*, or at least the music from *South Pacific* as Valley Hi sounds a lot to me like "Bali Hi."

Ellison put my father in charge of the new Tradewinds subdivision off SW Military Drive between Kelly and Lackland Air Force Bases. Company landscapers filled Lelani Street, the road in front of the four model homes, with rocks and boulders, suggesting a river instead of a street, constructing Japanese style bridges for prospects to cross as they toured the homes. Strings of electric Japanese lanterns hung between the houses, twinkling at night. A speaker system piped in Hawaiian and Polynesian music, "Sweet Leilani," "Lovely Hula Hands," and Martin Denny's new instrumental album *Quiet Village*. The four Tradewinds model homes and grounds looked like a Hollywood set.

The night before the grand opening, Tai Shan Restaurant catered a lavish Oriental buffet. Mrs. Rose Wu, matriarch of San Antonio's Chinese community, personally supervised. Miller and his salesmen wore tropical shirts with Tradewinds sewn on the pockets. Opening weekend, Miller sold twelve houses. He told us the front office staff applauded when he turned in the contracts Monday morning.

Ironically, many of the soldiers who lived in this pseudo–South Sea development left a few years later for the real thing in Vietnam, trading their home set in *South Pacific* for something closer to *Apocalypse Now*.

Today, the residents of Lelani Street live in one of the city's poorest neighborhoods. I wonder if anyone knows their street once looked magical, like a Polynesian Village, with little bridges crossing a river of boulders, piped in Hawaiian music, and Japanese Lanterns dangling in the breeze.

One afternoon, Miller pulled an ancient scrapbook out of the closet. "These are newspaper clippings my mother kept in the days when I played championship golf." The stories and photos from the 1930s and 1940s covered page after page. *Campbell makes Hole-in-One. Campbell and team to Indianapolis Championship.* My father looked handsome in black and white pictures swinging a golf club. *Campbell wins 1942 San Antonio Golf Association Tournament.* Looking at the articles he said, "Galleries followed the big match and applauded when I won. I've got some old clubs at Aunt Mamie's house. Let's go get them."

He found a beat up nine iron in Mamie's junk filled storage room. He put the club in my hands, showing me the golf grip. "This is how you hold a golf club and this is how you swing it." His demonstration looked like poetry in motion. "If you learn golf, Archie, you can meet people and make friends you would never know otherwise." After a few trips to the driving range, we started playing at Chuck Klein's par three course. The short holes looped around the San Pedro Avenue driving range.

The Accidental Critic

Ray Ellison gave my father Thursdays off. Our Thursday golf at Chuck Klein's progressed to Brackenridge Park, the city's public course and host of the PGA Texas Open. When we entered the old club house, the golf pro smiled and shouted "Welcome back Miller. It's been a long time." Suddenly, caddies and characters appeared out of nowhere to laugh about past golf matches and my father's wild adventures. A group of guys watched him tee off, averting their eyes when I slashed my ball a few yards sideways. My father relaxed completely, making the frustrating game look easy.

Brackenridge Park allowed students to play for 50 cents. I spent a couple of scorching summers knocking around the almost empty layout. The Texas heat made the ground so hard, the city built concrete tees, with rubber mats on top so a player could at least tee up a golf ball. Still, Brackenridge Park possessed charm. The National Youth Administration built beautiful stone bridges and walkways. Curving park roads ambled through the layout. Afternoons, the Butter Krust Bread factory next door baked hundreds of loaves of bread. The smell of fresh bread turned the links into an aromatic dream.

A group of women in the neighborhood sold sandwiches and cold drinks from a stand under a grove of trees next to the 12th green. A pimento cheese sandwich cost thirty cents, a grape or orange soda went for a dime. Beyond golfers, salesmen, truck drivers, and people from the neighborhood bought lunch at the spot everyone called "the 12th hole." Time and a highway erased this unique place, now cut off from the golf course by the 281 freeway. Sometimes, I wander back to look at the abandoned green and old tee box among the weeds. Occasionally, I run into another old-timer doing the same thing.

The Brackenridge links has always drawn unique characters. On one visit, I said hello to an old guy sitting on a bench near the back nine. He pointed to a grove of trees by the river. "See that pecan tree?" he said. "So many golfers have pissed on it, it grows salted pecans."

My father's golf tournament days

68
Life with Mother

My mother spoke with a Southern accent so thick it made people laugh. One afternoon, phoning a friend, the woman's husband answered. When Martha asked for his wife, he answered: "Yessum, I'll go git hur rat away. Dis here's de butlah speakin.'" The guy thought a friend put a strange woman on the phone just to poke fun at him. To my mother's credit, she found this funny. She kept her Southern accent as a badge of honor.

I fondly remember my mother reading to me *The Wind in the Willows*, and poems from Robert Lewis Stevenson's *A Child's Garden of Verses*. Her dream of two children and a house she loved ended when my father's business failed.

My Home Town

Now she taught first grade, juggled my sister and me, and inherited the role of strict parent. It did not help that my early teens coincided with the beginning of her menopause. She regularly burst into tears of frustration.

Every few years, we returned as a family to Athens, Alabama to visit her father, who sent cash for us to make the drive. Those riotous journeys took us on two lane highways through Louisiana, Mississippi, and Alabama. We spent the night in motels named Stonewall Jackson. Bouncing along the lousy roads with all the windows down in our worn out 1953 Plymouth, my mother drilled us on the rules and regulations of the old South. "Do not speak unless spoken to, say thank you, and do not do anything to upset Daddy or especially his wife Ruth."

As a sign of respect, everyone called my grandfather, William Ransom Hightower, "Mr. Will." He owned farms and real estate and a clothing store on the town square. He could talk a farmer just in from the country into buying a Sunday suit, leaving the farmer grateful in the process. He spoke with authority, walked ramrod straight, and looked you straight in the eye.

Athens, Alabama participated in the harsh segregation hard to imagine today. Drinking fountains, restrooms, and the railroad station waiting rooms divided into "White" and "Colored." I watched my grandfather give dollar bills to poor Blacks begging on the town square. I never heard him use the "N" word. In the 1920s the Klan asked him to join. He refused. Yet, he proudly voted for George Wallace for Governor and later President.

Mr. Will lived in one of the finest houses in Athens, Alabama. A large portrait of his first wife "Miss Pearl" hung over the mantle. My mother's mother died in the flu epidemic of 1918. Martha was only three. She told us she remembered the servants stopping the clocks, closing the curtains, turning the mirrors to the wall, and draping the front door in black. Miss Pearl lay in her casket in the living room, Mr. Will weeping by her side.

An equally large portrait of Mr. Will's second wife "Mother Anna" hung next to "Miss Pearl." Mrs. Anna Landis worked for a women's hat company and called on Mr. Will's store. He brought his new wife home as a "surprise" to his three children. My mother and her siblings lived in awe of Mr. Will. Unlike children today, they did not complain about the new mother. After fifteen years of marriage, Mother Anna suffered a stroke, lingered, and died.

A friend of my mother's older sister introduced Mr. Will to a never married Irish redhead in her late 40s. She tipped the scale at 300 pounds. Ruth worked as a home demonstration agent for the state of Alabama, traveling the back roads teaching farm women the basics of cooking, preserving, cleaning, and sanitation. Ruth excelled at cooking. Our trips to Alabama included some of the best meals of my life. Lunch arrived with one or two meats, three or four fresh vegetables, fresh baked rolls, biscuits, or cornbread, homemade pie, or cake with ice cream.

Martha never felt at ease around Ruth, the woman who ruled Mr. Will and his household. Ruth was harsh and judgmental. She gave my sister and me the evil eye, corrected us, snapped her fingers, and kept us in our place. Ruth often spit out the "N" word, especially complaining when her maid needed time off. One of the harshest things I heard Ruth say came when my mother asked about a newly engaged couple. "Well," Ruth sputtered, "she's NOT pretty." Ruth went on to criticize the girl's dress and pony tail and quiet manner. We swallowed our tongue in fear knowing Ruth said worse about us when we left.

Ruth trained a young Black woman "from the country" as her maid. Martha Horton arrived promptly at 7:00am, waiting at the back door. She and Ruth went to work. "Martha, sift the flour for the biscuits. Martha, fold in the lard, Martha, add the baking soda." Each step of the way, Ruth told Martha what to do, every morning for thirty years. We were required to compliment Ruth for the food, even though Martha Horton prepared it.

Breakfast was country ham, ham gravy, scrambled fresh eggs from the hen house, biscuits, fresh peaches, coffee, and prune juice. Martha Horton sat in the corner on a kitchen stool as we ate. The unwritten rule was: "leave something for Martha." She received the food left on the serving platters as her breakfast. She was not allowed to eat until we left the room. Mr. Will's house included a small bathroom next to the carport for the help to use. Martha never used the inside facilities.

At three in the afternoon, Ruth backed out her Pontiac to drive Martha to her unpainted shack in "Colored Town." Martha Horton sat in the back seat while Ruth drove up front. The two women never rode together.

One summer my mother's relationship with Ruth broke permanently. At breakfast, I asked for butter for my biscuit and Ruth insisted I take ham gravy. My mother said, "leave him alone." Ruth slammed her fist on the table, rose up, and screamed, "how dare you tell me what to do in my house?" Ruth charged out of the kitchen. Mr. Will trotted after her. Ruth barely spoke to us during the rest of the visit.

The next year, my mother stayed home, electing to have "female surgery." She sent my sister and me to Alabama. Mr. Will and Ruth acted like nothing happened. Martha never forgot.

My mother's "female surgery" occurred the year I turned 15. In Texas, in those years, 15 years of age qualified me for a driver's license. It took a couple of tries until finally I passed. With my mother laid up for the summer, I changed roles—from sparring partner to helper. I ran errands and grocery shopped. Her tears of frustration turned to smiles of thanks.

My father found a new way to cheer us up. He discovered a way to trigger the telephone bell. He told my mother and sister and me to answer the phone when it rang. We would pick up and he would pitch his voice to a high falsetto to imitate Ruth. Daddy, as Ruth, would tell my sister and me what horrible children we were and how glad she was to have us out of her house. "You chilluns be shore and never come back! Never!" We laughed and laughed and laughed at the pretend phone call from Mr. Will's wife Ruth.

69
Jefferson High

SOME HIGH SCHOOLS LOOK LIKE PRISONS, corralling students like inmates. My high school radiated beauty and inspiration. The Jefferson High School grounds include verandas, rose gardens, courtyard patios, and fountains. The building remains one of the most beautiful in the city, a Spanish palace topped by a domed tower. Opened in 1932, construction costs topped a million dollars, an amazing sum for the time. One elegant explanation portrays Jefferson as representing Depression hopes for future generations. A student project on the school's 50th anniversary successfully added Jefferson to the National Register of Historic Places.

Twentieth Century Fox used the campus as the setting for the 1940 "B" movie comedy *High School*. Jane Withers stars as a wise cracking teen sent from her father's ranch to Jefferson High to learn poise and sophistication. She overcomes early gaffs to win popularity by the film's end. Scenes of the campus appear throughout, including shots of groups of Jefferson students. Channel 5 ran *High School* at least once a year, usually on a Saturday afternoon. The school newspaper, *The Declaration*, alerted us to the showings.

When I attended Jefferson in the 1960s, about half the faculty started their teaching career there in 1932, when the school opened. Three thousand students attended grades ten through twelve. From the beginning, Jefferson excelled. Fans regarded the football team the way big cities worship an NFL team. Arts and performance lovers purchased tickets to school productions for their cultural value, whether their children attended or not.

The girl's drill team, the Lassos, appeared on the cover of *Life Magazine* in 1938. Lassos perform rope tricks, marching onto the football field, twirling ropes around their costumes of blue skirt, red blouse, jaunty neckerchief, white boots and Stetson cowboy hat. The sight of a hundred Lasso girls twirling and marching took your breath away. Every year, girls hoping to join the Lassos lined up on the practice field. Senior Lassos roped selected recruits. Those remaining suffered public humiliation, standing on the field un-roped.

A caste system ruled. Four sororities selected girls by secret ballot. The top club (Shakespeare) took the wealthiest, smartest, and most attractive. The next best sorority (The Martha Jefferson Randolph Society) attracted likeable popular all-around girls. Those elected or rejected learned their fate when the new member list posted on the main bulletin board for all to see.

For boys, the Hayne Club recruited star athletes and big men on campus. Well liked all-around guys joined the Senate (limited to 100 members, or Senators, get it?) One day a week the Hayne members wore deep red Hayne shirts. Senators wore white button-down shirts with Senate on the back. To my surprise, The Senate Club invited me junior year, thanks to a friend who put up my name. Once a member, I learned an "in" group produced a list of approved prospects. We voted accordingly. Our activities included taking care of the Senate patio on school grounds, plus occasional parties, dances, and after school outings.

In spite of the old school social exclusivity, Jefferson showed some forward moves. The school quietly integrated around 1957. My senior year of 1963-64, a Black student named James Jefferson led the football team as quarterback. The exclusive Hayne club extended their invitation to James Jefferson and several other Black athletes. Students called James "Mr. Jefferson." A charismatic, husky athlete, he walked the halls as the biggest of the big men on campus. I wonder if James Jefferson knows he showed the way for white kids like me to grow out of our parent's prejudice.

White kids and Brown kids mixed, despite an unwritten rule. My parent's generation warned white boys not to date Brown girls. Those who made that rule never got a look at Rebecca, whom I took to the movies three different times only to learn she was dumping me to go steady with Gilbert. The rule makers never got a look at Linda, with shapely legs and a spitfire personality. A beautiful Brown girl named Diana asked me to take her to the Senior Prom.

Jefferson allowed students to substitute an elective for gym—great news for near-sighted weakling me. My sophomore year, I marched in the band. The band included fun bus trips and good seats at football games. However, years of struggling with a clarinet after my embarrassing piano recital convinced me to listen to music rather than play it. The next year I tried photography.

Junior year brought bad news. Coming home from school one afternoon, my mother looked grim. "Your father is in the hospital. He had an asthma attack this morning. He collapsed on Mrs. Hill's porch."

Miller's asthma attacks brought on frightening bouts of wheezing, leaving him gasping for breath. He carried a glass atomizer in which he kept drops of dark medicine to spray into his throat. He treated his sinuses with nose drops, inhaled deep into his orifices. Upstairs in my room, I could hear him coughing and clearing his throat.

Martha made her way with my sister and me to St. Benedict's Hospital near the turn of the century King William District. Miller's allergist, an older no-nonsense woman, filled him full of fluids and medicine and kept him in the convalescent wing for a week. The doctor quietly diagnosed the asthma came on because of a panic attack, and suggested my father see a psychiatrist. My mother scoffed. I have a feeling she envied his week in bed. Miller returned to work as soon as they released him.

Business at Tradewinds slowed to a trickle. Miller sold one or two houses a month instead of ten or fifteen. Ray Ellison transferred Miller to a tract across Highway 90. He came home early one afternoon, with the same look as when the Mercury dealer fired him. This time he received $600 severance, his final check after selling Ray Ellison homes for four years.

Once again, my father would have to find a way to bounce back. His real estate license led him to other jobs selling new homes for various builders. At the age of fifty-five, Miller faced an exasperated wife, a son in high school, and a daughter in third grade. He excelled at golf, piano, painting, and hanging out. When it came to supporting a family, he struggled.

70
Fortune Smiles

"A funny thing happened to me at the Trinity Speech Festival. I was the best in the contest, but they gave me second prize." Arch Campbell's flair for comedy got him a second place in the after-dinner speech division at this highly competitive contest.

S PEECH CLASS OPENED THE WORLD TO ME. Our teacher, Betty Ann Janert, stood out from most of the faculty. Not quite 30 years old, she started her career at Jefferson after working her way through San Antonio College and Trinity University.

Miss Janert laughed. She told funny stories. She talked about her life and some of the productions and plays she worked on in college. She taught elements of speech: an interesting open, an action step, and a clear conclusion—the same instructions Bert Shipp gave me later at WFAA—TV when he told me how to produce a news feature.

We received our first assignment: the after dinner or humorous speech. I remembered the previous summer. As

I cut grass on one of my many lawns, the mower threw a jagged rock into my leg, severing the tendons about halfway up my calf, knocking me to the ground. Our family doctor checked me into the Baptist Hospital, where he stitched me together, and put a plaster cast on my leg.

My speech described the accident, my stay in the hospital, and jokes about bed pans, hospital food, and hopping around on a plaster cast, in a nightgown that exposed my backside. The class laughed. Miss Janert laughed and gave me an A. The laughs and the grade gave me confidence.

I loved walking to the podium, notes in hand, giving a speech. Full of myself, I approached my friend Robert Lozano. "Let's perform a two-man comedy act for the school talent show." We signed up for try outs. Miss Jean Longwith, chairman of the Speech and Drama department, approved the acts. An imposing middle-aged woman, she could project her voice from the stage to the top balcony of the auditorium. This formidable woman took some of the toughest kids, turned them into stage hands, and made them cower in fear of her.

MISS JEAN M.
LONGWITH
University of Iowa,
M.F.A.
Masque and Gavel
Spotlighters
Speech

We waited for our audition, suffering through dance numbers, a gymnast, and a bunch of pianists. Finally, we walked on stage and told our jokes. Nobody laughed. Jean Longwith beckoned us to her chair in the auditorium. She stood up, stretched to her full height, and looked down through cat eye glasses at us. Her withering look told us everything. Then she turned to me.

"YOU. I want YOU as my emcee."

I gulped and said, "OK."

The next day Betty Ann Janert

motioned me to her desk. She whispered: "Starting Monday, instead of going to your first period study hall, you will report backstage to Jean Longwith and work on the talent show. You'll have study hall during sixth period instead of this class. It won't affect your grade." Miss Janert smiled and winked at me.

Monday morning, I joined a dozen classmates in the wings of the school auditorium. Miss Longwith arranged us in a circle. "Ok, kids, what are we gonna do for the talent show?" We bounced ideas off each other, settling on a sideshow or carnival setting. I pitched various jokes and nobody, including Miss Longwith, shot me down. Our group pitched as Miss Longwith typed the script.

The curtain would rise, music would play, revealing characters dressed as carnival workers. I would burst through the curtain wearing a black cape with a bright red lining and deliver a line like Bela Lugosi's, "Good evening…" I would follow with a few lines about fate, and the wheel of fortune and introduce the first act.

I would stand off stage during the first performance and return to the front of the curtain to introduce the next act. Sometimes Miss Longwith required longer material to give the stage hands time to set up behind the curtain. During one change over, a heavy chain hit the floor with a CRASH, pushing the curtain toward me. I ad-libbed, "back, Igor, back!" referring to Dr. Frankenstein's hapless assistant in the classic movie. The laughter at my ad-lib sounded like a stadium cheering a touchdown.

The morning of the talent show, just before I went on stage, Miss Longwith pulled me aside and gave me a basic rule of comedy and speaking:

"When you tell a joke, and deliver the punch line, let your audience know it's their turn to laugh." Then, she opened her hand and swept her arm toward the imaginary crowd. It worked.

After the show, I washed off my make-up, hung up my cape, and raced up the stairs to second period economics. When I walked in, the class applauded. The teacher, Miss Julia Oliphint, smiled and said, "Archie, I saw you this morning and you were very good. Congratulations."

After that morning, when a school event needed an emcee, they called me. My hospital speech won a prize in the Trinity University Speech contest. I performed stand up at graduation parties and for a campaign party for a cool junior running for student council president (he lost). When I crossed the stage of the Municipal Auditorium to receive my high school diploma, I received an ovation. Speech class and emceeing the Talent Show changed my life.

The Talent Show required two performances, one for students in the morning, and a second show at night for parents and a panel of judges. The chairman of the San Antonio College Speech and Drama Department was one of the judges. A few days later, Jean Longwith told me to call him. Ron Lucke offered a personal tour of the San Antonio College Theater Department. As we walked around the performing arts complex, he pointed to a control room behind the stage with the equipment for the campus radio station WSAC. Something clicked in me as Professor Lucke revealed Jean Longwith was moving from Jefferson to San Antonio College to teach radio and television.

Back in speech class, Betty Ann Janert pulled me aside. "You have the gift of gab. You ought to go into radio." I knew I would follow Jean Longwith to San Antonio College, and study broadcasting and theater. Two teachers: Jean Longwith and Betty Ann Janert put me on the path I would follow the rest of my life.

71
San Antonio College

Locals called San Antonio College "Sack," a fond nickname for our town's community college. I joined twelve thousand students taking classes. Most of us lived at home, too broke or immature or not quite smart enough to enter a university, much less leave town. SAC wasn't exactly college, but it fit me. I studied the basics—English, history, math, and science.

My high school performing experience prompted me to declare myself a drama major. Besides Jean Longwith's radio and television class, I signed up for Ron Lucke's Speech class. Professor Lucke connected me to my first announcing job: calling the preliminary races at the San Antonio Drag Raceway. On Saturday nights in the summer of 1964, for five bucks, I spoke into a speaker system, and threw the switch for hot rod Chevys, or souped-up Fords to roar up a race track in time trials. In the past, I cut grass all morning to earn five bucks. Now I received the same money for merely talking into a microphone.

That fall, Professor Lucke directed *Macbeth*, casting me as King Duncan. If you know the play, you know Duncan gets bumped off in the first act. In other words, not much of a part, but it put me on stage. I loved hanging around the green room, and the oddball students studying drama. Our Stage Manager, Jay Trevino, ran the back stage area for most productions. Jay threw cast parties at his shotgun shack near the stockyards. We crowded in, all of us underage, drinking and smoking and acting like actors, choking down sloe gin over ice.

In the spring, Professor Lucke directed *Our Town*. He cast me as Professor Willard, the nerdy teacher who explains the history of Grover's Corners to the audience. Later in the play, I spoke as an old man in the graveyard. In rehearsal, Professor Lucke polished Emily's line, "one more look." The line comes before her big speech about the beauty of life. "One more look" has great meaning for me as the people and places and things I love vanish.

Years later, I met Thornton Wilder's nephew when he consulted a production of *Our Town* in Bethesda, Maryland. Tappan Wilder and I talked at length about his Uncle's play. We also discussed actors performing small roles. Like me, Tappen Wilder played Professor Willard in a production of *Our Town*. Except Tappen performed on Broadway, while I performed at San Antonio College.

I loved acting. However, I grew up in a home where commission sales bobbed us along like a rowboat in a storm. I wanted a steady job in life, and I wanted creative work. I focused on broadcasting. In class, Jean Longwith tossed aside the textbook, telling us stories about her life and career.

A San Antonio native, Jean Longwith earned both a Bachelor's and Master's in Theater and Speech at the University of Texas at Austin. Returning to San Antonio as World War II began, she stepped in to lead a local theater company when the male director left for the service. She also produced radio plays during the war. Once the conflict ended and the director returned, and Jean looked toward the new medium of television.

The University of Iowa built one of the first educational television facilities in the country and developed a media studies program. Jean signed up for a PhD. She worked as a director at the new station. She beamed telling us about her work in television's early days. She hadn't quite completed her PhD when her mother suffered a health crisis. Jean told us she settled for an MFA instead of a PhD and returned

My Home Town

home. She took a job as an advertising copywriter, and quit dramatically when she thought a salesman took credit for a jingle she wrote. She moved to teaching, taking over Jefferson's Speech and Theater program.

Jean stood tall, and spoke directly. Her shoulders were slightly off. One hung somewhat lower than the other, a condition that I think caused a certain amount of pain. She smoked, tearing through a pack of Kent cigarettes daily. I believe Jean possessed the brains and fierceness to head up a network or film studio in another time.

Local radio announcers, ad agency people, and television station managers spoke to our class. The question of opportunities for women always came up. The answer usually reflected 1964 values. "Well, they can work as a secretary or do something in the business office." Jean would roll her eyes and glare at the hapless speaker, raising our consciousness for women's rights in the process.

I learned how to operate the WSAC controls, and pulled a regular shift at WSAC radio. Opportunity almost knocked. A classmate told me about an announcer opening at a Stereo FM station. KEEZ-FM played lush music in old school studios in the Tower Life Building. I interviewed, read some copy, and was told to report that night for training. When I arrived, a nervous announcer much older than me oozed resentment. Between his attitude and my lack of experience, the audition went downhill fast. At one point, I lifted the needle off the record playing on the air, throwing the station into silence. The guy blew up and told me to leave.

I really wanted that job. I came home depressed, fearful that broadcasting might not work out for me.

72
The Greatest Store

Joske's of Texas anchored downtown San Antonio in a five-floor art deco building holding everything anybody could possibly want. More than a hundred departments included—tires, saddles, furniture, clothes, jewelry, toys, books, records—everything. Customers wore their best to shop at Joske's.

Founded by a German Jewish immigrant after the Civil War, Joske's thrived. By the 1930's the store covered a city block in a building so large, people called it "the Big Store." Joske's adopted the slogan: "the Largest Store in the Largest State."

In 1959, Alaska joined the union, making Texas the second largest state. Joske's made a one-word change. They changed "largest" to "greatest." The new slogan sounded like poetry: "Joske's of Texas, by the Alamo, San Antonio. The Greatest Store in the Greatest State."

Shoppers glided from floor to floor on escalators, among the first in Texas. Joske's staged civic events in the store auditorium. Joske's sponsored beauty pageants. My attractive Jefferson High School classmate Kathy Weir became "Miss Teena Texas," or Teen of Texas, modeling clothes for Joske's her senior year. At Christmas, "Fantasyland" featured a life-sized train taking kids to see Santa. Women in white gloves paused their shopping for refreshments in "The Camilla Room," Joske's tea room.

I ran into my high school friend Richard Doerr at SAC. He told me he worked at Joske's and that they hired a bunch of students for the summer. "Go fill out an application and I'll fix the rest." Richard's father sold jewelry, and I think supplied Joske's jewelry department. The connection helped

Richard win a plum job in the advertising department. The job came through. Joske's called offering temporary work at $1.25 an hour, telling me to report to Budget Furniture.

The guy who ran Budget Furniture was in his early thirties, a little gruff but funny. At first, I climbed shelves in a warehouse writing down inventory numbers on unsold furniture. After a few days, I stayed in the show room and ran errands. Budget Furniture's staff included a witty woman in her 60's and an old guy who appeared half Jewish and half Mexican. I think he spoke Spanish and handled Spanish speaking customers. The old man and old woman laughed and bickered. One morning the old guy came in talking about drinking. "I tell ya," he said, "they ought to call tequila 'to kill ya.'"

Richard told me the guy who worked in the advertising morgue was leaving. I could have this plum job. Advertising people called the room that housed the archives of Joske's newspaper ads "the morgue." Richard started in the morgue and worked his way to composition. After climbing around stacks of furniture, the morgue sounded great.

I reported to the lavish third floor office of advertising chief executive Miss Carolyn Shelton. She wore an expensive suit and spoke with a European accent. She told me Richard recommended me, and I would start the next week. She told me to wear a coat and tie and waved me out of her office.

I learned Miss Shelton moved to San Antonio from Washington, D.C. where she managed advertising for Garfinkel's, another legendary department store. Later she won acclaim for her work as a watercolor artist. She designed several of the posters for San Antonio's annual Fiesta. Many consider Carolyn Shelton's watercolors collector's items.

The advertising manager, a nice guy named Bill, showed me the morgue, a room full of newspaper sized books. Each book covered a month. In the morning I was to cut all of the Joske's ads from the previous day's editions of *The San Antonio Express, The San Antonio Evening News,* and *The San Antonio Light,* pasting them in order starting with the A section.

Around 1:00pm, the papers sent proofs of the ads—a "test" page to see how they looked-for the next day. My job included delivering those proofs to the various buyers in the store for approval. The ads would not run without a buyer's and the manager's approval. Our morning coffee break came at 10:30pm and lasted fifteen minutes. Lunch break: noon to 1:00pm. The afternoon coffee break began at 2:30pm. My last stop of the day came when I delivered the approved ads to the gruff executive who managed retail sales.

Richard took me aside my first day and said, "look—we all take our afternoon coffee break together. Stamp the time clock with your out time at 2:30pm but don't stamp your return time. Bill will write in that number, so we can all visit as long as we want." The afternoon coffee break lasted up to an hour.

Pasting the ads in the big archive books didn't take long. Cutting them out was fun. Roaming the store was even better as I searched for the buyer in various departments. I waited for the buyer's signature. Sometimes I would drop the ad off and return when paged. All afternoon the intercom announced: "Arch Campbell, report to…"

Buyers checked those proofs carefully because printers loved to play jokes. The best accidental on purpose misprint on my watch came in an ad for Girl's Sportswear. Bobbie Brooks manufactured a line of culottes called Bobbie Brooks Bobbies. The printers added an "o" and dropped a "b" making them Bobbie Brooks Boobies. The buyer, a young woman just a little older than me, started giggling, and so did I, even though we were both a little embarrassed. On the other hand, if the mistake went through, she might have lost her job.

Most of the buyers worked in little offices hidden behind the sales counters, generally places the departments stored inventory. One afternoon I looked for the buyer in women's foundations. Without thinking I walked through the hall by the dressing rooms. The buyer rushed up to me shaking, "what are you doing? Women are trying on girdles in there!" Ironically one of my high school friends was in one of the rooms struggling to try on a girdle. Melinda stuck her head out from behind the curtain to say, "Hi Archie." I was completely embarrassed. Whenever that buyer saw me, she gave me the stink eye.

A group of fun creatives worked in Joske's Advertising Department. The staff artist, a sophisticated woman in her 40s, sketched in the southwest corner of our offices where the sun poured in. She looked elegant in her smock as she drew ladies' underwear hanging on a manikin. A display window designer lived a block away in an apartment over the San Antonio river. He told me he didn't own a car, adding "On the weekend I catch the bus and ride to the Alamo Heights Swimming Pool. It's my day in the country." Then he threw his head back and laughed.

Downtown San Antonio filled with excitement as work began on HemisFair '68, the World's Fair planned for the acres just south of Joske's between Commerce Street and Durango. New restaurants and clubs prepared to open in the empty spaces under the buildings along the San Antonio River Walk. I loved lunch hour, strolling downtown, and eating a sandwich at Shilo's Delicatessen, or trying the new pizza place on the riverwalk.

Every afternoon at 2:30pm we punched out and gathered at a long table in the Camilla Room, where we drank coffee and ate cake and traded funny stories. That summer of 1965, Joske's merged with the other big downtown department store Wolfe and Marx. Joske's wanted Wolfe and Marx's suburban location at the new North Star Mall. Amazingly, Joske's folded most of the Wolfe and Marx staff into the new combined company.

One of the Wolfe and Marx copywriters told the story of the Wolfe and Marx Texas state flag. To mark an annual sale beginning the week of March 2nd, known as Texas Independence Day, Wolfe and Marx draped a gigantic Texas flag over the entire front of their eight-story building. When the merger happened, somebody made off with the flag. "Imagine all the bird shit on it," the copywriter said, and we laughed and laughed.

Joske employees received a ten per cent discount. As I made my rounds I also shopped. On payday, employees received their money from the top floor accounting office in an envelope with cash inside, down to the penny. We joked that between the discount and the cash, some of the employees were broke by the time they made it to the parking lot.

Joske's stayed open until nine one night a week, Thursday. Other days, the store closed at six. Many of the stern men and women executives headed next door to the Menger Hotel bar. Historians say Teddy Roosevelt recruited the Rough Riders for the Spanish American War in the Menger Bar. I found it funny that this was where the severe adults to whom I delivered ad proofs drowned their frustrations after work.

The regular shifts at Joske's and the money I tucked away from various odd jobs gave me enough to buy a four-year old MG Midget. For $800 bucks, I received transportation barely a step above a motorcycle. I remember Texas charged a license plate fee based on weight. My license plate cost 4 bucks. I think it cost 3 bucks to fill the gas tank. For heat in the winter, I opened a valve that let the engine heat blow on my feet.

I began to think about advertising as a career. I loved the people. I loved the culture. Then, Jean Longwith called.

"I want you to work as my Program Director. I'll pay you $1.25 an hour for 20 hours a week under the work/study program. You'll run WSAC and help me with my classes."

I gave Caroline Shelton two weeks' notice. She turned up her nose and said, "you just got here," and waved me out of her office. Richard found somebody else to take care of the morgue. I hated to leave that job, one of the best I ever had. However, Jean Longwith offered me a path toward the life I wanted.

My summer at Joske's came at a crossroads. Customers began to skip downtown stores for the malls in the suburbs. In the 1980s, a renovation connected a hotel and shopping mall to the store. Because of the construction, Joske's announced a temporary closure. However, the grand old store never reopened. A different department store, Dillard's, took over a few floors. Some years later, a developer turned the once beautiful art deco building into a food court. Tourists walk in with no idea of the style and excitement this space once represented.

"Joske's of Texas, by the Alamo, San Antonio. The Greatest Store in the Greatest State."

It's only a memory now, a beloved memory to me.

73
Radio

Arch Campbell, station manager, signals to Albert Kennedy that Radio Station WSAC is on the air. Broadcasting on a six-hour schedule, the closed circuit radio station provides Student Center listeners with music and news.

THE CAMPUS radio station and studio teaching space behind McAllister Auditorium became my domain at San Antonio College. As Jean Longwith's assistant and WSAC Program Director, I earned my $25.00 a week, going on the air and scheduling students for air shifts at WSAC. I filled in for Jean in class, handing out assignments while she worked on her big idea.

Jean persuaded the administration to build an on the air educational FM station. She used her formidable powers selling the idea. She found a grant, hired an engineer, drew up plans, and got the ball rolling for one of the first educational FM stations licensed to a community college.

The campus station nicknamed WSAC wasn't exactly a radio station. The control room sent music and our voice into the San Antonio College student union. The school's President, Dr. Wayland P. Moody, blew a gasket the year before Jean Longwith arrived. Dr. Moody walked into the student union and heard a Beatles record. He and the previous instructor got into a fight over music and the instructor left, creating the opening for Jean. She loved to fight, but preferred her dream of an FM station to an argument over music.

My job, as her assistant, included making sure WSAC didn't play anything that would disturb Dr. Moody. To avoid the President's wrath, our speaker played at the lowest volume possible. Basically, WSAC's listening audience boiled down to the one or two students who happened to be standing next to the speaker.

WSAC needed record albums. The school found a few dollars to buy some albums of middle of the road music—Henry Mancini, Andy Williams, Barbara Streisand, and similar artists. It dawned on me the FM commercial stations in town changing from mono to stereo might have some mono albums to give away. I called around, got brushed off by a few stations, and made an important connection.

The Program Director of KITY-FM, John Walk, invited me to the station. Johnny was a friendly guy about ten years my senior. He gave me a stack of albums and asked that I write a thank you letter to the station owner, Jack Roth. I sent the letter. A month later John Walk called. "We need a weekend announcer. Do you want to do it?"

KITY FM shared spotless studios with the city's major top 40 station KONO-AM in a 1930s building on Arden Groove Street behind KONO-TV. The control room hummed with top-of-the-line equipment, transmitting with the strongest signal allowed, 100,000 watts. Unlike my earlier experience, the announcer training me had a vested interest in my success. He wanted to stop working weekends. The KITY control room equipment was simple to operate. John called during my training. The guy showing me the ropes gave his approval. Over the phone, John offered $2.25 an hour for two shifts, 6:00pm to midnight, Saturday and Sunday.

FM radio broadcast a static free signal superior to AM radio. The arrival of television overshadowed FM and its technical benefits. AM remained the established favorite. In the early 1960s FM received its "ah-ha" moment—the introduction of stereo LP records. Radio engineers developed a method to broadcast dual channels or "stereo" on FM. Hi fidelity fans noticed and began buying FM receivers.

By 1965, KITY-FM was attracting a surprisingly large audience. As an announcer, I read news headlines on the hour, played two cuts of music, announced the titles, introduced myself, noted the time and temperature and played a commercial. Following the commercial, I introduced the next two songs. Good ratings verified our successful format, two songs in a row, some talk and information, a few commercials and headlines on the hour.

The Roth family owned KITY FM and KONO AM. The family patriarch "Papa" Gene Roth built KONO as a hobby in his garage in the 1920s. The station, one of the first in town, morphed into a commercial success, featuring country and western music and live performances. In the 1950s KONO switched to top 40 music. Teenagers and transistor radios and rock and roll made KONO a powerhouse. KONO and KITY combined attracted almost a third of all radio listeners in San Antonio.

"Papa" Gene's sons monetized the business. The Roth family won the license for the city's third major TV station KONO-TV. The family ran the AM/FM/TV facility like a Swiss watch, with son Gene Roth in charge of television and son Jack Roth in charge of radio. KONO radio disc-jockeys earned top dollar, $800 to $1000 a month. When a disc jockey's ratings fell, management showed no mercy. Personalities vanished overnight. The Roths ran a no-nonsense business.

My weekend shifts on KITY-FM and my weekday job as WSAC program director built up my savings and sharpened my work ethic. I slogged through math and science, and enjoyed history and English. In two years at San Antonio College, I earned an Associate of Arts degree.

The announcer who trained me moved to the sales department. John Walk offered me a weekday on-air shift. I would work late afternoons and Sunday mornings, and receive a raise to $3.25 an hour. The schedule worked perfectly with my class schedule.

I told Jean Longwith my new full-time job would interfere with my work for her. I resigned as program director. She didn't like it, and glared at me. "Well, you have to manage your time, and that opportunity pays more than I can." She charged ahead building her FM, and enlarging her department.

KITY FM's format fit my deep resonant voice. I didn't shout and scream like the top 40 jocks. I announced. I worked with professionals, including a delightful woman named Nancy Terry. She hosted the eight to midnight shift, and gained attention as the only female radio voice in town. A dark-haired sophisticate in her 40s, she returned to San Antonio after working in New York. I loved hearing her stories when she joined us for gossip in a local beer joint. At age 20, I was working with grown-ups, keeping an adult schedule. I made good money and accumulated professional experience. I felt like I had found my place.

Jean Longwith's station signed on the air in the fall of 1966 as KSYM-FM. The call letters KSAC and WSAC already existed, so Jean chose KSYM to stand for "symposium." She planned to produce educational programs using college faculty. Over time, KSYM launched careers and grew into an important voice as well as an outlet for regional music. Promoted to Radio/TV Department Chairman,

Jean hired additional teachers, added classes, and retired as Professor Emeritus in 1986. In 2005, San Antonio college constructed a Radio/TV/Film Center. The college named it the Jean Longwith Radio Television Building.

74
I'll Be Back

In 1966, only two Texas Universities offered a Radio/TV degree—the University of Houston and the University of Texas at Austin. I chose UT Austin, only eighty miles from San Antonio and a major school. As a state resident, my tuition cost $60 a semester.

At KITY-FM, the owners fired John Walk, the Program Director who hired me a year earlier. A new schedule eliminated my weekday shift, cutting me back to weekends. The loss of my weekday job made leaving for UT easier.

At home, my mother continued to regale us with her story of coming to San Antonio on vacation and never leaving. Her friend Smitty often dropped in. He and my mother relived their days working at Fort Sam Houston, and the year the families lived next to each other in Martha's duplex on West Cincinnati Street.

When I could, I rode along with my father on his "errands" to mail a letter, or stop at a drug store for five cent coffee and pick up medicine. His asthma attacks increased. A new doctor prescribed a form of cortisone. The drug curved Miller's spine. The man I remembered jauntily walking like Fred Astaire, now moved bent forward with a slow step, even as he laughed and joked.

Miller stayed in the real estate busines, working for several builders, including E. H. "Cotton" Jaroszewski, who built custom homes in different subdivisions around town. Cotton hired Miller as his chief salesman and put him on a regular salary. In the model home, Miller brought out his paint brushes and created small display signs extolling the virtues of the house for sale. He read Almanacs, learning various statistics and facts for fun. Despite his poor health, he kept a golf club nearby to work on his golf swing, even though he hadn't played in years.

My sister Marti was growing up. Now a teenager, she bonded with a group of girls who became lifetime friends and extended family. The father of Laurie and Tessie Hill owned a painting and decorating company. Martha liked the Hill family, and hired Mr. Hill's company to paint our house inside and out, and replace the old wallpaper. When they finished, the house on West Mistletoe looked as good as the day in 1951 when Martha got out of the car, took one look, and told the realtor she'd buy it.

San Antonio tugged at me. My radio job opened a grown-up world. I discovered "only in San Antonio" places. Hipp's Bubble Room sold beer in a soda glass for a quarter. The only light inside came from strings of Christmas tree bubble lights. The juke box propped up a Christmas tree year-round. Bob Wills sang "San Antonio Rose." The Sons of the Pioneers sang "Cool Water." Eddie Arnold offered "Cattle Call." The house specialty—Shy Poke Eggs—was a crispy tortilla with white cheese and a round piece of yellow cheese in the middle on top of a jalapeno pepper. Once out of the broiler, they looked like a fried egg, instead of their true self: a world class nacho. A Lionel train went round and round on top of the bar. Hipp put his slogan on the menu: "like the inside of a Christmas package."

One year my mother's brother Baylis and his daughter Nell came to visit. My wealthy Aunt Georgia held open house every Sunday morning, so we dropped by. Aunt Mamie never missed those Sunday morning occasions. Mamie took notice of my uncle's pretty daughter Nell. She immediately arranged for her shy grandson Jack to take Nell to the movies. Then Mamie added, "oh honey, the Pan American Council will hold our summer celebration Tuesday night on my lawn. Come on over about seven."

The big night, we turned up Park Hill Drive to find the street choked with cars. Mamie's house lit up with strings of colored lights and live music. A crowd jostled for space in her front yard. Mariachis played while matrons in summer dresses served cookies and punch. The music and the people and the night air made a heady mix.

The band played a flourish. All heads turned toward the porch as Aunt Mamie stepped to the microphone on a portable stage.

"Good evening everyone, and welcome to our little lawn party. Tonight, we are graced by the presence of a beautiful young woman who has just returned from California. Please welcome, Rosita Fernandez."

Rosita walked on stage smiling at the applause. She wore a beautiful Mexican peasant blouse and skirt. Her thousand-watt smile dazzled.

"Oh thank you, Miss Mamie. I have been performing in New York, and I just finished filming a segment for Mr. Walt Disney on his television show, 'Sancho, the Homing Steer.' I loved meeting Mr. Disney, and working in California and New York."

And then Rosita paused.

"But, ahhhhh…San Antonio."

The crowd burst into a combination of laughter, appreciation, and applause. The band began her music and Rosita sang the Mexican ballad of lovesickness "Cucurrucucu Paloma," the song of the mourning dove.

Rosita stayed in San Antonio, performing every summer on the downtown Riverwalk spectacle *Fiesta Noche del Rio*. She performed her grand finale standing by the arched bridge over the San Antonio River leading to La Villita. In recent years, the city named the bridge "Rosita's Bridge."

Thanks to that memorable night in Aunt Mamie's yard, whenever I return, I whisper, "ah, San Antonio."

August 1st, 1966, former Marine Charles Whitman rode the elevator to the 27th floor observation deck of the University of Texas tower. Armed with a rifle and other weapons, he started firing, killing 13 people and injuring 31 others. Watching the coverage on the national news, it never occurred to me to change schools nor did the event bother my parents. We shrugged it off.

At the end of the month, preparing to move to Austin, I packed my faded red MG Midget with my clothes, some sheets and towels, my records, and stereo equipment. My mother and father came out to the driveway. I climbed into my car, looked up, smiled and said, "I'll be back."

75
UT Austin

UT Campus life snapped back to normal a month after the Tower shooting. Forty thousand students jammed classes, cheered the football team, drank beer, and searched for connections to the opposite sex. UT closed the Tower observation deck that fall, and reopened it a few months later.

My mother insisted I join "rush," the annual Fraternity pledge week, about which I knew nothing. Hundreds of mostly 18-year-old boys gathered in Gregory Gym, signing up to visit various fraternities in the hope of receiving an invitation to join. Martha wanted me to join the fraternity her brother joined at Washington and Lee in the 1930s. Her brother wrote and his fraternity invited me to a party in Dallas, where I drank too much and made a fool of myself. Thinking I was "in" I signed up to visit during the first of three rounds of invitations. When the second-round invitations arrived, the group cut me. I ran into some of them later and they laughed at me. My childhood friend Sam Goldfarb spoke up for me at his fraternity, Lambda Chi Alpha. I joined, even though I never quite fit.

My high school friend Eric Shaw and I split an apartment near campus for $89 bucks a month. Sometimes to save money, we walked up alleys collecting glass soda bottles, worth 2 cents when you turned them in. With thirty bottles, we could score a package of hot tamales sold at convenience stores. Looking our oldest, we often managed to buy a six pack of Old Milwaukee on sale for $0.89. Eric joined Lambda Chi Alpha. Our monthly dues bought us lunch and dinner, alcohol fueled parties, and a few friendships.

I passed the basic classes in English, history, science, and math at San Antonio College. To complete a degree, I only needed a few broadcast credits, some electives, and to somehow find a way to finish four semesters of Spanish.

The University combined Journalism, Radio/TV, and Speech for the new School of Communications. With only a few students and not many professors, the place felt like a small town, surrounded by the gigantic UT Campus. Professor Ernest Sharpe taught advertising. Dr. Sharpe was an unusually kind man who showed a genuine interest in his students. Professor Glen Phillips, who taught while working on his PhD, anchored the news before coming to Austin. He took an interest in my talent. Both became trusted mentors. I think they took their cues from Dr. Dewitt C. Reddick, who presided over the Communication School with a kind and gentle hand.

Years later, I interviewed columnist Liz Smith about her just published memoir. Liz Smith graduated in journalism from the University of Texas in the late 1940s. The cameraman assigned to the interview was running late, so Liz and I talked and visited and traded memories of the University and especially of Dr. Reddick. An hour went by and our chat made it feel like five minutes.

I registered for a class in TV production, as well as a broadcast news lab where we wrote copy and delivered news on the University's radio station KUT-FM. The instructor, Phil Miller, anchored the 6:00pm and 10:00pm sports on KTBC Channel 7. He told me KTBC-AM needed a weekend announcer. That tip led to a four year connection.

76
KTBC Austin

Every radio and TV station I worked for came with quirks and oddities. However, few broadcast outfits possessed the array of eccentricities of KTBC in Austin.

The President of the United States controlled the station. Technically Lyndon B. Johnson's wife Lady Bird owned KTBC. Nevertheless, President Johnson's personality and position hovered over everything. KTBC AM/FM/TV commanded respect, and a certain amount of fear in Austin.

Friends in high places assured the organization's success. KTBC-TV Channel 7, licensed as the only VHF station in town, affiliated with all three networks. Let me explain. Channel 7 was the only VHS channel over the air. It carried all three networks ABC. CBS, and NBC. KTBC monopolized TV in Austin. Period.

Every thirteen weeks, KTBC TV chose the top programs offered by the networks. In the mid 60s, a competing station with a weak UHF frequency signed on. That station KHFI-TV, could only air programs KTBC didn't want. A cable system, Capitol Cable, brought stations from San Antonio into Austin. The Johnsons owned Capitol Cable.

I made an appointment to meet KTBC's Radio Program director, Joe Roddy, at the studios just off Congress on 10th Street. Roddy, a rumpled guy in his mid-40s, led me to a microphone in an adjoining studio. I read some copy and he waved me back to the control room. "You're hired!" Roddy grumbled. KTBC paid $2.00 an hour. I told him I made $3.25 in San Antonio. Roddy said $2.00, but if it worked out, he would arrange a raise.

For a time, Roddy managed a station for Gordon McLendon, the legendary broadcaster credited with inventing the Top 40 format. Joe Roddy regaled us at announcer meetings with stories of Gordon McLendon and the stunts created to promote his stations. One spring, McLendon's station in San Antonio, KTSA, touted an Easter Egg Hunt. On Easter Sunday, the station announced a $1,000 Golden Egg hidden somewhere in San Pedro Park. Thousands of listeners, including my father and me, responded to the "KTSA Easter Egg Hunt," tearing the historic park near downtown to shreds. Roddy told us LBJ hired him to revive KTBC radio. "We're gonna shake up KTBC the way McLendon shook up San Pedro Park."

KTBC AM carried a nine-minute CBS Radio newscast on the hour, followed by five minutes of local news, and a five-minute CBS feature on the half hour. Arthur Godfrey, a throw-back performer from radio in the 1940's and television in the 1950's hosted a one-hour radio variety show from 10 to 11 am, crooning and telling stale jokes. The KTBC control room held a scratchy collection of outdated "big band" albums. The night time announcer, a UT student, tracked albums while he studied. At a time of great changes in society and in radio, KTBC AM stayed firmly stuck in the past.

KTBC provided home base for a favorite son, Richard "Cactus" Pryor. President Johnson anointed Cactus his favorite master of ceremonies, calling on him to emcee events and parties at the White House and LBJ Ranch. A gifted comedian with a style like Bob Hope, Cactus could have achieved success on a national level. I think he preferred the life of a big fish in a small pond. Cactus hosted a weekday morning radio show from 8:15am to 9:30am with "Packer Jack" Wallace, an older announcer with a full-grown beard who also appeared as a side kick on KTBC-TV's afternoon kid's cartoon show.

My Home Town

The Cac and Jack Show followed an early morning news block that included the daily announcement of the school lunch menu. "Today the Austin school district cafeterias will serve roast turkey, buttered beans, potatoes, salad and a fruit cup." Joe Roddy tried to eliminate the school lunch announcement. Howls of protests kept it on the air.

Once a week, the receptionist opened the intercom announcing, "the EGGS have arrived. The EGGS from the LBJ Ranch have arrived." Ranch hands brought fresh eggs from Johnson's hill country property to sell to employees, along with fresh butter, and rings of smoked turkey sausage. A stampede to the lobby followed the egg announcement.

The Johnsons maintained an apartment on the top floor of the building. One afternoon, as I came into the lobby, a stocky take charge woman with a head full of grey hair looked at me and said, "you. Get my luggage." I picked up bags belonging to Liz Carpenter, at the time, Lady Bird Johnson's press secretary. I followed her into the elevator. Liz Carpenter pressed the Penthouse button and up we went. I lugged her bags to the guest room. She did not offer a tip.

"EASY" ARCH CAMPBELL

Arch, a native of San Antonio, brings to KTBC-Radio a fine background in broadcasting. His relaxing style travels with you wherever you go in Central Texas, each weekend. In addition to his Radio 59 duties, he also has a regular show on KTBC-FM. Arch is studying for a Masters Degree at the University of Texas.

LISTEN TO THE "EASY" ARCH CAMPBELL SHOW ON RADIO 59 AND KTBC-FM

The Accidental Critic

I was working on the air Sunday night March 31, 1968, when President Johnson delivered a speech on the war in Vietnam. At the conclusion, he announced, "I shall not seek, and I will not accept, the nomination of my party for another term as your president." From the newsroom I heard several people shout, "WHAT?" The news people screaming knew the announcement meant Lyndon Johnson would return to Texas and micromanage KTBC. After he left the White House, I often saw the former President enter the building through a side door, opening into a seldom used radio studio. LBJ was big and tall and fearsome; with long hair curling at his neck. Employees averted their glance, knowing never to make eye contact with the former President.

One morning in the garage next to the building, a soft voice behind me said, "you. Over there. Come help me." The voice belonged to Lady Bird Johnson. She stood outside her new Chrysler station wagon. The headlights remained on. "I can't get my lights to shut off." I stepped into the car and figured out the system had a delay switch, to keep the lights on until the driver safely exited. I flipped the switch to the off position and the lights cut off. "Thank you," Mrs. Johnson said as we walked into the station. I opened the door for her and turned to the left toward the control rooms. The switchboard operator told me Mrs. Johnson turned to her and silently mouthed the words, "who's that?"

KTBC radio remained stuck in the past while Top 40 and other formats gained listeners. Joe Roddy wrangled the go ahead to try to transform KTBC Radio. He offered me a full-time job working nights for $400 bucks a month. The job made it possible to trade my rattle trap MG Midget for a new '67 Ford Mustang.

Joe Roddy added more contemporary music and hired some announcers with top 40 experience. Every now and then Cactus, who held the title Program Manager, would object to a record he didn't like and make a big show of denouncing and breaking the record on the air. Cactus came of age in the 1940s and 1950s and preferred the music of those years.

I completed my degree in Radio/Television/Film with one glitch. I flunked the last semester of Spanish, throwing me into summer school for another six weeks. A kind instructor took pity and gave me a D minus, just enough to finish. That year, 1968, I was among a handful of students graduating with a Bachelor of Science in Radio/TV/Film. In the years to come, hundreds of students would earn Radio/TV/Film degrees from the University of Texas at Austin every year. The year I graduated, eight of us received Radio/TV/Film degrees.

77
Grad School

I MISSED SAN ANTONIO. NO PLACE IN AUSTIN compared to Hipp's Bubble Room; although I did spend a good bit of time in Schultz's Beer Garden, where they rarely checked IDs. If you showed them your driver's license on your 21st birthday, Schultz's gave you a free pitcher of beer, an Austin rite of passage.

Every few months, my Dad drove up for dinner and a visit. The newly completed Interstate 35 made the drive from San Antonio an easy hour and fifteen minutes. Naturally we met at the Night Hawk on South Congress Street, the sister restaurant of his favorite spot in San Antonio. We also favored the Hoffbrau on East Sixth Street, where they served T-Bone steak, white bread, fried potatoes, and salad drenched in olive oil. Customers called to reserve one of the limited number of steaks cooked each night.

My father wanted to hear all about my job at KTBC. He loved that I worked in radio, the technology that fascinated him as a boy. He nicknamed me "the Voice." Letters from him begin ,"Dear 'Voice.'" He supported everything I found interesting. I could relax completely when he visited. Ever the night owl, he drove back to San Antonio after we finished dinner, arriving back home at 11:00pm or midnight. When I came home to visit, often leaving after my night shift and arriving around 2:00am, I'd find him waiting in the kitchen, with a fresh cooked hamburger.

The School of Communications added graduate studies. Dr. Ernest Sharpe, my teacher and friend who taught advertising, asked me to sign up for the new Master's program. I think he listened to me on KTBC Radio, and liked my voice and jokes. Frankly, the new graduate school needed students. I held a good job in Austin and tuition was cheap. Given the cut-throat nature of radio, I hoped a Master's might pave the way for me to return to San Antonio College and teach in Jean Longwith's expanding Radio/TV department.

Because of my experience at KITY FM, I researched the history of FM radio for a class. My initial interest turned into a Master's thesis: *The Development and Current State of FM Radio Broadcasting in America*, published August 1971. I correctly predicted the move of audiences from AM to FM. In 1971, many radio professionals scoffed at the idea.

The KTBC business office installed a Xerox machine, highly advanced equipment for the time. I crept in late one night and photocopied my FM history. One of the station executives walked in and growled, "what are you doing?" Thinking quick, I brightly said, "I've done some research on FM radio and I want to give a copy to Roddy." The next day I delivered my pages. Roddy read it and sent a note transferring me to FM three days a week and AM Saturday and Sunday.

Leaving nights on AM was a bit of a demotion. One of the rock announcers complained to Roddy that my voice was too deep and my pace too slow. However, moving to FM gave me an opportunity to reprogram the station. Years earlier, Cactus staffed KTBC-FM with female British announcers. He gave the ladies a stack of lush albums and little else. They received no new music or direction for years. Now I could update the station.

I wrote record companies requesting new promotional albums, signing my letters, "KTBC Music Director." Recording companies, seeking air play, happily complied. Stacks of new albums arrived addressed to me at the station. The new music, by Peggy Lee, Tony Bennett, the Tijuana Brass, and others improved the sound and the ratings. The female British announcers gradually left, replaced by a mix of male and female announcers. Within a few months, KTBC-FM replicated the success of KITY-FM.

Change came easily to KTBC-FM; not so easily for KTBC-AM. Cactus Pryor and Joe Roddy possessed the same levers of power. Cactus could undo anything Roddy decreed. When the News Director left for a business opportunity, Roddy asked to take over news, promoting his associate Al Mustin to Radio Program Director. Cactus, Program Manager, and Mustin, Program Director, didn't like each other. In May of 1969, General Manager J.C. Kellam announced Al Mustin would fill the new position of Promotion Director.

Cactus and I maintained a distant but friendly relationship. I think Cactus liked the improvements I made on FM. With Al Mustin gone, Cactus told me to take over the AM radio midday shift, schedule announcer shifts, and provide the music for KTBC AM. A month later, KTBC named me Program Director, with a generous salary of $650 a month.

As Program Director I attended weekly staff meetings chaired by J.C. Kellam, the General Manager and longtime LBJ loyalist. Kellam and Johnson worked together in the 1920's at Southwest Texas State Teacher's College in San Marcos, and later at the Texas headquarters of the National Youth Administration. When Johnson won election to Congress in 1937, he deputized Kellam to watch over his interests in the state.

Everyone addressed J.C. Kellam as Mr. Kellam. He wore black suits, white shirts, and black ties. Nearly 70, with a shock of white hair, he reminded me of Mr. Potter, the villain in *It's a Wonderful Life*. When Mr. Kellam heard a complaint or sensed something wrong at KTBC radio, his secretary called me to report to his office. A summons to Mr. Kellam's office felt like a visit to the school principal.

Now staffing both FM and AM and because of turnover, I hired replacement announcers. Several times, Mr. Kellam called me on the carpet to complain about announcer's salaries. Mr. Kellam required his managers to work Saturday mornings. Cactus failed to inform me of this policy, so I earned more of the old gentleman's ire when he couldn't find me on a Saturday.

One morning, the early announcer, Paul Jones, scheduled to sign on at 5:00am, overslept. Cactus told the transmitter engineer to call me at home the next time Paul didn't make it. I would be expected to rush to the station and sign on until Jones arrived. As a result, I was routed out of bed several times. Cactus liked Paul, so firing the tardy announcer wasn't an option.

A talented professional named Bruce Williamson took over the afternoon shift. Bruce won Cactus' approval to host a progressive-rock show, Saturday nights on KTBC-FM. I didn't share Cactus' enthusiasm because I didn't want to tamper with the successful middle of the road FM format. Cactus gave the go ahead anyway. The show aired a few weeks. The ratings jumped. One morning Mr. Kellam's secretary told me to report to his office.

"Campbell, what is this show on FM Saturday night?"

"Oh," I said, "Cactus told Bruce Williamson he could play progressive music Saturday nights if it was in good taste." I don't remember exactly what Mr. Kellam said after that, only that he threw the words "good taste" back at me and started yelling he received a complaint and what was going on down there and that show had better never return. Later, I learned Lady Bird Johnson turned on KTBC FM, and heard Screamin' Jay Hawkins "Constipation Blues." Cactus and Bruce's idea blew up. The shrapnel landed on me.

Cactus blew a gasket when he heard a song by the Youngbloods on KTBC-AM. He charged into the control room and grabbed the 45. He called me into his office, furious, and broke the record in two. Ironically, the song was "Get Together."

I don't think Cactus or Mr. Kellam really knew what they wanted to do on KTBC radio. The television station made so much money, radio hardly mattered. I have a feeling not upsetting anyone in the Johnson family remained top priority. When something did go wrong involving radio, the Program director (me) provided an easy fall guy. My big promotion didn't feel so big anymore.

As a graduate student, I took a couple of classes a semester. Glen Phillips, the former news anchor, gathered ten of us to help him research his PhD on the importance of Presidential speeches, focusing on the 1943 Detroit riots. Research took me to the University stacks in the tall building in the middle of campus known as the Tower—the location of the Charles Whitman shootings in 1966. Every night, I would look through books and magazines for quotes. I found the key quote in an issue of *The Nation*, imploring Franklin Roosevelt to make a speech on the riots. Glen Philips practically kissed me when I turned the quote over to him.

At night, in the stacks, after a few hours study, I rode the elevator to the observation deck. Stepping out into the cool evening air, I looked out over the city. Sometimes in the distance, I thought I could see my future.

78
Exit Stage Left

THE PHONE RANG in the KTBC control room while I was on the air. "Arch, you have a long-distance call, it's an emergency." Myrtle Harris, one of my mother's fellow teachers at Ben Franklin Elementary, came on the line. "Arch, they've taken your father to the hospital. It's serious." I heard a commotion and then my great uncle Cecil, whom everyone called Bubba, said, "let me talk to him." Bubba came on the line and said flatly, "you'd better get down here, Miller's gone."

I felt a pain in my stomach and a pounding in my head. I was on the air, juggling this phone call and my radio show. The record ended and I played a couple of commercials while cradling the phone and starting another record. I told Bubba, "I'll drive down as soon as I can. I'll be there this afternoon."

I found the announcer scheduled to follow me and asked him to take over an hour early. When he arrived, I made my way to my desk in the music library. Cactus Pryor and Joe Roddy crowded into my office. The switchboard operator tipped them something was up. Roddy said, "what's wrong?" I took a deep breath and said, "my father died. I'm going to have to leave for a few days." Cactus said, "we'll put Bruce (the afternoon announcer) in charge." Roddy put his arm on my shoulder and mentioned his own father's death, looking genuinely sad for me.

The short drive from Austin to San Antonio went by in a blur. Cars surrounded the house on West Mistletoe. A half-dozen teachers who worked with my mother at Ben Franklin Elementary huddled in the living room. I unlocked the front door. The women stopped talking. I looked at them, and asked, "where's my mother?" They pointed upstairs.

I knocked on her bedroom door and found her lying on her bed, ashen faced. We hugged and I asked what happened. "He died," she said. "Just like that." We sat in silence for a long time letting it sink in.

I remember my father's death as a shock, completely unexpected. In truth, my mother, my sister, and I overlooked the obvious. Miller's health broke during my high school years. In October of the previous year, he suffered a heart attack. His doctor checked him into the Santa Rosa hospital for a week. For that episode, I drove home as fast as possible, visited him in intensive care, and exhaled when he appeared to recover. The next summer, a month before he died, he returned to the hospital with a second heart attack.

Miller made a lot of noise—coughing, clearing his throat, groaning. He sat down in a rocking chair in the den off the kitchen. Nearby, my mother noticed a sudden silence. She went into the family room and found him slumped in a chair, the same way he found his mother a generation earlier. He died at age 62, the same age his mother died.

Martha panicked, running next door to our neighbor Mrs. Hill, a former nurse, who came into the house, took his pulse, and shook her head. Martha called an ambulance, then called Aunt Mamie screaming, "Miller's dying, get over here." Martha didn't especially like Aunt Mamie, yet Mamie was the closest thing Miller had to a mother. My mother and sister jumped into the ambulance so rattled they forgot to put on shoes. They arrived at the hospital barefoot. Daddy arrived DOA.

Back at the house, Mamie went into full funeral mode. She worked Martha's address book, phoning with the news, inviting over friends, including Mrs. Harris who called me. Martha's lifelong friend Smitty, the man who encouraged her to move to San Antonio, came to the house and drove Martha to Porter Loring funeral home to make arrangements. When I arrived that evening, Smitty drove me to the mortuary with clothes for my father to wear in his casket.

Possibly because of the death of her mother, Martha shielded my sister Marti and me from funerals. Neither my sister nor I had ever attended a funeral, or experienced death up close.

The house filled with friends and relatives. Evelyn Hanson, a lifelong friend and member of Jefferson Methodist church asked Smitty what the ladies guild could do. Smitty didn't skip a beat. He told them to provide lunch on Monday after the service.

My Great Uncle Bubba came up to my room. He started telling stories about my father, especially the years in the early 40s when Miller and Bubba and Mamie's son Peppy shared a bedroom.

"He took care of his clothes and looked great in his suits and ties. He talked about you all the time. He went on and on about how proud he was of you. I tell you this: you've lost your best friend."

I never paid much attention to Bubba, an old bachelor with a funny nickname living with his sister. Over the years I came to learn Bubba, a retired lawyer, was the backbone of the family. I wish I could tell Bubba how much that conversation meant to me.

We went back to the funeral home Saturday night for a viewing. My mother arranged the cheapest funeral possible. The vinyl covered casket sat in a tiny room, with space for only a few people. A young Hispanic man, the architect at "Cotton" Homes stood next to the casket weeping. Aunt Mamie noticed and said quizzically, "he's really upset." Then she looked at my father and said, "he looks like he's about to sit up and tell a joke."

My father was a salesman, much like Willy Loman in Arthur Miller's *Death of a Salesman*. If you know the play, you know Willy talks about the beloved drummer whose funeral was the largest and grandest event of the year. At the end of the play, only Willy's wife and sons attend his funeral. Which do you think my father received: the lonely goodbye, or the death of a salesman?

Miller received the glorious death of a salesman. The morning of his service, we discovered a crush of friends, neighbors, and relatives at the funeral chapel. Astonished, Uncle Harold exclaimed, "they're setting up extra chairs!"

Our minister from Jefferson Methodist Church, one of the most boring speakers ever forced on a Methodist congregation, rose to the occasion, genuinely moved by the outpouring adding, "what can you say to this wife, this son, and this daughter?"

Miller often talked about the family plot in Mission Cemetery south of downtown. His grandmother and aunts purchased more than a dozen burial lots together. I remarked to Mamie how much Miller loved the family plot. "He wants to be buried with the family." Mamie quickly insisted there was only room for her and Bubba. I kept repeating Miller wanted to be buried there. Mamie started insisting we buy two plots somewhere and pay for them by the month. I screamed: "we need one plot. He wants to be buried with the family." No one checked, so no one knew, four plots remained. Mamie was wrong.

Mamie's daughter heard the argument. She confirmed the extra cemetery lots, and made the arrangements. Mamie didn't like or forget the way I spoke to her. I didn't forget this slight either.

We buried Miller in the family plot in Mission South Cemetery. As they lowered his casket, I noticed my family history, right at my feet. There they were, all the people from Miller's stories, laid out in the manner of the last act of *Our Town*. My grandfather Archie Alexander Campbell, the glad-handing talker, next to his shy wife Eddie Miller Campbell. Just above them, I saw the stone for Great Uncle Zollie Campbell, Archie's big brother who drove cattle on the Chisholm trail and joined the Texas Rangers. The family matriarch, my great grandmother Mattie Goode Campbell Russey, born 1849, occupied the exact center, surrounded by the boisterous family she melded into a tribe.

After the burial, about forty relatives and close friends filled the house for the lunch Smitty assigned the church ladies. Friends talked about Miller's golf game, his talent playing piano, and the time he played bridge with his toes. I noticed women weeping, including his "kissing cousin" Genna and a family friend named Jean, whom he dated before he married my mother. Someone told the story of Miller at church day camp in the country, slipping on a rock crossing a little stream and yelling, "goddammit," in front of all the little Christian children.

An insurance man arrived with a small benefit check. He unsuccessfully tried to sell me a policy. I brought the gruff builder Miller worked for a few of my father's papers relating to the business and one of his yard signs. A hard man, he shook his head saying, "I never had a cross word with him." He quickly added that Miller hadn't sold anything recently, and there would be no additional salary.

Jean Longwith and I hadn't spoken since I left SAC. I called, asking to visit. In her living room I told her about my father's death, and my troubles at KTBC. She reminded me I grew up with advantages. "A lot of your friends don't have a nice family like you. Sounds to me like you don't like your job. You need to figure out your path. You have the skills to do it." After that visit, Jean became a mentor. We traded letters, and I sent Jean tapes of my performances for the next forty years.

I attended my father's funeral in a trance. If I could, I'd go back and deliver a son's eulogy. I think I would say because my father had the soul of an artist, he struggled with ordinary life. He was almost 40 when I was born. I carry his name: Arch Miller Campbell. I go by Arch; he went by Miller.

He loved classical music and opera. He sang opera for comic effect while he worked around the house. He played piano by ear without sheet music. When the film biography of George Gershwin, *Rhapsody in Blue*, aired on television, he sat at his upright piano and performed along with the film. His musical ear extended to language and puns. "A guy goes to the hospital for gas pain. His treatment includes an enema every hour. Whenever he hears a knock on his hospital room door he says, "friend? Or Enema?'"

He loved theater and movies. Laughing in a crowded auditorium, friends heard his laugh and shouted his name "Miller!" He possessed a magnificent temper, cursing at cars that wouldn't start, ice trays that refused to come unstuck, tools that didn't work. My dad played golf at the highest level. He painted signs and lettered displays. He hung around railroad stations and chased trains leaving town.

People liked him. He died in debt leaving a tiny amount of life insurance. He left me this legacy: I love classical music, movies, and the arts. I love trains, golf, and a good joke. People tell me they recognize my laugh in a crowded movie theater. I curse. I enjoy life. My father, you are with me still.

79
Fast Forward

AND THEN MY LIFE WENT INTO OVERDRIVE. In less than five years, I moved to Dallas, married Sheila, transitioned from radio to television, found my place as a feature reporter, and skyrocketed sixteen hundred miles north to NBC in Washington D.C.

My mother stayed in her beloved house on West Mistletoe Street, even as the neighborhood struggled. Martha taught first grade until she turned 65. On retiring she faithfully attended Jefferson Methodist Church and chaired the Tuesday lunch bunch for senior citizens. My sister Marti, graduated from Jefferson and studied advertising at the University of Texas. After working a few years in Houston, she moved to D.C. in 1980 to work in sales and marketing.

Bubba died in 1975. Mamie buried him next to Grandmother Russey. A few years later, Mamie visited Washington, staying at the home of a retired doctor hoping to write her biography. I found Mamie surprisingly diminished. For a few minutes she confused me with my grandfather Archie. The family buried Mamie in the family plot in 1982. Martha told me the packed congregation at Travis Park Methodist Church sang "Jesus Loves Me."

I came home every year, returning to Jefferson High School for my 20th class reunion in 1984. I wrote Betty Ann Janert, the Speech teacher who pointed me toward broadcasting. We visited on a bench in the Jefferson hallway, trading stories, and catching up. I reminded her she told me to go into radio, and we laughed about my time in her speech class. Miss Janert taught at Jefferson 34 years. She sponsored the class that performed the work adding the Jefferson campus to the National Register of Historic Places.

80
Goodbye, Part 1

Jean Longwith (L) and My Mother (R)

MY MENTOR, TEACHER, AND FRIEND JEAN Longwith retired from San Antonio College in 1983. For years I sent Jean tapes of my performances on WRC-TV, receiving detailed criticism in return. SLOW DOWN! BREATHE! LET IT OUT! She appreciated that I managed to review films and theater, combining broadcasting with the fine arts, two of her personal interests.

Jean stayed active. She consulted the cable system, and coached talent for on air positions. Jean maintained her interest in women performers. She appreciated my wife Gina, an ordained United Methodist minister, and her ability to preach, speak, and perform liturgy.

Ironically, my mother Martha and Jean joined the same bridge club. Martha and Jean became fast friends. Jean told me she loved my mother's sense of humor.

One day at the bridge table, Jean suffered a spell. Her speech slurred as she slumped forward. It was the beginning of Parkinson's. This once powerful woman lived her last few months wheelchair bound, then bedridden. She died in January 2003, age 85.

The Accidental Critic

That same year, a bond issue funding San Antonio College included money to construct a new Radio/TV Building. I wrote the College President, reminding him Jean created the department and brought the idea for station KSYM-FM to the school. Many others wrote as well. On a spring day in April, 2005 I attended the dedication of the Jean Longwith Radio/TV Building at San Antonio College.

Professor Terry Tackett, chair of the department, asked me to share emcee duties with Sunny Melendrez, the local San Antonio radio personality. I suggested Sonny do the introductions as most people in town knew him and not me. I asked to deliver a speech on Jean and her life. A crowd of about two hundred stood at the corner of Courtland and Main in front of the new Jean Longwith Radio, Television, and Film Building.

I gave this speech at the Jean Longwith Building Dedication at San Antonio College in April 2005:

> *I had a dream about Jean Longwith. I dreamed I went over to her house on Quentin Drive—the way so many of us did—and I said "Jean, they built a big new Radio/TV building at San Antonio College and named it for you." In my dream, Jean looks at me and says, "what took them so long?"*
>
> *Jean would probably say that. She spoke her mind, and we loved her for it. She had a theater background and presence. She could project her voice to the back row of an auditorium or a classroom. And she had a look. If Jean Longwith didn't like something you did or said, she had a look that burned through you like a laser.*
>
> *She also had a gift. She could really SEE her students. In the months since she died, I've heard dozens of stories of students she pulled aside to say,*

"you should announce, you should report news, you should direct, you should teach, or write, or go into sales or management." Once she sized you up, she made it her mission to help you unlock your potential.

She taught me her final year at Jefferson and her first two years at San Antonio College. I witnessed the beginning of her vision for this school. She got this job because the President of the college walked into the student union and heard a Beatles song on WSAC, the school radio station. He hated the Beatles. He blew his stack and proclaimed, "no more rock and roll on the campus station." The guy who taught the radio course quit and Jean arrived.

Most of us would have taken the job prepared to fight over music. Jean never backed away from a fight. In fact, she LOVED a good fight. But this time, she went along because she had a bigger vision. Jean talked that same President into building a real radio station—an on the air educational FM station. Jean went after it, arranged a grant, filed the application, hired an engineer, and within two years signed KSYM on the air. Once KSYM established, students poured into this school because they sensed something special at San Antonio College.

One year I stopped into SAC to visit. Jean told me NPR wanted to affiliate with KSYM. Before I could say a word, she said, "they've got too many rules—they'll come in here and take my station away from my students. I'm not gonna let them have it." Now when I return to San Antonio, I turn on KSYM and I hear a unique creative free voice—one that reflects Jean Longwith's vision for her students.

I want you to know one other thing about Jean. She believed in equality—especially for women. In those early days in the mid-1960's, she called in everyone she knew working in broadcasting to talk to our class.

The question always came up: what about jobs for women? The speakers gave the 1965 answer. "She can get a job in the front office as a secretary." Jean would fold her arms and roll her eyes and let out a groan, traumatizing the poor guy who just answered. With her gestures, she planted a seed in all of us that everyone, men and women, deserves an equal chance. She gave us a life lesson.

Jean Longwith never married. She never had children. She put her heart into this department at San Antonio College. I think today on the dedication of this building named for her, she would say "Students and teachers: USE this building. Unlock your potential. Follow your dream." As one of her many former students I ask you: when you come into this great new space, remember the woman who started it all—our teacher Jean Longwith.

After I spoke, Betty Ann Janert, the Jefferson High School teacher who taught me how to give a speech, came up and gave me a kiss. My mother, Martha, no longer able to drive, tipped off her friend Smitty that I would be speaking. He came up as well, my mother's lifetime friend. Mine, too.

81
Goodbye, Part 2

My mother stayed in the house she loved 45 years, from 1951 until 1996. Arthritis and a mild stroke persuaded her to move to a graduated care facility.

For a decade, she lived in her own apartment nearby at Morningside Meadows on Babcock Road. She arranged bridge games and rarely missed services at Jefferson United Methodist Church.

When Martha reached 90, my sister Marti and I hosted a birthday party at the Meadows. Smitty gave a speech, remembering Martha as a young woman in Nashville, and taking credit for introducing Miller to Martha and remembering Miller as a great guy.

In the years that followed, a series of small strokes slowed Martha down, forcing a move to assisted living. Sixteen hundred miles away in Washington, D.C., I thought about the humor and sacrifice of a Southern Belle who never quite received the rescue she desired. I began working on a eulogy, which prepared me for her final night, Friday, October 23, 2009.

The following Sunday afternoon, childhood friends, relatives, and acquaintances gathered in Jefferson United Methodist Church chapel. By this time, Smitty lived in graduated care. He called to ask for a ride. Gina and I drove to Patriot Heights where Smitty was waiting at the curb, walker in hand. During the service, as I rose to speak, I noticed Betty Ann Janert, the teacher who taught me how to deliver a speech, in the congregation.

Here's what I said that day in my tribute to Martha Hightower Campbell, October 25, 2009:

> *As an adult, I love to tell stories about growing up in San Antonio with Martha as my mother. After a while friends say, "she sounds like a character out of a book." I tell them they don't know the half of it.*
> *Martha Hightower Campbell: like a character out of a book. With a twinkle in her eye and the thickest Southern accent any of us will ever hear, she could have come straight out of the pages of Gone with the Wind.*
>
> *One year on a visit my sister and I laughed and laughed as her report of a distant acquaintance's shotgun wedding. We laughed some more and then Martha added, "well, at least we know she wasn't on the pill." That stopped the show because I didn't know that Martha even KNEW about the pill.*
>
> *She did know that life requires a sense of humor. In 1918, when Martha was three, her mother died in the flu epidemic of that year. Martha told us this story often: Servants stopped the clocks in the house, turned the mirrors to the wall, pulled the drapes and covered the front door in black. Her mother lay in*

a coffin in the parlor, her father beside it weeping. As a teenager, Martha begged her older brother and sister to tell her what they remembered of their mother. They couldn't help her. I believe she missed her mother every day of her life.

My mother grew up well to do in the little town of Athens, Alabama. Her family lived in a big house in town on three acres with a barn, horses, a cow, a chicken house, a vegetable garden and a rose garden. A maid and a butler served the family. Her grandparents moved in after her mother's death. Martha's grandmother, a woman born during the Civil War, raised Martha.

She left for Vanderbilt University in Nashville for her senior year of college and graduated in 1935. My mother took great pride in her Vanderbilt degree. She did not want to follow the path of most educated woman of that time and teach school. She majored in English and French. Sometimes she spoke a little French to my sister and me for fun. She arrived in San Antonio to visit friends in 1942. She loved saying she liked it so much here that she decided to stay. "I sent for my things." Her friends found her a job at Fort Sam Houston where she met my dad Miller. They married in January, 1944. They loved to drive my sister and me by their first apartment at Belknap and Ashby streets. After the war, they bought a duplex on West Cincinnati Street. They rented the apartment next to them to their friends Dorothy and Smitty Smith.

One summer night, Martha and Dorothy sat on the front porch, laughing and talking and smoking. Yes, Martha smoked back then, just not in public. The children went to bed, the husbands went to bed,

Martha and Dorothy stayed on the porch. My dad got up early the next morning and they were still out there, laughing and talking. Smitty told me this story because he wanted me to know my mother could talk all night.[60]

She did love to visit. She loved bridge and bridge parties. She loved Bible Study Fellowship and Jefferson United Methodist Church. She attended services here for sixty years and came as recent as August of this year. She loved the Lou Ann platter at Luby's, onion rings at Tip Top, and soft chicken tacos (pronounced as "tacas") with tomatoes on the side at La Fonda.

How she loved our house at 2241 West Mistletoe. The real estate agent said the look on Martha's face was love at first sight. Martha bought her house with money from her mother's estate. She put the deed in her name. That house had her stamp. She crammed it full of big old antiques from Athens, Alabama, vitamin newsletters, religious books, magazines and ball point pens that didn't work. She loved the neighborhood, joining the group that helped build the walking path around Woodlawn Lake. She badgered the city to clean up the alley and complete other projects. She called about a median strip up the street with grass and a concrete planter so often we called the strip "Martha's Park."

Martha loved to lie in bed and read. When visitors or salesmen rang the front doorbell, they often got a greeting from the upstairs bedroom window, a listing Southern accent asking, "what is it?" I watched entire conversations between strangers on the porch and Martha in her upstairs window.

The one thing she insisted she did not want to do in life was teach school. But times got tough, so she taught; first grade, for almost twenty-five years. I believe she made a wonderful teacher. One afternoon at Osborne's Grocery Store, she noticed a display for Campbell soup featuring the Campbell kids. She marched right up to Mr. Osborne and asked for the display. She took it out of the store and put it in her first-grade classroom at Ben Franklin School. Her students became "the Campbell Kids." She studied for and received certification in the difficult bi-lingual program of the 1960's. Martha's instruction may explain the occasional San Antonio adult who speaks Spanish with a Southern accent.

Martha has another legacy. When she retired, she helped create the Jefferson Methodist Tuesday Lunch bunch for senior citizens. I understand she fixed them some wonderful meals. Her turn as a cook came as a surprise to my sister and me. We remembered her shortcuts cooking for us. Sundays she came home from church and put a cheap cut of meat into the oven, then went upstairs to read. The meat sat in the oven all day, melba style. About 4:00pm, she came down and threw a slab of frozen broccoli on the front right burner in a pot with a broken handle. She selected the lowest level of heat and went back to her reading. The broccoli turned to green mush. When my sister and I came home she would call down, "there's broccoli on the stove, and a roast in the oven."

One Christmas she took the turkey leftovers and poured a can of mushroom soup over them, grandly announcing turkey a la king in a cream sauce on toast. I don't remember exactly who—it might have been me or might have been my father—one of us looked at it and said, "who vomited?" Oh, what a fury that caused. I want you to know I apologized for that wise crack this year. Martha accepted. She almost, but not quite, conceded we had a point.

She did the best she could for my sister and me in her unconventional manner. Martha had a good time in life but she didn't have an easy life. She grew up without her mother. She and my father faced economic hardship. She lived on her own as a widow for 40 years. In her final years she endured physical pain. When she went into the nursing home she couldn't walk, or dress herself, or even feed herself. I remembered how much she loved the chocolate covered peppermints Luby's sold at their cash register. I brought some, broke them up, and fed them to her. She looked at me and said, "I've never had it so good."

She gave me optimism, a love for San Antonio, and an appreciation for good manners.

"If you have good manners," she often said, "every door will open for you."

She was right. I do not know what heaven brings, but for Martha, I hope it brings reunion—with her father, her family, her husband, her friends, and most of all with the mother she never knew.

I have a message for St. Peter. Brace yourself. We are sending you Martha. And she is like a character right out of a book.

The day after her service, I made a discovery about my mother.

The last few years she taught at Ben Franklin Elementary her principal was a no-nonsense Black woman. I have described Athens, Alabama and the harsh segregation and Martha's thick Southern accent and Scarlett O'Hara ways. When we spoke long distance in the years she was teaching,

Martha told me she feared her principal, adding, "when I open my mouth, she knows where I came from."

When Martha died, Morningside Meadows asked to hold a service in the facility in her honor. Martha made many friends, and tickled the head administrator inviting him to lunch on one occasion. During the meal she told him, "I wanted you to have lunch with me so you could experience just how lousy the food is here."

At the service, my sister Marti and I noticed a ramrod straight woman whom we guessed might be a Salvation Army officer. The woman got up to speak.

"I was Mrs. Campbell's Principal," she said. My sister and I looked at each other, our jaws dropping.

"Mrs. Campbell kept her class in good order. When we had faculty-meetings she made us laugh. When she retired, she left a hole in our faculty that we couldn't fill. We missed her. We really missed her."

A final surprise from my mother.

Warfield "Smitty" Smith and my mother at her 90th birthday party

82
Family Reunion

HERE THEY ARE: THE CAST OF MY FAMILY story. Mattie Goode Campbell Russey, (1849–1932). She's in the middle, next to her son, Bubba, Harry Cecil Russey (1893–1975). My great aunt Mamie Dial (1890–1982) lies in the row above, next to her husband Preston Dial (1890–1931). The names endure on headstones in Mission South Cemetery.

The Campbells gather to Mattie's right. Archie (1876–1938), my grandfather and grandmother Eddie (1879–1942). Next to Eddie, her father, Robert J. Miller (1849–1926). Daddy told me Mr. Miller passed away while visiting, and that the old man's ghost appeared every now and then in the house where they lived on Roseborough Street.

My great Uncle Zollie Campbell (1874–1947) shares a headstone with the wife he married, divorced, and remarried Kathryn (Aunt Katy) (1892–1967). The family matriarchs moved the body of Zollie's second wife, Mary, shoving her to the side to make room for Aunt Katy. For 82 years Mary Campbell lay in an unmarked grave. In 2023 I bought a headstone. Now next to Katherine lies Mary L. Campbell (1884–1940).

On the other side, my great aunt Georgia's first husband Ezra Beach (1872–1914) anchors the group. Ezra's death by "hunting accident" might have prompted the purchase of these plots. Thirty-eight years later Ezra's daughter Jean Beach McWiggins (1910–1952) joined the assembly. When great aunt Georgia (1879–1966) died, her husband Harold buried her in the Kayton family plot, leaving two spaces. My father Archibald Miller Campbell (1907–1969) received his resting place thanks to my argument with Mamie during his wake. My mother, Martha Campbell (1914–2009) completed the family assembly.

It rained buckets the day we buried my mother. Mamie's son, Judge Preston Dial, stood next to me as six strong men struggled with Martha's casket. Watching the water come down in sheets, and the men slogging through the mud, Judge Dial turned to me and said, "we never complain about rain in Texas."

I knew some of these characters in their sunset years, others by reputation. Here they are—the players who bind me to San Antonio and Texas. Whenever I leave, I promise to come back.

Left:
Zollie Campbell
Cowboy/Lawman

Below:
Great Aunt
Mamie
Dial

Archie Campbell and his cigar salesmen

Archie Campbell
On the road in about 1925

MY PLACE

83
Return

Ten years after I left Channel 4, WRC's promotion department sent an email. Would I join Bob Ryan at the station to record a few stories about Doreen Gentzler? The National Academy of Television Arts and Sciences was inducting Doreen into the Silver Circle, honoring veteran local broadcasters. Delighted at the opportunity, I called Bob. We agreed to go back together.

Bob met me outside the front door with a big smile. We laughed at the sight of each other. "This'll be weird." Once inside, a young guard with a shaved head handed us a clipboard and asked to see our driver's license. A senior woman came out of the security office, waved the young guy off, and hugged us both. "What are you two doing here? You don't have to sign anything. Go right in."

A fresh-faced promotion guy in his mid-thirties met us in the lobby. He would supervise our tape session, and show us around after we finished. To my delight, we stepped into Studio A. I stood in this space often when I worked here, just to feel the history. President Eisenhower dedicated Studio A in 1958 as the first television studio designed exclusively for color broadcasting. During the live broadcast, the home picture changed from black and white to color.

Studio A hosted the second of the four Presidential debates in 1960 between John Kennedy and Richard Nixon. I worked with stage managers and engineers who staffed that broadcast. One crew member told me Nixon was friendlier than Kennedy, and a better debater.

Friday afternoons, John McLaughlin and his panelists, including Pat Buchanan and Eleanor Clift, gathered in Studio A to tape the nationally syndicated *The McLaughlin Group*. One Friday I set up an interview with Buffalo Bob Smith, host of *Howdy Doody*, the pioneer kids show in the early days of TV. Buffalo Bob happened to arrive during McLaughlin's tape session. As a gag, I led the old performer into Studio A to meet McLaughlin and his pundits, with my cameraman recording the encounter.

McLaughlin boomed, "hello Buffalo Bob, thanks for your work with the young people of America." I suspect McLaughlin had no idea of Buffalo Bob or T*he Howdy Doody Show*. Eleanor Clift giggled. The promotion guy's eyes widened as I laughed about introducing John McLaughlin to *Howdy Doody's* host Buffalo Bob.

"Did you know Jonathan Demme shot some of the scenes of *Silence of the Lambs* in Studio A?" The promotion guy's jaw dropped. "*Silence of the Lambs* was shot here?"

"Yeah," I said, "he used Studio A for the scene where the

Senator begs the kidnapper to release her daughter. He used Studio B for a newscast scene featuring George Michael as Gene Castle. Demme liked George's Sunday Night *Sports Machine*, so he gave him a cameo in his movie."

George Michael taped *The George Michael Sports Machine* in Studio A. I hosted *The Arch Campbell Show* for five years in front of a live audience in here. *Meet the Press* broadcast from Studio A since the building opened in 1958.[61]

The camera rolled and Bob and I ad-libbed a greeting congratulating Doreen. We remembered the night Bob added, "…and he's not wearing any pants," to Doreen's introduction to me.

I mentioned Jim Vance, Doreen's co-anchor, the Dean of Washington TV newsmen. Management required years to find someone strong enough to hold their own alongside Vance. On Doreen's first night, she jumped into a conversation between Vance and George Michael, letting them know the anchor desk was no longer a "boy's club." She won their respect in that instant.

We finished and a couple of engineers came out to say hello. Bob and I asked to look around. Next door, electronic locks guarded the giant doors leading to Studio B, the local news studio. Pat Lawson Muse, anchoring the midday news, looked up during a break and shouted, "oh my God, Hello!" The break ended and Bob and I tiptoed out to let her work.

In our time, on Thursday nights, the Studio B stage manager, Maurice Javins, wearing elegant white gloves, served Meyer's Dark Rum and Coke to the anchor team. The stage manager position no longer exists, eliminated during years of cost cutting and automation.

A young woman ran up and hugged me. "Do you remember the first week I started here and I was in the tape library and you started turning the handle that shoved the tape files together not knowing I was in there?"

"Oh yeah," I said, "you started laughing and squealing."

"That's how we met," she said.

We walked into the new digital newsroom. News Director Mike Goldrick came out to shake hands. Mike told me he used to run my movie reviews on a station in Florida.

"It's so quiet," I said.

"Yeah," Mike answered, "all of our people listen to their computer wearing headphones. They edit news video right at their desks."

"It wasn't quiet in the old newsroom," Bob said grinning. "How about the time George Michael threw a coffee pot across the room after a fight with the News Director?"

I added, "just another day at Channel 4. Before computers we had three teletype machines typing wire copy non-stop plus the sound of a dozen typewriters going all at once and people yelling."

Bob added, "throwing paper wads and cigarettes at each other like grenades. It was different then."

The News Director blanched. It felt like time to go. We told the promotion guy we knew the way out.

Bob and I moved through the building like ghosts. I noticed side glances as if to say, "hey, isn't that?" The people who said hello seemed happy to see us. The station felt busy and energetic. We walked to the parking lot, grinning all the way, happy to return yet ready to move ahead.

A few months later, a newsroom manager left an urgent call on my home phone. "Can you come into the station as soon as you get this? Jim Vance died."

84
Jim Vance

THE NEWS OF JIM VANCE'S DEATH ON JULY 22, 2017, touched off cell phone bulletins and Twitter storms. Radio and television stations interrupted programming with the news.

Vance checked into Georgetown hospital a few weeks earlier. At first I heard, "no visitors allowed," followed by a string of uncertain messages. Finally, I called Bob Ryan and said, "we're going over there." Early in July, 2017, Ryan and I marched into Georgetown Hospital. The visitor's receptionist recognized us and said, "go on up."

Officially his doctors brought Vance in for "tests." I knew what "tests" meant. I watched Vance chain smoke for decades. During his last year on the news, his breathing was shallow, his voice less robust.

The anchorman who towered over everyone, looked small and thin in his hospital bed. He lit up when Bob and I walked in, pushing out his go to greeting: "my man." We both hugged him as he got up and made his way to a chair.

My Place

"Tell me all about podcasting," Vance said to me. I had just begun a podcast with *Washington Post* critic Ann Hornaday. "I want to start one when I get out of here," Vance added.

Vance and I stayed in touch after my exit from Channel 4. Every few months we would meet for breakfast at the American City Diner, a now vanished 1950s style short order place we both liked. Vance knew I missed my old home. He almost moved to Channel 7 during more than one contentious contract negotiation. I attended a small station dinner celebrating his 45th anniversary at WRC as well as several gatherings at his house in the Spring Valley suburb of Washington, D.C.

The day he died, and the week after, Channel 4 devoted their evening newscasts to highlights and stories of Vance's career. Doreen Gentzler, his professional partner of twenty-eight years, anchored the Saturday night 6:00pm report. Doreen interviewed Bob Ryan and me for the late news.

I pointed out how much Vance loved going against the grain. When he didn't like a manager's suggestion, he did the opposite. Consultants especially tried to tone down his appearance. Vance often grew a beard, just to annoy them.

Remembering Jim Vance the night he died

Vance carved his own path. In the 70s, prisoners in the D.C. jail demanded Vance mediate a dispute during a prison riot. News management feared for Vance's safety. He went anyway. In the 80s, D.C. Mayor Marion Barry, caught with crack in a downtown D.C. hotel, called Vance to come to his house and counsel him. Management told Vance not to go, but he went anyway, even as the visit called attention to Vance's stints in rehab for drug abuse.

Despite his iconoclasm, Vance stayed at one station 48 years. He anchored during local television's most influential era. His salary exceeded seven figures, reflecting the value of his longevity, and personality. Vance made his Cancer diagnosis public during a commentary in May 2017. Nevertheless, his death shocked the city. *The Washington Post* ran his obituary on the front page.

Following a family service in Philadelphia, and a private burial service, WRC-TV arranged a public televised memorial service at the Washington National Cathedral on September 12, 2017. The Cathedral filled with a cross section of the city, including D.C.'s broadcasting and print best known names of the past fifty years. Speakers included Vance's on-air partner, Doreen Gentzler, and NBC network anchor Craig Melvin whom Vance mentored. College friends from a quartet Vance joined in college reunited to perform doo-wop hits. Maurice Javins, the stage manager everyone fondly remembered returned, as did Katie Couric, Susan Kidd, and Susan King. Outside the Cathedral, a long line of motorcycles gleamed in the sun reflecting Vance's love of motorcycles. The crowd, many of whom only knew Vance as viewers, stood outside the building following the service, talking and visiting for hours.

Washingtonian Magazine asked for a few thoughts on my friend. Here is what I wrote:

My Place

I don't know how tall Jim Vance was but he towered over me and everyone else, so of course, I remember him as bigger than life. A guy this big only required one name: Vance. I met him in 1974 when I came to work as a reporter at Channel 4. He was not the usual white bread middle of the road TV Anchorman. Vance had edge and loved upsetting viewers in a business that feared edge. He took the measure of the people he worked with and took his time deciding if he respected you or not. It took a while, but once Vance accepted you, he was your friend for life. In 1980, I talked a News Director into letting me review movies on the 6:00pm news. Vance gave me his seal of approval when I finished. "My man," he said, and made my career possible.

Vance loved to talk about his early years at NBC. He asked David Brinkley, the legendary NBC anchor, how to succeed as an anchorman. Brinkley told Vance to be himself. He took Brinkley's advice. Be yourself is the secret of Vance's success. When managers and news consultants told him to play it safe, he pushed the envelope. When they told him to cut his hair, he grew an afro. When they told him to shave his moustache, he added a beard. The consultants feared angering viewers, and Vance delivered regular commentaries leaving no doubt of what he thought or whom he despised. His uniqueness kept him on the air and made him vital to the success of NBC4. He also spoke truth to power, and never hesitated to complain about decisions or directions he found wrong. I believe Vance's complaints prevented managers or consultants from harming the station's unique character. His presence made Channel 4 unlike any other newscast in the country.

He had bigger than life flaws, including drug and substance abuse that almost ended his life. He shared that struggle and our town loved him for it. One morning in the early 80's he called me at home.

'Arch, I've been playing poker with Marion Barry and I owe him a couple of hundred bucks. Can you lend me the money?' 'Sure,' I said, 'Come on over.' A half hour later, a couple of really bad dudes pulled up to my house and Vance came to the door. I gave him a check and forgot about it. A few months later, Vance left for the Betty Ford Center. I found a check for the exact amount in my mail box. We never talked about it until a celebration of his 45th year at NBC4. Vance got up and discussed his relationship with each person in the room. When he got to me, he mentioned that morning and how I never brought it up, and how much it meant to him.

Vance's office—in the days when anchors had offices—was like a private club. He kept the overhead light off, using only a couple of lamps. The place was thick with cigarette smoke billowing out the door. In my office two doors down I could hear Vance and George Michael smoking and laughing and cursing various people they didn't like. Vance kept a state-of-the-art stereo system playing cool jazz non-stop. One of his legacies is the music Channel 4 uses at the end of the 6:00pm news on Fridays when they run credits. The cut is "My Mood" by MFSB. Our News Director in 1975 told Vance he needed some great music to end the newscast. Vance picked "My Mood." Over the years various consultants and managers tried to change or drop the music, but viewers always noticed and complained, and it always came back. As long as "My Mood" ends the 6:00pm news on Fridays, Vance's spirit endures at NBC4.

My Place

*Washingtonian Published July 23, 2017
(Reprinted with permission from Washingtonian magazine)

85
Whatever Happened to Arch Campbell?

In 2020, Gina and I traveled to Texas for a stay in Marfa, the hip artistic community in the desert near the Davis Mountains. We flew home to D.C. March 13, 2020, as news emerged of a new virus: COVID-19. A few days later, the world changed.

The threat of a national pandemic shuttered most of the places where crowds gathered. The Uptown Theater closed. Few noticed the loss of the location regarded as the best place in D.C. to watch the latest blockbuster. I stood on red carpets at the Uptown countless times to interview stars and celebrities at gala premieres.[62]

Entertainment accelerated to streaming services, where viewers binge series of eight to ten episodes, or settle in for sixty-episode epics, or watch the traditional two-hour movie. My Smart TV gives me access to almost every classic film, and most new ones as well.

The news of Willard Scott's death in September 2021 brought a flood of tributes, reflecting Willard's years on national television and his final gig, celebrating seniors turning 100. WRC assembled a tribute, using footage and interviews from the series Jim Vance produced in 1979, the week Willard left for *The Today Show*.

I last saw Willard at Jim Vance's funeral. He did not look good. Confined to a wheelchair, Willard lacked his usual energy and smile. When he died, *Washingtonian Magazine* asked me for a few memories. I told them about the rollicking dinners, adding that Willard usually invited newsroom rookies and newcomers—his way of reaching out and connecting.

My Place

When he first joined WRC, Jim Vance received the same dinner invitation from Willard. That helping hand formed the beginning of a lifetime friendship. In their tribute, Channel 4 included a clip of Vance talking about Willard's final WRC newscast before moving to New York. Vance recalled Willard arriving with a jar of something that looked like water. He poured some for Vance and a good dose for himself. The two of them knocked back moonshine. Vance laughed, saying he didn't remember much about the news that night. I watched at home, and remember those two on their last night choking back tears as they said good bye.

A few months after Willard started at *Today*, WRC sent me to New York to interview him. He had the crew laughing and the backstage people in the palm of his hand. During the interview he sat me on his lap. When the tape stopped rolling, Willard told me he thought my movie review gig would really work out for me. And then, he pinched me on the ass.

The exchange of Willard Scott for Bob Ryan made possible one of the longest friendships of my career. Bob Ryan and I drag out the same stories with glee year after year. At WRC, Bob Ryan became the most successful and highest paid weatherman in Washington television history.

WRC called in May 2022. Would I join a celebration of Channel 4's 75th anniversary? Bob Ryan and I returned once more to trade memories with Doreen Gentzler. The three of us gabbed for more than an hour. I remembered the blizzard of '79, and raising Spot the Pig, and the year everyone left including Willard Scott. Bob talked about moving from *The Today Show* to Washington and I mentioned the snowstorm he correctly predicted in his first few weeks. We talked about the team concept and how it served the station for a generation.

GE sold NBC and its stations, including WRC, to the cable giant Comcast. The new owners launched a reconstruction of the NBC building. The network news bureau, headquartered on Nebraska Avenue since 1958, moved to studios near the U.S. Capitol.

Back on set for Doreen's retirement.

Doreen Gentzler, Jim Vance's co-anchor and successor, announced her retirement. WRC recognized her prominence with a private dinner the week before her final broadcast. Bob Ryan and I shared a few stories of Doreen's first night, and of the times one of us did something to break her up. Doreen represented the final link to our "dream team" of the 80s and 90s.

Pat Collins, the legendary crime and feature reporter, announced his retirement the next month. My old friend worked 36 years at Channel 4, preceded by stints in Chicago as well as Channels 9 and 7 in D.C. Earlier in 2021, Wendy Rieger concluded a 33-year career at Channel 4. Her death from Cancer the next year, shocked those of us who remember her exuberant spirit. Pat Lawson Muse celebrated 40 years at WRC, and stepped away a few months later. Barbara Harrison concluded 40 years at the station. I think of all of us as members of the second generation of TV news. The departures cleared the path for the third generation.

The one and only Wendy Reiger

A recent invitation gave me the opportunity to see the renovations of the NBC building at 4001 Nebraska Avenue. The new design hollowed out the building, allowing architects to redesign from the inside out. The grand reopening celebration September 24, 2024, took place just about 50 years since my first day at WRC in 1974.

A hallway lined with historic pictures, a mural of Jim Vance, and a video history of WRC-TV leads to an open area the size of a football field. The new high-tech newsroom accommodates dozens of young people writing and editing on computers. Construction replaced the east and south walls with glass, filling the space with natural light. Open stairways rise to second floor management and support offices. My old newsroom, the row of anchor offices, the golf course we fashioned at night in the hallways—have all vanished.

Studio A no longer exists. Renovations carved it into three spaces: a studio for Channel 4 News, one for Spanish language channel Telemundo, and a third to be determined. The new construction anticipates the future.

I worked in newsrooms where people shouted and smoked, slammed phones and banged on typewriters. Bosses said, "what the hell, let's try it." I loved the noise, the jokes, the passion. My generation owes a debt to those who came before us and shared their wisdom.

In the 1980s, I produced a series on Washington TV pioneers; the first generation of local performers. NBC staff announcer Mac McGarry recalled announcing commercials and performing interviews live in the days before video tape. "Pick" Temple relived his days as host of an afternoon children's program, *Pick Temple's Giant Ranch*, complete with a studio full of kids and a live pony.

Inga Rundvold Hook, a statuesque Danish beauty, entered local television in 1951 as host of a daytime interview program. She began her professional life as a model, then a fashion journalist for *The Washington Times-Herald* before moving to the new medium of television. Retired, and in her 60s when we talked, Inga dazzled with a Zsa Zsa Gabor touch in speech and manner.

"Oh Archie," she said, "the day you leave television, your jokes are no longer funny, your conversation is no longer interesting, you are no longer cute." At the time, I thought this quote hilarious and repeated it often. Now, I get it. I still think it's funny.

So I'm smiling as I leave you, not quite as funny or interesting and certainly not as cute as when these stories happened. That's OK. I've moved into the audience. I'm watching the next generation, and applauding.

86
"What's Your Favorite Movie?"

Blockbuster days at the Uptown Theater

I GET THAT A LOT. I LOVE HEARING THE CASES people make for their all-time favorite. My stock answer evades the question. I answer a favorite reflects how you felt and where you watched and who you were with, and what you remember, and that favorites change over time. But since you asked—OK.

The Godfather, or *Godfather 1* and *Godfather 2* combined.

I grew up in the 50s when TV stations showed movies from the 1930s and 40s., I like the movies of my father's time, the atmosphere, the clothes, the storytelling. I like film noir classics and thrillers. I like *Casablanca, The Maltese Falcon, Citizen Kane, Notorious, The Third Man, It Happened One Night, It's a Wonderful Life, Double Indemnity, Sunset Boulevard, the Wizard of Oz.* Those films led me to *Rear Window, Vertigo, North by Northwest, Psycho,* and later *Chinatown, Paper Moon, the Last Picture Show, Heaven Can Wait, In the Heat of the Night,* and *Being There.*

In 1980, I listed my ten favorites of the year. I've done it ever since. Some haven't aged as well as others. The lists reflect a mix of art and audience favorites. Here we go, help yourself, you are welcome to disagree. I've added notes, mea culpas, and additions I overlooked. Hey. Nobody's perfect.

1980:

The Empire Strikes Back, Being There, The Great Santini, Raging Bull, All That Jazz, Ordinary People, Close Encounters, The Elephant Man, Airplane!, The Shining

(I should have included *Caddyshack,* so here it is. Most of these hold up. I count *Being There* among my all-time favorites.)

1981:

Raiders of the Lost Ark, Breaker Morant, Atlantic City, Body Heat, Arthur, The Four Seasons, Chariots of Fire, Whose Life is it Anyway?, Melvin and Howard, The Great Muppet Caper

(I doubt that A*rthur, The Four Seasons,* and *Whose Life?* work as well today. *Body Heat* gets better every year, as well as *Chariots of Fire.* I marveled learning that Dodi Fayed, Princess Diana's boyfriend, produced *Chariots of Fire.*)

1982:

E.T., An Officer and a Gentleman, Tootsie, On Golden Pond, 48 Hours, Diner, Diva, Missing, The Verdict, Poltergeist

(You can't argue with *E.T.,* can you? I doubt *The Poltergeist* is very scary.)

My Place

1983:

Terms of Endearment, Risky Business, War Games, A Christmas Story, Local Hero, La Traviata, The Grey Fox, The Right Stuff, Star Wars: Return of the Jedi, The Big Chill

(I never tire of *A Christmas Story* even when it plays 24 hours in a row. *War Games* looks ancient today.)

1984:

Amadeus, Places in the Heart, A Soldier's Story, Bizet's Carmen, The Cotton Club, Romancing the Stone, The Natural, The Karate Kid, Country, Beverly Hills Cop

(I'm a sucker for *Places in the Heart*.)

1985:

The Color Purple, Back to the Future, The Killing Fields, Mask, Witness, Silverado, Prizzi's Honor, Sweet Dreams, George Stevens: A Filmmaker's Journey, Cocoon

(Recently TCM has programmed George Steven's tribute to his father—well worth watching.)

1986:

A Room with a View, Little Shop of Horrors, Aliens, Hannah and Her Sisters, Crocodile Dundee, Children of a Lesser God, Peggy Sue Got Married, The Color of Money, Stand by Me, Star Trek IV: The Voyage Home.

(*Star Trek IV* was a big deal in 1986—time hasn't been too kind.)

1987 :

Fatal Attraction, Hope and Glory, Roxanne, The Last Emperor, Full Metal Jacket, Tin Men, Dirty Dancing, The Princess Bride, Broadcast News, Jean de Florette/Manon of the Spring

(*Broadcast News* still gets me. *Fatal Attraction* inspired decades of revenge films. *Dirty Dancing* and *The Princess Bride* have achieved cult classic status.)

1988:

Big, Babette's Feast, Bull Durham, Who Framed Roger Rabbit?, Moonstruck, The Accused, Crossing Delancey, The Thin Blue Line, A Fish Called Wanda, Working Girl

(*Moonstruck*—better than ever. *Babette's Feast* never gets old. Not so sure about *Working Girl*.)

1989:

Field of Dreams, When Harry Met Sally, Sex, Lies, and Videotape, Batman, Lethal Weapon, Do the Right Thing, Dangerous Liaisons, Indiana Jones and the Last Crusade, Driving Miss Daisy, Steel Magnolias

(*Field of Dreams* never gets old. *When Harry met Sally* might be the best romantic comedy ever. *Do the Right Thing* gets more powerful every year. *Driving Miss Daisy* and *Steel Magnolias* capture the South I remember on tense visits to my grandfather.)

1990:

Avalon, Cinema Paradiso, Dances with Wolves, Presumed Innocent, Memphis Belle, Ghost, Goodfellas, The Godfather: Part III, Postcards from the Edge, The Hunt for Red October

(Please forgive me for *Godfather III*. I got carried away. *Goodfellas* ranks with the first two *Godfathers*. Barry Levinson considered *Diner, Tin Men,* and *Avalon* his Baltimore trilogy.)

1991:

Silence of the Lambs, Bugsy, Truly Madly Deeply, City Slickers, Dead Again, Boyz n the Hood, The Commitments,

My Place

Rambling Rose, The Vanishing, Barton Fink

(Nothing scarier than *Silence of the Lambs*, not even *The Vanishing*, which is very scary.)

1992:

A League of Their Own, Unforgiven, Fried Green Tomatoes, Aladdin, The Crying Game, Malcolm X, Howard's End, The Player, Glengarry Glen Ross, A River Runs Through It

(I recently watched *Howard's End* and *Fried Green Tomatoes*—good as ever.)

1993:

Schindler's List, Like Water for Chocolate, The Joy Luck Club, The Fugitive, Strictly Ballroom, What's Love Got to Do with It?, Benny and Joon, Sleepless in Seattle, Much Ado About Nothing, Groundhog Day

(Amazing how often writers and reporters refer to *Groundhog Day* all these years later.)

1994:

Forrest Gump, Hoop Dreams, Four Weddings and a Funeral, Ed Wood, Quiz Show, The Shawshank Redemption, Speed, The Lion King, Clear and Present Danger, Pulp Fiction

(*Quiz Show, The Shawshank Redemption,* and *Pulp Fiction*: timeless. *Ed Wood* still makes me smile. *The Lion King*, like *the Dude*, endures.)

1995:

Apollo 13, Nixon, The American President, Sense and Sensibility, Babe, Toy Story, The Brothers McMullen, The Postman, Heat, The Usual Suspects

(Give me *Babe, Toy Story,* and *The Usual Suspects* any night.)

1996:

Big Night, The English Patient, Ransom, Fargo, The Spitfire Grill, Secrets and Lies, Shine, Mr. Holland's Opus, Dead Man Walking, Twister

(*Fargo* gets better every year. I love me some *Big Night*. *Twister*'s about as good as last month's forecast-skip.)

1997:

Contact, Wings of the Dove, L.A. Confidential, Shall We Dance, Face Off, Eve's Bayou, Amistad, As Good as it Gets, Air Force one, the Full Monty

(Forgive me for *Contact, Face-Off* redefined outrageous.)

1998:

Saving Private Ryan, Shakespeare in Love, Smoke Signals, Elizabeth, The Impostors, A Bug's Life, Simon Birch, Slam, Waking Ned Devine, The Truman Show

(*Saving Private Ryan* got robbed for best picture, *The Truman Show* came true, add *The Big Lebowski* to this list—it gets better every year.)

1999:

American Beauty, Being John Malkovich, Buena Vista Social Club, The Green Mile, The Limey, Toy Story 2, October Sky, The Insider, The Straight Story, The Sixth Sense

(Give me *The Sixth Sense* any night—just don't give away the ending.)

2000:

Gladiator, Crouching Tiger, Hidden Dragon, Traffic, East is East, Remember the Titans, Girl on the Bridge, Almost Famous, Billy Elliott, Erin Brockovich, Meet the Parents

(*Gladiator* rocks, *Almost Famous* still amuses, as does the original *Meet the Parents*.)

2001:

Shrek, Memento, The Man Who Wasn't There, In the Bedroom, Ghost World, Harry Potter and the Sorcerer's Stone, Amelie, The Royal Tenenbaums, Bridget Jones' diary, Monsters, Inc.

(A good year for animation.)

2002:

My Big Fat Greek Wedding, Road to Perdition, Adaptation, Real Women Have Curves, Standing in the Shadows of Motown, Igby Goes Down, The Rookie, Antwone Fisher, Monsoon Wedding, Chicago

(Gotta love *My Big Fat Greek Wedding*. I thought of *Real Women Have Curves* when America Ferrara received raves for her speech in *Barbie*.)

2003:

Mystic River, Lord of the Rings: The Return of the King, The Fog of War, Bend it Like Beckham, Whale Rider, Swimming Pool, Lost in Translation, Pirates of the Caribbean: The Curse of the Black Pearl, Finding Nemo, Seabiscuit

(Not sure the *Lord of the Rings* series will pass the test of time. Same with *Pirates of the Caribbean*. *Lost in Translation* gets better every year.)

2004:

Sideways, Finding Neverland, The Aviator, Million Dollar Baby, Ray, Garden State, Eternal Sunshine of the Spotless Mind, Harry Potter and the Prisoner of Azkaban, Dodgeball, Maria Full of Grace

(Watched *Sideways* recently—better than ever. Given today's immigration problems, *Maria Full of Grace* deserves another look.)

2005:

Capote, Good Night and Good Luck, Brokeback Mountain, Syriana, Crash, Walk the Line, The Wedding Crashers, March of the Penguins, The 40-Year-Old Virgin, Cinderella Man

(*Crash* upset *Brokeback Mountain* for Best Picture. Another Academy mistake. I'm a fan of *Good Night and Good Luck*.)

2006:

Little Miss Sunshine, The Queen, Dreamgirls, A Prairie Home Companion, The Departed, Letters from Iwo Jima, Borat, The Illusionist, Happy Feet, Cars, The Devil Wears Prada

(I could watch *The Devil Wears Prada* every week.)

2007:

No Country for Old Men, There Will Be Blood, American Gangsters, Juno, Atonement, The Kite Runner, Ratatouille, Into the Wild, Charlie Wilson's War, Michael Clayton, The Lives of Others belongs on this list—an overlooked German Big Brother Spy/Thriller/Romance.

(*No Country for Old Men* and *There Will Be Blood* win the intensity award. My friend Ann Hornaday considers *Michael Clayton* a perfect thriller.)

2008:

The Curious Case of Benjamin Button, Slumdog Millionaire, Frost, Nixon, Wall-E, Revolutionary Road, Doubt, Tropic Thunder, The Dark Knight, The Visitor, Iron Man

(I'm a fan of *Benjamin Button*. *Iron Man* launched a franchise.)

2009:

Up in the Air, Julie and Julia, Precious, The Hurt Locker, Inglorious Bastards, The Hangover, The Blind Side, Up, 500 Days of Summer, Invictus

(*Up in the Air* hasn't aged, nor has *The Hurt Locker*. *Up* remains a gem. *The Blind Side* might be a tough watch.)

2010:

The Social Network, The King's Speech, True Grit, The Girl with the Dragon Tattoo, Toy Story 3, Inception, The Kids are All Right, Get Low, The Fighter, Waiting for Superman

(Hollywood remade *The Girl with the Dragon Tattoo* from the original quite good Swedish version. *Get Low* will surprise you thanks to Robert Duvall and a charming script.)

2011:

The Descendants, The Help, Harry Potter and the Deathly Hallows, Bridesmaids, My Week with Marilyn, Midnight in Paris, Moneyball, The Artist, Martha Marcy May Marlene, Drive

(*The Descendants* ranks among George Clooney's best. *Bridesmaids* remains hilarious. Little known *Martha Marcy May Marlene* will scare you silly.)

2012:

Zero Dark Thirty, Lincoln, Argo, Moonrise Kingdom, The Master, Silver Linings Playbook, End of Watch, Looper, Skyfall, Ted

(*Argo, The Master,* and *Silver Linings Playbook* work for me.)

2013:

American Hustle, 12 Years a Slave, Gravity, Philomena, Nebraska, Enough Said, Blue Jasmine, Saving Mr. Banks, The Great Gatsby, Lee Daniels' The Butler

(*Philomena* and *Nebraska*—surprisingly good.)

2014:

Boyhood, Selma, Birdman, Whiplash, Gone Girl, The Lego Movie, Guardians of the Galaxy, The Grand Budapest Hotel, Nightcrawler, Life Itself

(Every movie fan should watch *Life Itself*—the story of critic Roger Ebert's life. TV News people need to watch *Nightcrawler*.)

2015:

Brooklyn, Spotlight, Inside Out, Carol, Room, The Martian, Mr. Holmes, Ex Machina, Me and Earl and the Dying Girl, Bridge of Spies

(*Brooklyn*'s timeless. *Bridge of Spies* deserves another look.)

2016:

La La Land, Manchester by the Sea, Moonlight, Hell or High Water, Jackie, Loving, O.J. Made in America, Sully, Paterson, A Bigger Splash

(*La La Land* and *Moonlight* are now remembered for the Oscar mix-up. *Hell or High Water* is amazingly good. *Paterson* will pleasantly surprise.)

2017:

Lady Bird, Get Out, Phantom Thread, I, Tonya, The Post, Darkest Hour, Three Billboards Outside Ebbing Missouri, The Lost city of Z, The Big Sick, Wonder Woman

(*Lady Bird* and *Get Out* rate among my all-time favorites.)

2018:
    Roma, Green Book, A Star is Born, Black Panther, Won't You Be My Neighbor, If Beale Street Could Talk, A Quiet Place, Blindspotting, First Reformed, First Man
    (At a screening for *First Reformed,* one of the audience members said out loud, "this is weird." Gotta love that.)

2019:
    Once Upon a Time in Hollywood, The Irishman, Parasite, JoJo Rabbit, The Farewell, The Last Black Man in San Francisco, Ford v. Ferrari, Queen & Slim, A Beautiful Day in the Neighborhood, Little Women
    (Tarantino and Scorsese did what they do best in *Once Upon a Time in Hollywood* and *The Irishman.* Parasite's a first rate thriller. *Queen & Slim*—overlooked crime gem.)

2020:
    Nomadland, Minari, Ma Rainey's Black Bottom, Soul, Mank, The Trial of the Chicago 7, Hamilton, News of the World, Promising Young Woman, Kajillionaire
    (I watch *Mank* because I love the era. *Soul* remains a delight. *Promising Young Woman*—a great thriller.)

2021:
    CODA, The Power of the Dog, Licorice Pizza, Belfast, Nightmare Alley, Summer of Soul, West Side Story, Passing, The Card Counter, The French Dispatch
    (*CODA* is hard to beat. *Passing* and *The Card Counter* stand out.)

2022:
    Top Gun: Maverick, Tar, Knives Out: Glass Onion, All Quiet on the Western Front, Emily the Criminal, The Fabelmans, Elvis/Babylon (epic double feature), *The Outfit/*

Phantom of the Open (Mark Rylance double feature), *Weird: The Al Yankovic Story*, *Vengeance*

(Aubrey Plaza in *Emily the Criminal* made me her ardent fan. *The Phantom of the Open* and *Weird: The Al Yankovic Story*—both delightfully hilarious.)

2023:

Oppenheimer, Past Lives, The Zone of Interest, The Holdovers, Nyad, American Fiction, Barbie, Still, Killers of the Flower Moon, Maestro

(*Oppenheimer, Past Lives,* and *The Zone of Interest* stand out.)

2024:

So far, I like *Wicked, The Brutalist, Conclave, Inside Out 2, Thelma, A Complete Unknown, Ghostlight, Emilia Perez, His Three Daughters, Remembering Gene Wilder,* and all the great movies to come.[63]

Acknowledgements

MANY FRIENDS READ, CORRECTED, AND added suggestions to these chapters. Ellie Maranda of Opus Publishing shaped, encouraged, and made this project possible. Sayan Ray helped out with the editing.

My WFAA colleague and UT classmate John Sparks helped shape some of the Dallas stories. Good friend Michael McCarthy, formerly of the A.H. Belo Corporation, sharpened my memories of WFAA-TV personalities. Texas writer Jan Jarboe Russell donated an afternoon helping me understand the politics and quirks of my home town. Longtime pal Roy Neel read many of these stories, always offering improvements and encouragement. My WRC-TV colleague Joel Albert confirmed facts and gossip about WRC-TV in the 70s and 80s. Kathy McCampbell Vance shared many stories about her life with her husband Jim Vance. Washington writer Stephen Moore contributed to chapters on Katie Couric, Donald Trump, and Glenn Brenner. Stephen inspired many rewrites which I hated at the time but came to appreciate. Andrew Beaujon of *Washingtonian Magazine* has generously read my material, occasionally printing my work. Gary Waxler gave permission to use his amazing clay figures on the cover. WRC-TV Vice President of News Mike Goldrick and WRC-TV General Manager Jackie Bradford have graciously opened the doors of 4001 Nebraska. My wife Reverend Gina Campbell contributed many hours clarifying this work. I am grateful to Gina's high school English teacher, the late Mrs. Nancy Coward of Sylva, North Carolina, for giving Gina a firm grasp of the rules of grammar and punctuation. I'm most grateful to Gina for our life together.

The Writer's Center:
I began this memoir as a student at the Writer's Center in Bethesda, Maryland. Founded in 1975, the Center offers a variety of classes and workshops, and access to many dedicated teachers. I am most grateful to Ellen Herbert, Cheryl Somers Aubin, and Marilyn Smith for their guidance and encouragement. Ellen Herbert's group sessions led to several friendships and the formation of a writer's group, where we shared our struggles and cheered each other's success. I especially remember the late Jane Oakley, a former national television show producer. I miss her input and sunny personality.

Arch Campbell

ARCH CAMPBELL (BORN APRIL 25, 1946, SAN Antonio, Texas) is an award-winning Washington, D.C. broadcast critic, television feature reporter and show host. *The Washington Post* describes him as a, "local legend," and "iconic broadcaster." He is best known for his affiliation with NBC Television and their owned station WRC-TV where he worked thirty-two years. In 2007, he joined the staff of WJLA-TV, retiring in 2014. In the years since he has hosted several major podcasts including "At the Movies with Arch Campbell and Ann Hornaday," and "The Arch Campbell Podcast."

A graduate of San Antonio, Texas public schools, including Jefferson High School and San Antonio College, he completed a Bachelor of Science in Radio-Television-Film at the University of Texas at Austin in 1968. He received a Master of Arts degree in Journalism from UT Austin in 1971.

Professional honors include eight Emmy awards from the National Academy of Television Arts and Sciences, the Washington D.C. Mayor's Arts Award for television news arts coverage (2007), and the Ed Walker Lifetime Achievement award from the National Capitol Radio Television Museum (2017). *Washingtonian Magazine* selected him as a Washingtonian of the Year. (2015)

In 1994 he married Reverend Gina Gilland, an ordained United Methodist minister. Mrs. Campbell has served churches in the Washington area, including Concord-St. Andrews United Methodist Church in Bethesda, Maryland. In later years, Mrs. Campbell held the position of Director of Worship at the National Cathedral in Washington, D.C. For many years, she taught religion at Wesley Seminary on the American University campus in Washington, D.C. She works as a consultant for the United Methodist Church.

Courtesy Gary Waxler, Large Paw Productions

Endnotes

[1] Lee Salzberger moved from news to sales and ultimately ran the A.H. Belo station in Tulsa, Oklahoma. He finished his career as Vice President in charge of Personnel.

[2] I thought about calling this collection "Did You Fear for Your Life?" in honor of Bert Shipp.

[3] Other anchors paired with Bob Gooding during Murphy Martin's absence included Frank Gaskin and Jerry Taff. More station upset occurred when the morning show anchor, Gene Thomas, died in a race car accident, while shooting a feature story.

[4] Many of Don Harris' reports, including the opening day of Delta's metal detectors at Love Field, are posted on You tube. Southern Methodist University is gradually digitalizing years of WFAA news film from the 1960s and 70s on the site "G. William Jones Film & video Collection."

[5] Bruce had a secret that gradually leaked. He and Mary Ann were married. He kept their union secret to avoid conflict of interest problems for hiring her. An early invitation to Bruce's house revealed the arrangement.

[6] Andrea Mitchell became a revered NBC political correspondent. Susan King became Dean of the Hussman School of Journalism and Media at the University of North Carolina Chapel Hill.

[7] The Fines left WMAL for a long association with CBS News and Sixty Minutes.

[8] If you don't know what a newsreel is, watch the opening minutes of *Citizen Kane*. Newsreels showed films of important news events narrated by a voice over announcer. They usually ran prior to the feature film in a movie theater.

[9] Betty Endicott became the first female News Director in Washington, at WTOP-TV and later WTTG-TV, where she became General Manager. See: Brennan, Patricia, "Betty Endicott," The Washington Post (May 31, 1987)

[10] Yeah, I suggested that to Mrs. Rinker, but she loved the idea and really went with it.

[11] Richard, Paul, "A Campbell for all U.S. Campbells," The Washington Post (November 23, 1974)

[12] Forty years later, my second wife Gina—a member of the worship department at the Washington National Cathedral—helped arrange the annual Kirkin' of the Tartan of the St. Andrews society, an annual blessing of various Scottish family clans. I attended. A St. Andrews society member recognized me and brought up the painful evening in 1974. He remained unamused.

[13] Before video tape, stations presented reports in the field on 16 mm film. To create a reporter package, stations invented the simule-roll, in which the audio including reporter on camera stand ups, played on one track, the "A" roll. The simultaneous track, the B-roll, held the visual cover shots. Stations synchronized two projectors to air a simule-roll news package. Stations referred to the visual track as B-roll, a term still used today.

[14] Mann, Jack, "The Great Big Shadow of Little Warner Wolfe," The Washington Post (April 30, 1978)

[15] Shales, Tom, "Willard!" The Washington Post (December 30, 1979)

[16] The National Observer was a feature oriented weekly newspaper published by Dow Jones, owners of The Wall Street Journal. The paper operated from 1962 to 1977.

[17] Martin, Judith, "Tuneful Talent, Gone to the Dogs," The Washington Post (March 7, 1975)

[18] I went back to visit a couple of times. The first time I returned, Spot noticed me and run full speed into my arms. I swear this happened. Some months later I called and learned Spot ran out on the highway, where a truck turned him into Spam.

[19] Shales, Tom, "The News to Amuse," The Washington Post.

[20] The job of Editorial Director provided Bryson Rash a prestige position as he neared retirement age.

[21] "Around Town", The Washington Post (1978)

[22] I visited the WFAA newsroom a year after I left. Marty Haag introduced me to the young guy who took my place. Bill O'Reilly thrust a folder at me. It held some of my notes and a list of ideas. "What's this?" He snarled. "Just some ideas," I said. O'Reilly snorted and walked away.

[23] Founded by George Stevens, Jr. to show and preserve classic films, the AFI shared headquarters with Los Angeles, home of the film industry, and Washington, D.C. where Stevens kept his home, and where the AFI lobbied for government support.

[24] The Pedas Brothers became one of the largest property owners in Washington. They made a fortune in real estate. They also supported the Washington film community. They formed Circle Releasing in the 1980's and helped produce and finance the Coen Brother's earliest films including *Blood Simple,* and *Miller's Crossing.*

[25] Davey reviewed films on Channel 9 from 1970 to 1987. He left Washington to teach theater and playwriting at the University of Nevada Las Vegas. He died in 2004. His son Oliver Jones writes about entertainment for People and other publications and lives in Los Angeles. Oliver introduced himself to me on the red carpet outside the 2007 Oscars. We've been friends ever since. He's a regular on a podcast I host, and one of my favorite people.

[26] Judy Bachrach reviewed on Channel 4 for about 18 months, until NBC cut-backs laid off the part time commentators. Years later, after I established myself as the town's go to movie guy, she and I ran across each other at an event. We locked eyes for about a second, both of us taking a breath thinking about saying something. Neither of us said anything.

[27] Kresnak, Jack, "Bruce MacDonell: Journalist traveled a lot, enjoyed his job," Detroit Free Press (April 16, 1999)

[28] Paris went on to work for NBC and ABC in New York. Willard Scott knew Paris from working with her in the 1970's. Willard's wife Mary died in 2002. Paris and Willard very quietly became a couple some time later. Willard and Paris married in Florida in 2014.

[29] Without fail, anything new that happened overnight showed up on the 5:30 am WMAL radio newscast.

[30] Valentine, Paul, "Huge Snowfall Shuts Down D.C. Area," The Washington Post (February 20, 1979)

[31] I always liked Paul Anthony. He has deep roots in radio and television. Not long after this, Channel 9 hired him to report weekend weather. He continued a very successful voice over career, in both local and national commercials, and as the voice and pledge drive host for Washington's PBS affiliate WETA-TV.

[32] Carmody, John, "Now Here's the News," The Washington Post (February 26, 1979)

[33] You can watch Willard and Ed at work on YouTube listing "Joy Boys Radio Show." Willard and Ed remained life-long friends, working together occasionally. Ed Walker continued to perform on radio and television and was inducted into the Radio Hall of Fame in 2009.

[34] A veteran employee remembers some of Willard's eggs came from his chickens, while others might have come from a store – possibly Safeway – in packages labeled Willard's Farm.

[35] It transmitted still pictures by wire, mostly for newspaper clients. This is how it worked in the age before the internet.

[36] Still don't know what a newsreel is? Watch the opening scene of *Citizen Kane*.

[37] Washington Post television stations faced pressure during and after the Watergate scandal from the Nixon administration. In 1975, the FCC banned cross-ownership of a newspaper and television or radio station in the same city. The rule did not extend to concentrations already existing. The rule was never extended to current concentrations. Regulation relaxed in the 1980s. As it turned out, The Post didn't need to exchange stations with Detroit.

[38] Peterson later told me he ran into the judge, who told him he didn't want to change channels. Maybe he was kidding, but I wonder.

[39] Shales, Tom, "Willard!" The Washington Post (December 30, 1979)

⁴⁰ J. Fred Muggs was a chimpanzee added to The Today Show in the 1950's as comic relief.

⁴¹ Kelly, John, "The first *Star Trek* film took off from an unlikely launchpad: Washington", The Washington Post (November 30, 2019)

⁴² Carmody, John, "Sportscaster Mike Wolfe dismissed from Channel 9", The Washington Post (March 22, 1977)

⁴³ The American Film Institute showed *The Shining* February 4, 2023. The sold-out audience gathered to celebrate my friend Count Gore DeVol's 50th anniversary as host of Creature Feature. Watching *The Shining* again in a theater 43 years after opening night, I can report it still packs a punch. The slow pacing ups the tension. Jack Nicholson's descent into madness still creeps me out. I loved the contrast between Nicholson and the innocent Shelly Duvall and their little boy played by Danny Lloyd. I understand Lloyd became a college professor. No more acting for him.

⁴⁴ "Greaseman" angered listeners in January, 1986 with a joke about the shooting of Martin Luther King suggesting the shooting of four more civil rights leaders would lead to a week off. Angry criticism followed. A similar remark a few years later lost him a high paying job, effectively ending his career.

⁴⁵ Kathy McCampbell became Jim Vance's third and final wife.

⁴⁶ Steve Moore contributed to this chapter.

⁴⁷ The Museum of the American Indian opened fourteen years later on September 21, 2004.

⁴⁸ Madonna brought a camera crew that night to film her for her documentary *Truth or Dare*. When you see the scene of her walking into the Dick Tracy premiere, you clearly see me waving a microphone mouthing the words, "Madonna, Madonna." I'm told people yelled out, "Arch" during screenings.

⁴⁹ Wellington, "Stephanie Mansfield", The Washington Post (November 17, 1981)

⁵⁰ The nephew of Madame Wellington's late in life companion told me this story not long after she passed away.

[51] In another irony, Gina preached the homily at George Michael's funeral in 2010 at Washington National Cathedral. As a result, the Dean of the Cathedral asked her to join the worship staff.

[52] Kelly, John, "An insider solves at least one mystery connected to the infamous Evelyn Y. Davis", The Washington Post (May 23, 2021)

[53] Steve Moore contributed to this chapter.

[54] Farhi, Paul, "WRC Cuts change Face of Local News", The Washington Post(November 29, 2006)

[55] Maynard, John, "Arch Campbell to leave WRC by Year's End", The Washington Post (November 29, 2006)

[56] Let's Talk Live was a talk show on Channel 7's cable station located in the same building complex.

[57] Mr. Miyagi is the character in *The Karate Kid* who inspires Ralph Macchio to excel at karate by making him do menial chores including waxing his car.

[58] Patton remarried actress Meredith Salenger. They are raising Patton's daughter with Michelle.

[59] In Stephen Spielberg's 2022 film about his childhood, *The Fabelmans*, he and his family attend a screening of *The Greatest Show on Earth* in 1952. They drive to the movie in a 1955 Plymouth, a model not produced until three years later. The mistake ruined the film for me.

[60] I referenced the talking all night story and Martha's love for her house earlier. I used them in her eulogy because they helped define her.

[61] NBC moved the network newsroom and *Meet the Press* staff to offices and a studio near the U.S. Capitol in 2020.

[62] The Washington Post reported October 7, 2024 news of a group planning a high-tech renovation of the Uptown. No opening date set.

[63] List incomplete at publication time